Paul Frère
My Life Full of Cars

Paul Frère

My Life Full of Cars

*Behind the wheel with the world's
top motoring journalist*

Haynes Publishing

First published in October 2000

British Library Cataloguing in Publication Data:
A catalogue record for this book is available from the British Library.

ISBN 1 85960 670 9

Library of Congress Catalog Card Number 00-134251

Haynes Publishing, Sparkford, Nr Yeovil, Somerset, BA22 7JJ.
Tel: 01963 442030 Fax: 01963 440001
Int. tel: +44 1963 442030 Fax: +44 1963 440001
E-mail: sales@haynes-manuals.co.uk
Web site: www.haynes.co.uk

Haynes North America, Inc.
861 Lawrence Drive, Newbury Park,
California 91320 USA

Designed and typeset by G&M, Raunds, Northamptonshire
Printed and bound in Great Britain by J.H. Haynes & Co. Ltd, Sparkford

Contents

Preface

THE TITLE OF this book was suggested by my friend Shotaro Kobayashi, the former editor of the superb Japanese car magazine *Car Graphic*, to which I now have been a regular contributor for 33 years. I have been interested in cars since my childhood, and my career as a motoring journalist began in 1945. Testing has been a large part of my activity ever since and I have been a witness to the evolution of the motor car over more than three-quarters of a century, a fantastic experience. Many people have suggested that I should write the story of my varied experiences with cars, as owner, journalist, racing driver and consultant,

Signing copies of my first book, On the Starting Grid, *on the* Autosport *stand at the Racing Car Show in 1957. Looking on, seemingly sternly, is Archie Scott-Brown.* (LAT)

as well as having been a member of the Technical Commission of the FIA and involved with people responsible for the development of the automobile. But it was Shotaro who managed to make me sit down and write the story, initially for the readers of *Car Graphic* in the form of separate instalments; later these were gathered together and published as a book by Nigensha, publisher of *Car Graphic* as well as of many other magazines dealing with automobile, aviation, arts, and many other subjects.

Since my children and grandchildren, their families and most of my friends are just as unable to read Japanese as I am, I was anxious to have *My Life Full of Cars* printed in a language they could understand, and fortunately Darryl Reach of Haynes Publishing, publisher of several of my earlier books, thought that my new story would find a sufficient number of readers to warrant printing it in English, for which I am most grateful.

This book is by no means an autobiography. Except for the early years, which serve as a background for later happenings, you will not find any details of my private life. This is a book about cars, motor sports and car people. Even though my fairly short career in motor sport has been dealt with in other books, several chapters of this book are devoted to it. This is not surprising, as the years when I was involved in top-level racing were not only a very exciting part of my life, but also a very important one, because the experience gave a great boost to my career as a motoring journalist and opened many doors in the motor industry.

The book is also not chronological. Each chapter is a short story on a specific theme. This may be a little confusing, but it makes it easier for readers not interested in any particular chapter's content to disregard it and move on to the next without losing the thread!

In addition to Shotaro Kobayashi, his colleagues at *Car Graphic* and the President of Nigensha, Mr Takao Watanabe, who together persuaded me to write this story and contributed some of the photographs illustrating it, I would like to extend my thanks to all those who helped me with many of the other illustrations, particularly my dear friends André Van Bever, whose collection is worth its weight in gold, and Bernard Cahier, as well as the many anonymous correspondents who sent me photos that are now part of my collection, from which many illustrations were extracted.

Finally I would like to thank my wife Suzanne for her patience as I wrote far into the night, and for the time she took to read my manuscript and make suggestions to improve it.

Paul Frère
Monaco
June 2000

Chapter 1

Childhood

I WAS BORN at 7am on 30 January 1917 in Ste Adresse, a suburb of Le Havre, Normandy, to which the Belgian Government had exiled itself during the First World War. My parents, who were Belgians, had settled there because Maurice Frère, my father, had been chosen by one of his former high school professors, who had become the Minister for Economy of the Belgian war government, to become his assistant.

I can remember nothing of my time in Le Havre. I left at the age of $2^1/_2$ and only once in my life did I return, quite recently, to have a look at my birthplace. My first memory is of the sleeping car in which we left Le Havre for good. My father was by then with the Committee for German Reparations in Paris, and before a suitable villa was found in Chatou, some seven miles from the centre of Paris, we stayed for some weeks at the Hotel Lotti, near the Tuileries Gardens, to which my mother took me to see and feed the goldfish. It is at the Hotel Lotti that I got the first big fright that I can remember. At lunch, nobody warned me that the waiter had poured sparkling water into my glass – when I drank it I was so frightened that I disappeared under the table!

The winter of 1919 turned out to be bitterly cold, and I well remember helping (at least so I thought) my father to lay a fire, and the birth of my brother in November. It was also in Chatou that, a few years later, I got my first taste of school. It was a small private school and the only other children in my class were a certain Charly and two Swedish girls called Else and Erna.

The railway station from which my father took the train to Paris every day was only five or six minutes' walk from our home, but after two years he thought that a car would be more convenient and I remember him discussing the matter with my mother. It was to be a saloon car and the choice was between a Citroën B2 and Fiat 501. The latter was a little more expensive, but, as my father rightly remarked, it had a four-speed gearbox (against the Citroën's three) and semi-elliptic springs all round. So the Fiat it was.

I will always remember the smooth, singing noise of its 1,460cc side-valve engine, good enough to propel the high-built car at 45mph (70kph). It had right-

> ### The Fiat 501
>
> *Designed by Carlo Cavalli, at the time Fiat's Engineering Director (he was actually a lawyer!), the 501 was the Turin company's most successful model of the immediate post-First World War years. It was first produced in 1919 and continued almost without modification until 1926, four-wheel brakes becoming optional in its last two years of production. Standard bodies were a saloon, an open four-seater, a two-seater roadster and a taxi.*
>
> *The 1,460cc side-valve, four-cylinder engine had a bore and stroke of 65 x 110mm and developed 26bhp at 2,600rpm. Cooling was by pump, a rare feature in small cars of the period. Transmission was through a multi-plate clutch to a four-speed sliding pinion gearbox, an enclosed propeller shaft and a conventional differential. The wheelbase was 2.65m and the track 1.25m. The saloon weighed 1,000kg.*

hand drive with a right-hand gear lever and handbrake, and the saloon body had only two doors, one front left on the passenger side, and one rear right, the front passenger seat being collapsible to allow access to the driver's seat and, if required, to the rear compartment. The car was quite modern for its time, electric lighting and starting being standard. I rode quite often in the front passenger seat because my mother often chose to sit in the back as the seat was more comfortable or because she had to take care of my little brother.

Of course I loved it, but it was not without danger. In those days chickens were usually left to go where they wanted and used to run wild across the road as cars approached. Several times in the year we drove from Chatou to Brussels where most of my family lived. The 190 miles was a full day's journey, and during one such trip, near Laon in France, my father braked hard on the slippery dirt road to avoid a chicken; the car, having only rear-wheel brakes, skidded and hit a house. The plain glass windscreen broke (I probably hit it) and splinters got into my eyes, which hurt very much. We struggled on to Laon where we had to stay overnight to get the front axle straightened. I was taken to an oculist to make sure my eyes were all right. My mother had actually managed to remove all the splinters.

The roads in northern France were still in a very bad state from wartime damage. Asphalt was unknown at the time and only main roads were surfaced with 'macadam'. Horse-drawn carriages were numerous and horseshoe nails abounded on the road, causing punctures. On one journey from Paris to Brussels we suffered no fewer than five! As we had only two spare wheels, three times the tyre had to be removed from the rim and the inner tube repaired on the spot. And be assured that removing and fitting beaded-edged tyres, which were the norm at that time, is not an easy job!

As with many others at the time, the Fiat engine still had four little taps over its cylinder head through which a few drops of fuel could be injected into the cylinders to help starting on cold days. Once, during the early life of the car, the engine was not running too well and my father called in a mechanic. It was a beautiful day and the car was attended to in the garden, with me of course watching the proceedings. To find out which cylinder was misfiring, the mechanic opened all the taps in succession with the engine running. It made such a noise that I was scared stiff and ran away as fast as I could!

Although the car was kept in a wooden, albeit unheated, garage in the garden, starting in winter was frequently a problem, and as often as not my mother, the housemaid and myself were summoned to participate in the early morning push start!

The Fiat was nevertheless a valiant little car, and when climbing up Mont Valérien on the journey back from Paris its four-speed gearbox, which was not so common in cars of that class, paid off, the most frequent victims being De Dion-Boutons.

For its time the Fiat was also a fairly reliable car, but it had no shock absorbers and broken spring leaves were not uncommon. One year my parents went on a trip to the centre of France, the Côte d'Azur and Italy with a couple of Italian friends and came back with the front axle welded – it had not been equal to the assaults of the potholed roads of the Massif Central and had broken in the middle!

The Fiat wound up 25,000 miles in two years. It was still going well, but my father, who from the beginning of car ownership had subscribed to *La Vie*

My parents' Fiat 501 in 1923. My father is at the wheel and the children are my younger brother Jean and myself.

Automobile, the chief editor of which was the famous Charles Faroux (I still have an almost complete collection from 1922 to the Second World War), was now tempted by something more powerful from the 2-litre class. After due consideration the final choice lay between a Georges Irat and a Ballot. This was in 1924, and both were modern cars with four-wheel brakes. The Ballot's overhead camshaft engine was considered a plus (the Georges Irat had pushrod overhead valves), but my parents tried both cars. What really won the day for the Ballot was when, at 50mph (80kph), the driver demonstrating it took his hands off the steering wheel and the car proceeded unperturbed on its straight course.

The Ballot was bought as a chassis and delivered to a coachbuilder called Girand de Rumigny with a workshop in Bougival, on the banks of the Seine; the building still exists. The body my father ordered was a very conventional six-light, four-door saloon with a spare wheel on either side of the scuttle and a folding luggage rack at the rear. As with most quality French cars of the period, the Ballot had right-hand drive, central gear and handbrake levers, and Rudge centre-lock wire wheels. The brake pedal operated the front and the hand lever the rear brakes by confidence-inspiring rods. Later, a Dewandre vacuum servo, which had become standard on later models, was fitted to our car, and thereafter all brakes were operated simultaneously by the pedal.

It was in this car that my parents, my brother and I, together with my paternal grandmother, went on a tour to the south of France and the Côte d'Azur, and I quite clearly remember staying overnight in Aix-en-Provence, visiting the Roman baths of that town and having lunch on a terrace on the Promenade des Anglais in Nice. We also tackled a number of Alpine passes and I was amazed to see snow on the roadside in summer.

The Ballot may have been a fine car, but it also frequently broke spring leaves, a problem that was completely cured by fitting Hartford friction shock absorbers front and rear (originally the car had none). A more serious fault was that the body proved too heavy for the chassis, and the two longitudinal chassis members broke, one after the other, fortunately at a point where the two parts were still held together by the engine. This weakness was dealt with by welding and reinforcing. However, the chassis's lack of rigidity also did the steel-panelled wooden body no good. The problem was attended to by the Paris coachbuilders Merville & Garnier, who raised the entire body about 1cm above the chassis frame and supported it by a number of soft coil springs, a patented system that allowed the chassis to flex and twist without excessively affecting the body.

That first Ballot, chassis number 888, remained with us until 1927. By now I was 10 and we had moved from France to Berlin, where my father was involved in the Dawes Plan, an American-led report into Germany's post-war economic problems. The car was sold and finished its life as a taxi in the well-known resort of Villengen, in the Black Forest.

Undaunted by the problems he had faced, my father replaced it with another Ballot 2LT with a long-wheelbase chassis, number 1812, which was a much better car and had a much stiffer frame. It was fitted with a standard four-door, four-light body by Vanvooren, built under Weymann licence, with forward-facing emergency seats.

Weymann bodies were designed to deform. They had a light wooden frame whose components were joined by flexible steel strips and were fabric panelled. They were light and did not rattle, were immune to the deformations of the chassis of the period, and were very popular before the era of all-steel bodies. The

Left *My parents' first 2LT Ballot in the Alps in 1926.*

Right *The second 2LT Ballot in Stuben on the Arlberg Pass, with me, Jean, grandmother and father.*

car also had 'balloon' tyres on well-base rims, which were not only more comfortable but also easier to fit. In addition, Excelsior-AFA friction dampers were now standard.

The new Ballot was also our first car with provision for dipping the headlights. With our first two cars, passing another car at night was fraught with difficulty. In order not to blind oncoming drivers, the standard practice was to switch off the headlights and drive on what today we call the parking lights. Our new Ballot had a better system. Its two Marchal lights had different functions: the left-hand one (remember we were driving on the right-hand side of the road) had a wide, flat, non-glaring beam, while the right-hand one had a long-range beam. As oncoming cars approached, the long-range beam was simply switched off, to be replaced by the parking light, while the non-glaring left lamp remained on, providing sufficient illumination for the speeds of the time; even a quality car like the Ballot would barely exceed 65mph, a speed that was very seldom reached because of the time required to attain it and the mostly narrow and steeply cambered roads.

While my father's family did not have any motoring tradition, my mother's family were almost pioneer motorists. My mother often told me about her father's Minerva motor cycle, which he used around the turn of the century. Apparently it had no clutch, so when her father took her with him on the luggage rack (no pillion seat!), she had to be very alert and jump on to it with the bike running!

Around 1906 my maternal grandfather bought his first car, a Belgian-built FN tourer, which was mostly driven by my uncle, who was 16 at the time. All his life Uncle Bob (Robert Schimp) was very interested in cars, though he never owned very exciting ones. He was also a very competent driver and the only member of my parents' families who ever came to see me race. In his later years he spent a lot of time rebuilding very early cars, with which he then took part in oldtimer rallies. One car he rebuilt, a Vallée built in Le Mans in 1897, is now in the Le Mans Automobile Museum.

It was Uncle Bob who first took me to a motor race, the Spa 24 hours of 1926, won by André Boillot and Louis Rigal driving a 3.8-litre, four-cylinder sleeve-valve Peugeot. On the Sunday morning he took me to the circuit from the family home near Brussels in his Buick saloon, and we stayed on to the end, walking along the track to various corners. This and other visits to Spa, when the 1,500 and 1,750cc supercharged Alfas reigned supreme, considerably raised my interest in motor sport, and I often dreamed of racing those wonderful cars myself.

The family business on my mother's side was growing grapes in glasshouses in a village called Hoeilaart on the outskirts of Brussels. At the time it was a flourishing business and most of the grapes were exported to England. Apart from his Buick (he had three before the war, with a short-lived Auburn and a Packard 120 in between), for several years my uncle also had a 5CV Citroën in

Citroën 5CV: the first car I drove

The C-type Citroën, which went into production early in 1922 and was better known by its tax rating as the '5CV', was virtually a scaled-down version of Citroën's larger B2 model.

The four-cylinder, side-valve engine had bore and stroke dimensions of 55 x 90mm for a capacity of 856cc. As on the larger model, it had a two-bearing crankshaft, lubrication was by splash, and cooling by thermosyphon. At 2,100rpm, 11bhp was developed. The gearbox had three speeds operated by a central lever. The brake pedal worked on a large drum aft of the gearbox and the handbrake operated on the small rear drums.

The original duck-tailed two-seater weighed 545kg and was soon followed by a 'Clover Leaf' three-seater on a wheelbase increased from 2.25m to 2.35m, a cabriolet with dropping side windows, and even by a small wooden van, called the 'Boulangère'.

In contrast to the then current crude 'cyclecars', the 5CV was a real car, fully equipped with an electric starting motor and decent weather protection. It was an immediate success, especially with women, who until then had rarely been seen at the wheel of a motor car. Production ceased in May 1926, when Citroën decided to concentrate on its more profitable larger model, which, in 1925, had become the first European car with an all-steel body. In all, 70,000 5CVs were made.

My uncle's 5CV, the first car I drove, was a 1925 cabriolet. In 1950 I bought a well-worn 1925 'Clover Leaf', which was reconditioned and with which I took part in a few oldtimer rallies. I kept it until 1994 and it is now in good hands.

With my eldest daughter Marianne in my 1925 'Cloverleaf' 5CV Citroën during an 'oldtimer rally' in 1964.

I was less than 10 when I drew this copy of a photo. Even at that age I was a great admirer of the early Horch 8 designed by Paul Daimler.

which to travel to work. Once, when we spent a holiday with my grandparents, he lent the car to my father, who brought me home on the passenger seat. When he stopped the car in front of its garage to open the door, at 10 years old I was courageous enough to say to him, 'You know, I would be able to drive the car into its garage.'

'Let's see', he said. So I moved to the driver's side, stretching myself to the utmost to reach the pedals, selected first gear and took the car in, stopping in time so as not to hit the wall, and without stalling the engine.

'Wonderful – who taught you?' asked my father.

Nobody had taught me; not only had I observed how it was done, I was also an enthusiastic addict of Meccano and had once built a chassis complete with electric motor, gearbox, differential and all, so I knew perfectly well the various functions of the power train.

When he heard of my exploit, my uncle, who had often taken me on his lap to let me steer the car, was enthusiastic. He wanted a repeat performance, and from then on, when we were in Belgium on holiday with the family, he often used me as his chauffeur. He was a well-known personality in the region and was sure that if we were caught by a policeman he would get away with it – he knew them all! Legally you had to be 18 to drive in Belgium, but until 1966 no driving licence was required. As the Citroën had no synchromesh (no car had at the time), it was Uncle Bob who taught me how to double-declutch when shifting down.

By that time I had been a car owner myself for a long time. In 1923, I think it was, Father Christmas brought me a splendid Eureka pedal car with a pointed tail and working lights. My brother was still too small to reach the pedals, so I had it all to myself, and who knows how many kilometres I covered at its wheel in our garden!

Chapter 2

The road to
motoring journalism

As ALREADY MENTIONED, my father's career involved a move to Berlin in 1925, just after the period of huge inflation that had left Germany in a chaotic state. Unemployment, demonstrations and strikes were the order of the day, and communism was looming, but by 1925 the country had begun to recover, though the economic burden of war reparations certainly contributed to the development of the Nazi movement.

My father spoke acceptable German and my mother just about got along with it, but neither my brother nor myself spoke a word. Mother decided that she would be our schoolmistress, and had all the books and programmes sent by the private school that I had attended when we lived in France; as part of the programme it was she who explained to me how an internal combustion engine worked! An elderly German lady, Fraülein Dunkel, also came regularly to teach us German, so after two years we could be sent to a public school.

As it was important that we also continued to learn French, we were sent to the 'Französisches Gymnasium' (French College), a state school that had been established in the 18th century by Frederick II of Prussia, a great francophile, for the French Huguenots who had come to Prussia as refugees. In the lower classes all the lecturing was done in German, but there were up to nine hours of French per week, and from the third year a progressively higher number of lectures were given in French, so when they left school the German pupils spoke the language almost perfectly. It was a wonderful school with excellent teachers and only a small number of pupils per class.

In Berlin the car scene was completely different from that in France, with many makes unknown in the West and completely forgotten today. Only Opel, Audi and Mercedes-Benz (until 1928 two separate makes) are still with us. Not so, at random, Adler, Hansa, Steiger, Stoewer, Szawe, Simson Supra, Stolle, Brennabor, NAG, Protos, Presto, Aga, Apollo, Wanderer, Dixi, Dinos, Dürkopp, Ego, Elite, Fafnir, Ley, Mauser, Pluto (made under Amilcar licence), Rabag (a Bugatti licensee), Selve, Voran (the first front-wheel-drive car with homokinetic joints), Grade, Faun, NSU, Delta, Mannesmann, and such classics as Maybach,

This is as far as I could get in 1933 to making a working Meccano model of a Bugatti type 35/51 chassis. It has four-wheel brakes and the electric motor drives through a clutch, gearbox (four speeds and reverse) and differential.

Rumpler and Hanomag's 'Kommissbrot', which were all part of the scene. The list does not include such cars as Röhr and DKW, which came later only to subsequently disappear, and BMW, which added cars to its motor cycle production by acquiring Dixi.

I was completely fascinated by Berlin's double-decker Büssing and NAG buses and built a Meccano replica, which was updated every time a new model appeared. In addition, my running chassis, which now had a clutch, a four-speed-and-reverse gearbox, a differential and later independent suspension and four wheel brakes – all working – was steadily improved and eventually acquired a body.

Though the second Ballot was still running well, some time around 1930 my father, who had temporarily returned to Brussels, spotted a used Ballot RH3 straight-eight with an elegant four-light body by Albert D'Ieteren for sale by the importer Pierre Decrose, and bought it. The chassis was virtually identical to that of the 2LT, but with a longer bonnet to house the beautiful 3-litre engine. It had the same slow sliding-pinion four-speed gearbox as the 2LT, but its biggest fault was that the camshaft-driven fan was too small and too slow, so that in the Alps the car tended to overheat. We still had that car when my father was appointed as a Consultant to the Austrian National Bank and we all moved to Vienna.

In Vienna the Ballot broke a piston. These had an aluminium top and a cast front skirt to prevent cold-starting piston slap, and a skirt had broken away from the top. This did not prevent the engine from running properly, albeit noisily, so my father bravely decided to drive the car to the works to have the damage repaired; on the way to Paris another skirt broke – consistency indeed! By that time the Ballot company had been acquired by Hispano Suiza. The RH3 was out of production, but there were still some unsold chassis left. Instead of reconditioning the engine, the factory people suggested moving the body to a brand-new chassis, which was done.

This later model had a much better constant-mesh gearbox and a less elegant, but more efficient fan, belt-driven from the crankshaft, which solved the overheating problem. The car remained in the family until 1937, when it was sold in Vienna.

Before that, it was decided that my mother should have her own car. I was now sufficiently grown up to have my say in the choice of the family's cars and I persuaded my mother to buy a 5CV Amilcar 2+1 convertible for which, surprisingly, there was a dealer in Vienna. The Amilcar's outrigged front leaf springs looked very racy and the little 890cc side-valve engine was quite lively, driving the rear wheels through a rather noisy non-synchromesh three-speed gearbox.

It was in this car in Vienna, where the left-hand rule of the road still reigned,

My first competitive event in a car, in 1935, came with my mother's Amilcar in a gymkhana, which I won.

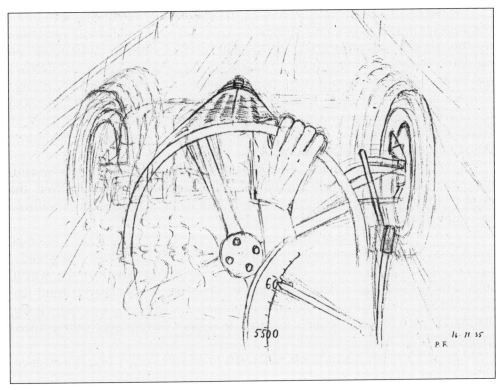

This 1935 drawing I called 'Speed'.

that, on 31 January 1935, just one day after my 18th birthday and without any previous schooling, I obtained my first driving licence. Six months later, still with that car, I won my first competition, a 'gymkhana' driving test event, which took place in the Austrian resort of St Wolfgang, where we were on holiday, and which included a slalom between trees!

Few people remember that in the early 1930s the rule of the road in Austria was to drive on the left. The Austrian Government then decided that the rule should be changed to match that of its western neighbours, but such a change would be very expensive because all road signs would have to be changed, tram lines rearranged and trams, cars and buses modified to have doors on the right-hand side. This represented a very big investment and Austria was not a rich country. As most of its large towns were in the eastern part, except Salzburg and Innsbruck, and western Austria bordered Germany and Italy, where the right-hand rule of the road was enforced, it was decided that the west of the country should drive on the right and the eastern part provisionally continue to drive on the left! And that is what happened. As you drove between the two regions, large signs invited you to change from one side of the road to the other! Of course, for the Nazis money was never a problem and as soon as they invaded Austria the right-hand rule was adopted for the whole country.

In 1936 I left Vienna to study for an 'Ingénieur Commercial' degree at Brussels University, but returned to Austria for holidays. A few months before my family finally returned to Brussels, I took the Amilcar from Vienna to Belgium and enjoyed it for a brief period before it was sold and replaced with a Fiat 1100, a type 508C pillarless four-door saloon, a wonderful little car. Until my parents returned to Belgium, while at university I stayed with my mother's family in Hoeilaart, from where I usually commuted to Brussels by train. However, my grandfather, who had now given up driving, owned a 1935 Buick 40 Sedan, and I found any excuse to borrow it. It had independent front suspension, very soft springing, and considerable final oversteer. One of the roads linking Hoeilaart to Brussels curved (and still does) through the Soignes Forest and was, at a time when traffic was still rather scarce, a wonderful training ground, especially in wet weather. There I readily learned how to control a car.

Following the 1936 Monte Carlo Grand Prix, won by Caracciola in abominable weather, Rodney Walkerly, alias 'Grande Vitesse', the sports editor of *The Motor*, wrote that 'while most other drivers spun or went off the road, Caracciola proceeded unperturbed, sliding and skidding, but always keeping his foot hard on the floor', or something to that effect. This cannot be true, I said to myself. Keeping your foot hard down when the rear wheels are sliding can only make things worse. I was determined to prove it, and on a rainy day, coming by a large cobbled place, I decided to prove good old Rodney wrong. I put the car on a curved path, put my right foot hard down and spun the car in a grand way. My conclusion: never believe a journalist!

At school in Vienna my English had left a lot to be desired, so for three years from 1934 my parents sent me to England to the East Coast seaside resort of Felixstowe as a paying guest with the Ransford family who accommodated a few foreigners anxious to improve their English. Most of them were French or German, so I spent a lot of my time speaking very little English. But I discovered those two famous magazines *The Autocar* and *The Motor*, which I continued to buy when I was back on the Continent. They were by far my best teachers, and at university I quickly became No 1 in English! I still have a complete collection of those magazines from 1935 to date, except for the war years when, for obvious reasons, they were unobtainable in German-occupied countries.

Those magazines had a considerable influence on my view of the British car industry, just at a time when, in Vienna, my father had decided to sell the Ballot and get a more modern car, asking for my advice. I was all for a Bugatti 57, a Talbot Lago or a Delahaye 135, but if those seemed too expensive or exotic, I suggested that he look at a 2½-litre SS-Jaguar. At that time, according to *The Motor* and *The Autocar* road tests, it was a very potent performer and apparently amazing value for money. Jaguar's Austrian importer was Georg Hans Koch, a real enthusiast who had driven a works SS1 in the Alpine Trial of 1935. My father had never heard of the make before and, though having ruled out my three first choices, did not even visit Koch.

However, one day, driving back from his office in the Ballot, he spotted, parked in the street, a car that he did not recognise, but one that struck him as very elegant and desirable. He stopped to investigate – it was a 2½-litre SS-Jaguar! He therefore rushed to Georg Hans Koch, tried one and signed an order. From then until his death in 1970, he always had a Jaguar in his garage. His last, a 3.4-litre Mk1 saloon, now rests, beautifully kept, in the Jaguar company's collection.

An interesting but sad interlude intervened in November 1938, when I lived in Brussels. A Czech girlfriend of mine who owned a Tatra 57 drophead (a Ledwinka-designed car with a 1,200cc air-cooled flat-four engine, a tubular backbone chassis, independent twin transverse leaf springs at the front and swing axle rear suspension) and who had spent several months in England, suggested that I should accompany her back to Prague. I met her in Boulogne and off we went, partly over snowbound roads in the Vosges mountains, through Switzerland and Germany to Prague. In Germany the atmosphere was very gloomy, with many military vehicles everywhere. We were happy to cross the border to Czechoslovakia where we arrived rather late and stopped in Pilsen for a last night before we proceeded to Prague. When we woke the next morning the streets of Pilsen were full of German military vehicles: Hitler had invaded Czechoslovakia. We nevertheless proceeded to Prague and the girl, who was Jewish, was ultimately clever and lucky enough to escape from the country before it was too late.

The 1.2-litre flat-four Tatra that I drove to Prague was slow but immensely robust, and had wonderful rack-and-pinion steering.

The Tatra was slow, though obviously very strongly built, but one of its features was a revelation to me: its rack-and-pinion steering. I had never driven a car with such light, friction-free and accurate steering.

At Brussels University I quickly made friends with other car enthusiasts and we soon made up a group of four, Henri Goldsmit, Pol Cox, 'Daddy' Marcq and myself, soon joined by Jean Dieudonné. The latter was the father of Pierre, who became a racing driver, winning the European Touring Car Championship of 1976 in a BMW before becoming a works driver for Mazda. Marcq shared a wonderful Talbot Lago 'Baby' convertible with his father and later had his own BMW 328, while Dieudonné, after running an old Studebaker, had been given a splendid Hotchkiss 3½-litre 'Paris-Nice' saloon for his 21st birthday. He was so performance-minded that, for some time, he had the body removed and drove it as a chassis!

Neither Goldsmit nor I had a car of our own, but soon after we met Cox bought a two-seater pointed-tail sports car, looking somewhat like a Bugatti, of a make we had never heard: a Delfosse, the only one I have ever seen. The factory was in the north of France, and the make was short-lived (1922–26). The car had a 1½-litre CIME ohv engine and was reasonably quick for its age. Of our group I was the one who best understood car engineering, and when it came to doing some maintenance work on one of the cars I usually took it home, which

'Practising' in fellow student Pol Cox's MG P-type in the Bois de la Cambre on the outskirts of Brussels.

provided an occasion for driving it. On one such occasion I took the Delfosse and unfortunately a big bang announced that a connecting rod had found its way to freedom. That repair was beyond my ability, and Cox had the car repaired and sold it. It later reappeared, in good condition, in some rallies organised by the Veteran Car Club of Belgium.

To replace the Delfosse, Cox bought a second-hand P-type MG Midget, a delightful little car that I borrowed as often as possible. Unfortunately I had far fewer occasions to drive 'Daddy' Marcq's BMW 328, which had wonderful performance for its time, though I never felt completely at ease at its wheel. That hair-sharp rack-and-pinion steering and the comparatively soft springing with a fairly large travel all seemed so unfamiliar. At the time I did not realise that the 328 really was the first sports car of a new era.

Sadly, both Marcq and Goldsmit, two very dear friends, lost their lives during the war.

In the winter of 1939–40, with France, Germany and Great Britain already at war, I bought the first car I could call my own since the pedal-driven Eureka. The opportunity came when another friend crashed his Belgian-made Imperia of which he was, I believe, the fourth owner, all of them students known to our group. He was offered 600 francs for it by a breaker; I could offer no more than 550 francs, but at least the car would not be broken up, and the deal was

The first car I owned was a Belgian-made Imperia GS with a 1.8-litre, six-cylinder, slide-valve engine. This is the car after I restored it, in 1945.

clinched. The car was about ten years old and was an 1800 GS model of which very few were made.

The Imperia works were located in Nessonvaux, near Liège, and after the First World War they produced a high-class, four-cylinder, 3.7-litre model with a single ohc and 16 valves. One of them had won the first Belgian Grand Prix in 1922, the first motor race to take place on the Spa circuit. However, Mathieu Van Roggen, Imperia's Managing Director, saw a better future in the manufacture of more popular models and called in an experienced engineer, Arnold Couchard, to design an 1,100cc car. This had a novel valve-less type of engine in which the valves were replaced by lateral slides, one on each side of the bore. The slides were actually part of the bore and were operated by twin camshafts located in the crankcase to open and close the inlet and exhaust ports. The system was desmodromic and did not involve any springs. Around 1927 a 1,650cc six-cylinder model using the same system had followed, later increased to 1,800cc.

The GS consisted of the 1,800cc 'six' fed by three Zenith carburettors, mated to the chassis of the four-cylinder model. Though I bought the car for next to nothing, the damage – mainly a bent front axle, a broken headlight and a crumpled front fender – was easily repairable. I knew that the rest of the car was in an acceptable condition, as I had driven it before its accident, so I had it towed to the workshop of my family's glasshouse business and, with the help of my uncle, it was soon straightened and made driveable. However, only a few days after I had driven it back to the garage of my parents' house in Brussels (completely illegally, with borrowed number plates!), Belgium was at war and the car was not used for five years.

During the war I did a lot of work on it, taking up play in the big-end bearings, improving a very scanty body and making the car look more attractive. A previous owner had replaced the three-carburettor installation with the single carburettor of the saloon models, but by visiting a few breakers I was able to lay my hands on an original intake manifold, complete with the three Zeniths, and fitted it to the car. However, by the time the war came to an end I had a family, and when someone offered me 55 times the price I had initially paid for the car, I let it go, having driven it probably less than six miles, again on illegal number plates.

Being a university student, my compulsory military service was postponed, but when Germany invaded Belgium, youths of my age were required to move to France and enrol in the Belgian Army in Toulouse. I therefore moved to France driving my mother's Fiat 1100, independently of my parents who left slightly later. My plan was to join my friend Goldsmit in Les Eyzies, a little town in the Dordogne, where we would join the army together as soon as we were called. However, this never happened because after two weeks Belgium capitulated and its army was completely disbanded and never remobilised. It took about 2^{1}/$_{2}$ months before the family, which was scattered all around France, could communicate and finally return to Belgium. With all the refugees moving to the

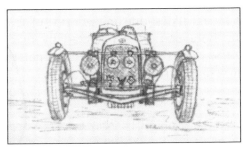

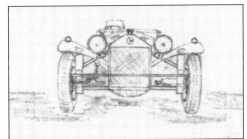

Drawings I did strictly from memory during the more boring lectures at Brussels University in 1939–40. Starting top left, the cars are Frazer Nash Shelsley, Ballot 2LS, HRG Le Mans, MG K3 Magnette, Mercedes-Benz SSK, Lancia Lambda, Lagonda LG45, Blower Bentley and Delahaye 135 MS.

South of France, the local garage was completely overwhelmed, so I decided to give a helping hand, which provided me with the first money I ever earned. Among the jobs I tackled was taking up and adjusting the main and big-end bearings of a Citroën C4 engine – perhaps not exactly as modern manuals would recommend …

The 'Commercial Engineer' degree I obtained at Brussels University was supposed to prepare its holders to become industry managers with a good insight into economics, trade and engineering – certainly not to become a racing driver! Neither was it my ultimate aim, though I was determined to dedicate my life to the automobile. To improve my chances of succeeding in my ambition, I spent a lot of time reading those publications that I could get in wartime, such as bulletins of the French SIA (the French equivalent of the SAE), to improve my knowledge of automobile engineering. Handling has always been a matter of major interest to me, but at the time I had never found any serious analysis of the comparative behaviour of front-wheel-drive and rear-wheel-drive cars. So I decided to find out for myself, using my knowledge in mathematics and trigonometry. The result proved to be quite interesting, so I decided to submit it to the famous Charles Faroux, a graduate engineer who, as a journalist, was very

This 'four', with me at the bow, was the Belgian Champion three times and the only Belgian crew selected to participate in the European Rowing Championships of 1947.

influential and was Editor of *La Vie Automobile*. He immediately published it, and it became my first published article.

As a result I further developed the article and decided to have it printed as a booklet, which, I thought, would help me into the car business when the war was over. And it worked. I went with the booklet to see André Laurent, Editor of *Belgique Automobile*, the only Belgian car magazine worth mentioning at the time, and he immediately wanted more articles. I had become a motoring journalist! That was certainly not enough to make a living, but it helped me to obtain jobs within the industry, first as service manager to the Kaiser-Frazer importers in Belgium, then with General Motors Continental's publicity department in Antwerp, and as service manager again to the Jaguar importers.

Most people have forgotten Kaiser and Frazer cars, which were in fact identical except for the badge and the fact that the Frazer was the more luxurious of the two. In 1947 they were the first American cars of post-war design, styled by Howard Darrin. Their shape was widely, if not always successfully, copied in Europe, examples being the Fiat 1400 and the Singer SM 1500. The company, which was in Willow Run, near Detroit, had been founded by Henry J. Kaiser who, in the war years, had built hundreds of Liberty Ships that had contributed strongly to the American war effort. Unfortunately, the cars, which were powered by a 3.7-litre side-valve Continental engine, were of very poor quality. Some of the engines almost pinked their heads off, cylinder blocks cracked between the valves, the steering was prone to shimmy, the gearshift mechanism frequently locked between gears, the overdrive kickdown refused to work, and after a few thousand kilometres the shock absorbers were as good as bicycle tyre pumps. The service manager's job was therefore not an easy one. Fortunately, most owners were only too happy to have secured a car at all at a time when most makes had enormous waiting lists, so were not too difficult.

However, Jaguar owners were, on the whole, more discriminating. They ranged from well-known personalities to the *nouveau riche* showing off in their elegant cars. I remember one of the latter, a wine merchant from St Nicklaas, driving into the workshop one morning in a green 2¹/₂-litre saloon, and complaining about horrendous oil consumption. The car was a 1949 model with a pushrod six-cylinder engine, the oil filler opening of which was on top of the cast aluminium rocker cover. So up goes the bonnet and the chief mechanic pulls out the dipstick, cleans it and puts it back. He carefully pulls it out again, looks at it incredulously, cleans it again, repeats the operation and finally has to believe his eyes: the oil level is about twice as high as it should be.

'I'm not surprised your car uses so much oil,' he says. 'The sump is grossly overfilled.'

'Strange,' is the owner's answer. 'When I add oil up there, it never overflows!'

Chapter 3

Getting into racing bikes and cars

HAVING SOLD THE Imperia, I needed transport. I first bought a 125cc Saroléa motor cycle from an acquaintance (who later became Belgium's Minister of Finances), but that was stolen after only a week. It was replaced by an ex-Wehrmacht (German Army) DKW 125, which was much more modern and a wonderful little bike. Changing it for an ex-Wehrmacht NSU 250, which had been brought back from Germany in parts by a friend, was a big mistake. The NSU was followed by an ex-British Army Triumph 350 ohv single, which I fitted with a higher-compression piston and telescopic forks from an ex-army Matchless. This was the best bike I had in that early period. But though it would do about 72–73mph, I felt it was not quite enough and I changed it for a new 500cc AJS single with rear suspension. For more than a year, during my time with General Motors, I commuted every day from my home in Brussels to Antwerp and back – about 60 miles – first with the Triumph, then with the AJS which, on one occasion, broke its crankshaft on the way to Antwerp. Amazingly it got me back home, the two parts of the crank being held together by the conrod's roller bearing.

But as I now had a family, I also needed a car. A new one was out of the question, and even the worst used cars were horrendously expensive. One day, when I visited the garage of Pierre Decrose, an importer for the Nuffield Group, I spotted a 1925 2LTS Ballot that he was using as a breakdown van. Decrose, whom I had known for many years and from whom my father had bought his Ballot straight-eight, had been a Ballot racing mechanic and works driver. He had kept the 2LTS mostly out of nostalgia and let me have it at a ridiculously low price. As it still had beaded-edged tyres, I had the Rudge wire wheels rebuilt with well-base rims to take more modern tyres, put a trunk and a spare wheel across the chassis members and, without any other service, except for an oil change, drove it to Italy and back with my first wife without any problem, except for the replacement of a front wheel bearing. Later I had a scanty four-seater body built to take the entire family. We also used the Ballot to drive to Lucerne, in Switzerland, when I was a member of the crew in a 'four oars' selected to represent Belgium in the European Rowing Championships on the Rotsee.

The Ballot 2LTS was basically identical to the two 2LT models my father had owned, except that the valves were in a 'V' configuration and were operated by rockers from the single overhead camshaft, which added 5–6hp. I sold it to a friend when I bought my father's 1939 2¹/₂-litre Jaguar.

Once I had a motor cycle, I became as interested in bikes as in cars. I started writing articles on bikes for two magazines, one of them a small club affair for which I invented the title *Motovox*. I was anxious to get more background information and regularly bought the British magazines *The Motor Cycle* and *Motor Cycling*, the editor of which was pre-war motor cycle ace Graham Walker. I also borrowed from two friendly fans hundreds of pre-war issues of those two magazines in order to get the proper background on techniques and riders like Stanley Woods. In the 1930s Woods had almost triggered a revolution by winning the 1935 Isle of Man Senior (500cc) TT (then the most famous race of all) with a rear-sprung Moto Guzzi, beating another top star, Norton rider Jimmy Guthrie, at a time when rear springing was considered 'unsuitable for racing'! Others were Freddie Frith, still one of the greats in the post-war years, Jimmy Simpson, Tim Hunt, Ted Mellors, Jock West and the German ace 'Schorsch' Meier.

When racing was resumed after the war, a few new names cropped up, such as Fergus Anderson, Les Graham, A. J. Bell, Bob Foster and Ernie Lyons, who created an enormous surprise by winning the 'Manx Grand Prix' on a racing version of a Triumph Twin, the only one in the race. But when the early 1950s came, the greatest of all was Geoffrey Duke, whom I had the very great pleasure to meet in 1998 when the Goodwood Circuit celebrated its 50th anniversary. My enthusiasm for motor cycles was such that I not only competed in a few races,

Spoils of victory at the 1946 Brussels Grand Prix after winning the 500cc class for Standard bikes on Robert Everts' pre-war Triumph Speed Twin.

hill-climbs and, on a higher scale, in trials, but once even flew to the Isle of Man in the late 1940s with a group of fellow enthusiasts to attend a Senior TT.

As to my own exploits, I entered my DKW 125 for a motocross and a speed trial, doing well in both, but though in those immediate post-war times no special bikes were used in motocross, I soon realised, after bending my NSU, that that kind of sport was not the ideal treatment for the bike you had to rely on to go to work the following day.

The first proper motor cycle race organised in Belgium after the war took place in 1947 in the Bois de la Cambre, on the outskirts of Brussels, five minutes' walk away from the flat in which I lived with my family. The event was international and comprised separate races for 350cc and 500cc racing bikes, but there were also two races – 350 and 500 – for standard bikes with full equipment. I just could not resist, and under the name 'Frépau' (for 'Frère, Paul') to keep it secret

Left *Under the pseudonym 'Frépau' and wearing a helmet borrowed from superstar Les Graham, I finished fourth in the 125cc class on an Austrian Puch at the 1948 Brussels Grand Prix.*

Right *With the Puch on the Jabbeke autoroute, where I broke the 125cc world record for the flying mile – but held it for only a few weeks.*

from my parents, I entered the NSU 250 for the 350 race, knowing that the bike was much too slow to have the slightest chance.

On the day before official practice, many riders were already on the spot and practising on the circuit, which comprised a stretch not normally open to motor vehicles (which was simply ignored) and a one-way stretch open to the (very thin) traffic.

I joined the fray with the NSU and met Robert Everts, a long-time friend, who had entered his pre-war Triumph Speed Twin for the 500cc class. His girlfriend, Marianne, who was also a keen motor cyclist, had timed him over several laps and, after exchanging impressions, he said to me, 'Have a try with my bike – I wonder how fast you would be.'

As it happened, I lapped about 10 seconds quicker than he had done. Whereupon he said, 'Well this is a waste of a good bike – why don't you ride it? And, if you agree, I'll take the NSU.'

Thanks to his generosity I raced the Speed Twin and easily won from another – but post-war – example. This set the ball rolling, and on many other occasions Robert lent me his bikes, mainly for hill-climbs and speed trials. He later had a Triumph 350 Twin, an Ariel 500 Twin and Square-four, and two Vincent HRDs, including a Black Shadow – no mean bike in its time.

In the following years, Albert Breslau, the official importer for Associated Motor Cycles (AJS and Matchless) and the Austrian Puch, lent me a 125cc Puch racing machine for the 1948 International Brussels Grand Prix on the Heysel

site, dominated by the Atomium, in which I finished fourth behind three very fast Dutch Villiers-engined Eysinks. Following some good results in trials with my Triumph, for two seasons running he provided me with a proper AJS trials machine with which I was reasonably successful. But when I got more involved in car racing, and journalism took up an ever increasing part of my time, the bikes had to yield to the pressure. I also had to give up the evening courses I gave on automobile engineering in a State Technical School in Brussels.

Car racing, if only on a modest scale, had been one of my ambitions for a long time, but fighting it out with the 'greats' seemed to me a dream that could never be realised. I would have been content to drive a small car at Le Mans or in the Spa 24 hours race, just to be part of it, in the purest Olympic spirit. So when, quite by chance, I spotted young Jacques Swaters, whom I had known as a schoolboy, at the wheel of a special MG that I had known for a long time, I saw the opportunity – the first post-war 24 hours race on the Spa circuit was only three weeks away. It did not take me long to persuade Jacques that we should

Left *In 1949, winning the 250cc class on a Puch in the Lamborelle Trial, which at that time was Belgium's most important trial.*

Right *Last-minute check-up before driving the 12-year-old ex-Bonneau MG PB to the starting grid for the 1947 24 Heures de Francorchamps.*

team up and enter the car. But before the race it would need some attention. As the owner, Jacques took care of this, entrusting the MG to a mechanic who, he thought, was reliable. It soon proved to be otherwise …

Jacques, who later became one of the world's foremost Ferrari importers and founded and ran the Ecurie Francorchamps, did not know the history of the car he had bought. But I did. When I was at university our group of enthusiasts had met regularly in the garage of a Singer importer, also an enthusiast, called Pierre Goldschmidt, where a certain Claude Bonneau also occasionally looked in. He had bought one of the last PB MGs made, and had entered it for the Paris-Nice Rally of 1937. Unfortunately he had suffered an accident with a lorry during the race and his beautiful MG, finished in British Racing Green, was destroyed. Luckily he had escaped unhurt and, undaunted, had ordered a new chassis from the factory, rebuilding the car with a light aluminium racing body. He had entered it for the 1938 Le Mans and, with Anne Itier as co-driver, one of the foremost lady drivers in France at the time, had finished 12th overall. He had entered the car again in 1939, but had to retire and, a few weeks later, in the Spa 24 Hours, had crashed spectacularly through a large advertisement panel after only a few laps.

During the war I had rediscovered the MG in Pierre Decrose's garage, where it was in danger of being spotted and driven away by some enthusiastic German officer. We had therefore decided to hide it in a friendly private garage where, from time to time, I poured some oil into the cylinders and gave the engine a few

turns. I had been tempted to buy it when the war was over, but now, with a family, I had to spend my money on less futile matters. Unfortunately, the owner, Claude Bonneau, who was French, had joined his army and had been killed. For some time the car disappeared, only to reappear in the hands of a certain Nicolaï, a garage owner, in the Brussels Grand Prix of 1947, one year before Jacques Swaters bought it.

Before our 24 hours race, very little was done to the car. The king pins were changed, the sump was dropped for inspection and cleaning, and – unfortunately – the cylinder head was lifted.

First practice was on a Thursday, and on the previous Tuesday Jacques generously lent his car to a friend to go to Louvain University where he was studying. When he came back the engine was making a terrible noise – all the bearings of the overhead camshaft had gone because some stupid mechanic had fitted the head gasket the wrong way round, and the little hole allowing the oil to reach the camshaft bearings and the valve gear was in the wrong place. Decrose had no spares for the 12-year-old car, so I took it to a friendly Kaiser-Frazer garage and worked with one of the mechanics late into the night, cutting and filing to shape a bronze tube to make new camshaft bearings. As a try-out, Jacques drove the car to Spa – at least we would not be non-starters.

The engine certainly did not run as it should, but it survived practice. On race day Jacques was very nervous and I was overjoyed when he suggested that I should take the start. At least, I thought, I would get a drive! But against all expectations, the little MG, though using a lot of oil, ran like clockwork through rain and fog and we finished the race 3rd in class behind dominant works entries from Fiat and Simca-Gordini.

Next morning, when Jacques tried to start the engine for the drive back to Brussels, it defeated all attempts, and the car had to be put on a trailer. When the engine was dismantled, hundreds of little bits were found where the piston rings should have been ... The car was then sold and all attempts to trace it have been in vain.

My next step towards serious racing was the 'Production Car Grand Prix' organised by the Royal Automobile Club of Spa, the first of which was staged in 1950. Classes were not by engine capacity, but by list price, and it was obvious that in the lowest-price class an 850cc Dyna Panhard just could not be beaten. By then I was already fairly well known as a journalist, and I went to see the manager of the Panhard import company to draw his attention to a good opportunity for publicity, adding that I would gladly drive the car. He agreed and took the matter quite seriously, a well-cared-for engine even being sent from Paris.

I had no problem winning the race, and the operation was resumed in 1951 with the same result. However, by that time I had become service manager to the Jaguar importers. Sports car enthusiasts were rushing to buy XK120s and several of them had entered their cars for the production sports car race. One such was Johnny Claes, the only Belgian driver regularly competing in Formula 1 races with his private Talbot Lago. The difference was that he had secured a works car, and that together with Grand Prix experience obviously resulted in some superiority. As I was on the spot, it was only natural that, apart from racing the Panhard, I would, in my role as service manager of the Jaguar importers, also take care of the XK owners. One of the latter, who shall remain nameless, could not accept that the best time put up by Johnny Claes was some 15 or 20 seconds quicker than his own best. He was convinced that his beautiful green Jaguar was down on performance and asked if I would mind trying his car. I certainly had no objection! 'But,' I said, 'to really find out I need three laps.'

'OK,' came the answer.

I knew the car very well and was sure it was all right, but what I really had in mind was to do a reasonably cautious first lap to find out where, with the much faster Jaguar, I would find bends that the little Panhard would just ignore. Then I would try two really fast laps to see what I could do with an XK, knowing that, on the last lap, I would have to brake before the timing strip in order not to overshoot the pit.

When I stopped, I heard the loudspeakers announce that I had done the fastest time of the day. The owner was therefore satisfied that his car was in order, while Johnny Claes did not even get another chance, as his works car had developed a gearbox problem. He nevertheless won the race, in which I was a mere spectator, on the following day.

In 1952 the main event was to be of two hours' duration for strictly production touring cars. The regulations were much tightened: stock specifications were

With this Dyna Panhard I won the small car class of the Spa Production Car Race in 1951.

ensured by the compulsory selection by a justice officer of one of each car entered from among ten identical models, following which seals were applied to prevent any dismantling while the cars were being run in. Any adjustment involving the breakage of a seal was allowed only in the presence of an official observer.

General Motors entered four Oldsmobile 88s, with Hydramatic transmission, and Chrysler entered two Saratogas with the brand-new Hemi engine. André Pisart, a former Chenard & Walcker works driver who had an Oldsmobile dealership in Brussels, was put in charge of the Oldsmobile team and immediately secured the services of Belgium's three most experienced drivers, Johnny Claes, André Pilette and Jacques Swaters, who, after his first experience with me, had bought a Veritas that he had run in several sports car events. There was a question mark over the fourth driver, and it was Jacques Ickx, Jacky's father, then a very influential journalist, who, remembering my 'pole time' in the Jaguar in 1951, suggested that I should be tried.

To cut a long story short, with a lot of luck I won the race coasting down from La Source hairpin to the finishing line with an empty tank.

Thereupon I was invited by the Royal Automobile Club of Belgium to take part in its Grand Prix – that year's Grand Prix d'Europe – if I could secure a suitable car. Remember that in 1952 and 1953 the World Championship was for 2-litre Formula 2 cars, which made the task slightly easier. In that class the British HWMs were reasonably competitive, though far behind the inaccessible Ferraris, and I knew that on some occasions the team had lent one of its cars to local

The three Oldsmobile 88s at the end of the first lap of the 1952 Spa Production Car Race. I am third here, led by André Pilette and Johnny Claes, but I eventually won the race with some help from Nemesis.

Oldsmobile team manager André Pisart with his drivers (from left): Johnny Claes, André Pilette, Paul Frère and Jacques Swaters.

drivers, for instance to Johnny Claes in 1951 when he won at Chimay. So I tried HWM.

This choice did not come entirely out of the blue. In 1948 a race had been staged in Paris's Bois de Boulogne on the occasion of the Salon de l'Auto. I was visiting the event, and went to watch the practice. It was all very informal and I had no problem in meeting John Heath and George Abecassis, the owners of H. W. Motors, who had entered an Alta for George. In practice, on Saturday morning, the Alta's timing chain broke. The chain was to British standards and to find a replacement on a Saturday afternoon was an almost impossible task, but I said, 'Give me the chain and I'll find you a spare.' The only possible sources were car and bike breakers, and I eventually found one. It was worn, but at least it allowed Abecassis to get his starting money.

Though he recalled the episode very well, John Heath's answer to my request for a car was kind, but negative. Not knowing anybody else likely to provide a car, I had given up the idea when I had a call from Heath who was in Chimay, having entered three cars for the Grand Prix des Frontières, a Belgian event of lesser status. 'As I wrote to you,' he said, 'I cannot give you a car for the Belgian Grand Prix, but if you can be in Chimay tomorrow, Saturday, at seven, I will give you a car for the race.' Needless to say, I was in Chimay next morning half an hour before the appointed time. One of the three cars was to have been driven by Peter Collins, but at the last minute he had sent a telegram informing Heath that he was to drive an Aston Martin in Monte Carlo and could not come.

There was only one practice session, and just as it began it started to rain. I was not used to the quick reactions of a Grand Prix car, and on my second lap I spun and ditched the car, damaging the tail. Heath was less than happy and kept the car in the pit to check that the tank had not been damaged. Meanwhile the rain had stopped and the roads were drying quickly. About half an hour before the end of practice, I went out again and found myself on pole!

Next day I was understandably rather nervous and made a mess of the start, having worked the pre-selector gearbox incorrectly, but progressively getting used to the car I picked up several places and finished up overtaking the leader, Ken Downing in a Connaught, at the last corner, 250 metres from the finish. John Heath was now more than happy. He immediately promised me the car I wanted for the Belgian Grand Prix at Spa, where I finished fifth, again ahead of all the other team drivers, Lance Macklin, Peter Collins and guest driver Roger Laurent.

The 500km race was run mostly in rain and I was pleased not only by my good

Driving an HWM, I finished fifth in my first World Championship event, the 1952 Belgian Grand Prix at Spa. (LAT)

performance (those ahead of me were all big names driving faster cars: Ascari and Villoresi, both in Ferraris, Manzon in a new six-cylinder Gordini, and Mike Hawthorn, who had a Cooper-Bristol), but also to be still alive. It had stopped raining and at the fast and dangerous Malmédy right-hand bend of the old circuit – where many drivers have been killed – I was trying a new line. Suddenly I lost the car and found myself proceeding at high speed completely broadside. I was expecting the worst, but the front wheels went on to the still wet grass on the inside, which was more slippery than the asphalt, so that even though the front grille just skimmed a little brick wall, the car straightened itself and proceeded unperturbed. That was probably the most dangerous situation in which I was ever to find myself during my racing career. But all's well that ends well, and for team managers I had become someone to watch.

Another race that had an important influence on my racing career was the Eifelrennen of 1953, which took place over seven laps of the Nürburgring in pouring rain. I had learned the 22.8km 'Ring and its 172 bends during the previous year, when HWM had entered me for the German Grand Prix; unfortunately, I had been forced to retire early in the race with gearbox trouble. This time the winner was the debonair Toulo de Graffenried driving a brand-new six-cylinder Maserati, who beat me by 1.7 seconds. But the highlight of the race was the wheel-to-wheel fight I had with my team-mate Peter Collins: for the whole of the seven laps we passed and repassed each other, and the show we put on did not escape the attention of Porsche team manager Huschke von Hanstein, who a few days later invited me to be part of the Porsche team in what was to be my first Le Mans.

Chapter 4

America, Mercedes and Aston Martin

BEFORE WE PROCEED with my racing years, let us make a flashback to 1947. Charles Follett, a former racer at Brooklands, mainly with Alvis and Railton cars, which he also sold in his Berkeley Square dealership in London, had added an HRG dealership to his business. The HRG company was founded in about 1936 by Ted Halford, Guy Robbins and Henry Ronald Godfrey, the 'G' of the GN make from which the chain-driven Frazer Nash evolved. In turn, the HRG was a later evolution of the GN, and was to all intents and purposes a Frazer Nash with a conventional gearbox and shaft drive instead of the multiple chains that the Frazer Nash had inherited from the GN. Though it was originally powered by a Meadows pushrod 1,500cc engine, performance was very good for the capacity, thanks to its light weight, the body being a typical aluminium-panelled British two-seater. A 0–60mph acceleration figure of around 18 seconds was good at the time and the car was very successful in English-type trials. One even finished at Le Mans in 1937 and 1939. I was quite impressed with its performance, its simplicity and its stark looks.

After the war the Meadows engine was no longer available and was replaced by a tuned single-ohc Singer engine of the same capacity, soon followed by an 1,100cc model. At the same time, the 'Aerodynamic' HRG was added, featuring an all-enveloping streamlined aluminium body that added weight and was not really suited to the harshly sprung, rather whippy chassis, though most people found it good-looking.

Somehow, I got in contact with Charles Follett, a bespectacled, rather big man with a good sense of humour and a lot of enthusiasm, and in 1947 he gave me the chance to accompany him in an 'Aerodynamic' to the Geneva Motor Show. The make was not present in the show, but he wanted to contact some possible dealers in the country. On a rainy day, early in March 1947, he picked me up in Brussels and gave me the wheel. I remember overtaking a funeral car in Overïjse, perhaps 12 miles from Brussels, and saying to Charles, 'Now, if something happens, we will quickly be taken care of.' Some 15 miles later the HRG lay in a field, upside down, me with my face in the earth, Charles rather worse off with lots of bruises.

Before Namur, the wet cobbled road surface wound its way nicely through the country and I enjoyed sliding the car around until a slightly tighter bend came up. We hit the small roadside ditch broadside on and the car just flipped over. We were taken to hospital in Namur where Charles remained under observation for a few days while I washed my face, now 'embellished' with hundreds of very superficial little cuts from stones embedded in the field in which we had landed. I then took a train to Geneva, my face causing no little curiosity among the train's passengers and people I met at the show.

The HRG was not too badly damaged, and was soon repaired. A few weeks later Charles entrusted me with the car again to drive to Switzerland in order at last to show the car to potential dealers, but this time, for his peace of mind, he went with his wife in a Bentley!

My parents had always been less than enthusiastic about my determination to make a career with cars, but they finally realised that there was little they could do about it. So one day my father said to me, 'If that is really what you want, you should go to America and see how they do it.' And to make this possible, he put some money at my disposal that would allow me to spend seven weeks in the United States.

Early in May 1949 I therefore crossed the Atlantic on a merchant ship on which I happened to be the only passenger, holding a letter of introduction given to me by Albert Dewandre, the inventor of the vacuum servo, who was a friend of my father and who well understood my ambitions. Another great help was Floyd Clymer, an enthusiastic American motoring writer, former motor cycle racer and also publisher of the Indianapolis 500 Yearbook. He had known me when I worked for the Kaiser-Frazer importers, whom he had contacted when preparing a book on touring in Europe. He had asked to borrow a car for himself

The Aerodynamic HRG that I crashed, with Charles Follett as passenger, en route to the Geneva Motor Show of 1947. A few months later he was brave enough to enlist me again as chauffeur for a trip to Switzerland, but this time he elected to follow me with his Bentley!

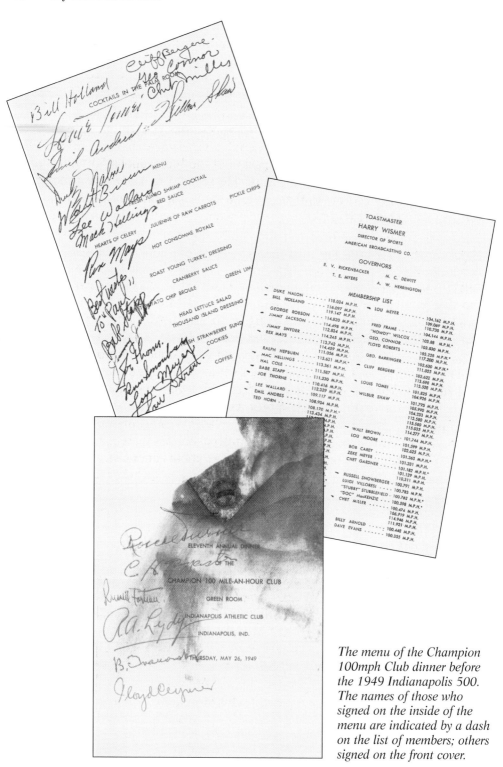

The menu of the Champion 100mph Club dinner before the 1949 Indianapolis 500. The names of those who signed on the inside of the menu are indicated by a dash on the list of members; others signed on the front cover.

and his wife, with someone who could show him around Belgium and Holland in a two-day marathon. I had been delegated for this difficult task and I still don't know how, in two days, he could have formed an opinion of two countries having such long histories and having produced so many famous artists. We stopped in the best possible restaurants where his orders for a steak with ketchup and Coca-Cola or a cup of tea produced the most incredulous looks from the *maître d'hôtel*.

But he was a most charming person who, when I came to the States, was a great help in directing me to the right people in the factories I visited. His help was particularly appreciated on the occasion of the Indianapolis 500 Miles race, which I attended at the end of my stay. He seemed to know everybody who mattered and introduced me to them as a 'great European journalist and racing driver'; the latter title I had earned from my drive with the MG! He got me the very top VIP passes for qualifying and the race, which was won by Bill Holland driving an Offenhauser-engined, front-wheel-drive 'Blue Flame Special'. He also took me as his guest to the dinner of the '100 MPH Club', to which were admitted only those drivers who finished the 500 Miles at over 100mph, still an impressive average in those days, and introduced me to many of the race's heroes. Another highlight was a meeting he arranged with one of my boyhood idols, Boris Ivanovski, who had won the Spa 24 Hours race in 1928 driving a supercharged 1,500cc Alfa-Romeo, co-driving with Attilio Marinoni.

In his younger years, Clymer had done a lot of motor cycle racing and, when I landed in New York, I found a letter from him with an introduction to the managing director of the Indian motor cycle company in Springfield, Mass. Since during my stay I was to visit many places – Washington DC, Detroit, Chicago, South Bend (Indiana), where Studebaker cars were made, and finally Indianapolis – I thought I would learn a lot more about America travelling by bike than by train, and it would also be cheaper than hiring or buying a car.

The first thing to do was to get an American driving license, valid for cars and bikes. On presentation of my International Driving Licence, I just had to fill in a questionnaire. I will always remember one of the questions: 'What must you do when preparing to turn left? a) Put you arm out of the window and hold it vertically. b) … hold it horizontally. c) Open the left door.'

After getting the licence I took a train to Springfield where Indian had recently launched two new models that were complete departures from the typical large-capacity American bikes. Except for the fact that they had the brake pedal on the right and the gear selector on the left, as is the case in cars and all today's motor cycles, they could have been taken for British bikes of the period. The models were a 220cc single and a 440cc vertical twin, the latter with a plunger rear suspension. Both were pushrod-operated ohv with an aluminium cylinder block and head.

I bought a 220cc demonstrator, and rather late in the afternoon headed back to New York, some 150 miles away, only to be plagued by a short that left me without lights on the darkest of all nights. Fortunately I found the cause of the problem. On the following day, a Sunday, a rear wheel bearing gave up the ghost and had to be replaced, so I lost a lot of time, and confidence. Finally, however, the little bike behaved quite well and in the six weeks of my ownership covered more than 3,000 miles, 500 of them in a single day.

Whether that first visit to the United States really served me in my later activities I am not sure, but it certainly taught me that it was another world, and what perhaps impressed me most was the Americans' hospitality. For example, the man who repaired my bike when the rear wheel bearing broke, and did so on a Sunday, invited me to his home to share his lunch. Many of the people I met in the factories also invited me to their homes, to share meals with their families and even to stay overnight. This experience was repeated on my next trip, eight years later, when after driving a Dauphine in the Sebring 12 Hours race for the factory, I borrowed a standard Dauphine to drive from Florida via New Orleans, Las Vegas and Arizona to Los Angeles, up to San Francisco and back to the East Coast across the deserts and past the Great Salt Lake, a long trip that was not without its problems with the car.

If, from 1952 onwards, I could devote more time to racing and, in winter, to motor cycle trials, it was because I had become much more free to organise my own time. After nearly two years as service manager with the Jaguar importers, I resigned to become joint editor, with Jacky Ickx's father Jacques, of *Royal Auto*, the official publication of the Royal Automobile Club of Belgium. This provided me with a fixed income independent of the industry and left me free to write for any other publication as long as it was not in direct competition with *Royal Auto*. In any event, it was not ethical to have journalistic activities while being associated with the industry, not to mention the lack of time to do everything properly.

Working for Jaguar had nevertheless been very interesting and useful. Before I started I had to spend about two weeks in the factory, still in Swallow Road, Coventry, to be made fully conversant with all the details of the cars' construction and with the most important service operations. I also learned how a big garage was run, how the spare parts stock should be kept and – most important for my future career – I was in close contact with the factory's service manager, who was none other than 'Lofty' England, who had just had motorsport added to his responsibilities.

Jacques Ickx is certainly one person who was a great help at the beginning of my career, both as a journalist and a racing driver. Just before the war he had been a Belgian Motocross Champion and had turned to cars to become one of the most respected and influential motoring journalists in Europe. Not only were his judgements usually spot-on, he also had a talent for turning rather indifferent events into fascinating reading. His book *Ainsi Naquit l'Automobile* ('This is how the automobile was born') may be partial, but it is nevertheless – perhaps because of that partiality – a masterwork. Once you start reading it, you can't stop.

Jacques had a great respect for my driving ability and, as I have related before, had been largely responsible for getting me a drive in the Oldsmobile at Spa in 1952. He also had respect for my technical knowledge and introduced me to several important personalities in the industry, such as Dr Giovanni Pestelli, Fiat's Public Relations Manager and his incredibly efficient and likeable secretary, Maria Rubiolo; to Daimler-Benz Managing Director Dr Könecke and his brilliant PR Manager, Gerhard Naumann; and also to Daimler-Benz Development Chief Rudi Uhlenhaut. Uhlenhaut will be remembered as the leading force in the development of Mercedes-Benz racing cars from 1937 up to the W195 of 1954–55. He was an invaluable asset to the Mercedes team as he was able to drive the racing cars as fast as the best drivers in the team and could thus get first-hand information about their behaviour.

I remember a cold evening in the winter of 1951–52, when Jacques and I were in Stuttgart and were supposed to have dinner with Uhlenhaut. At the last minute he had to cancel, but sent his colleague Kostaletzki to spend the evening with us. We talked a lot, not about racing cars as nothing had transpired about Mercedes's plans, then at the end of the dinner, much to our surprise, Kostaletzki took us in the dark, cold night to the factory, which had only just recovered from its wartime damage. In the greatest secrecy he took us to the experimental department, and there was a scantily bodied sports car built around mechanical components of the newly launched Mercedes 300: the prototype of the 300SL! He started it, took it out and drove first Jacques and then me as fast as he could (and he was no mean driver) around the factory blocks. It was just fantastic and highly impressive. Had it been today, Kostaletzki would have been fired the following morning, but those were other times!

Less than five months later, a 300SL, crewed by Karl Kling and Hans Klenk,

This Mercedes-Benz 300SL, with which Karl Kling finished second in the 1952 Mille Miglia, was one of two cars used by Mercedes at the Nürburgring for the 1953 drivers' test in which I successfully took part.

took second place in the Mille Miglia, and thereafter 300SLs finished first and second at Le Mans, Lang and Riess being the winners.

After the race I asked Uhlenhaut if he would entrust me with one of the race cars for an hour or two on the Monday to drive on the road. He immediately agreed and let me have the Kling-Klenk car, which had retired with some electrical problem that meanwhile had been fixed. It was a wonderful experience and I was most impressed with the accurate steering and the car's performance, which was better than I had ever experienced, except with the HWM single-seater. I even timed the 0–100mph acceleration, which was achieved in about 16 seconds, about the same as the heavier but more powerful production 300SL three years later.

The following year I had another chance to drive racing SLs (not to be confused with the later straight-eight W196 300SLR), which were narrower than the production model and had their slanted six-cylinder engine slightly offset to the right. This was when Daimler-Benz decided to return to racing in a big way, in Formula 1 with the W196 single-seater and in sports car racing with the very similar 300SLR.

For the long-distance sports car races Neubauer, Mercedes's famous team manager, needed more drivers and I was among the four who were tested at the Nürburgring. I later learned that in this case, too, not only Jacques Ickx but also Arthur Keser, Mercedes-Benz's legendary Public Relations Manager, who had succeeded Gerhard Naumann, had been at work. The other drivers were Hans Herrmann, Hans Klenk and Günther Bechem, who had been racing for Borgward. Two 300SLs were at hand, a gullwing coupé and a shorter-wheelbase open model. Each driver was first given three practice laps with one of the cars. Fortunately we were all on equal terms, each of us knowing the 'Ring perfectly. This was very important as it would have been impossible to learn the 22.8km course in the short time available. After this we drove the two cars in turn, several times, for three flying laps, each of them being timed.

After the lunch break the tests were resumed, and Klenk started first in the open model, followed after a 3-minute interval by Bechem in the coupé. When it became obvious that first Klenk, then also Bechem, were overdue, officials reported that Klenk had had an accident in the Aremberg bend leading into the 'Fuchsröhre'. Coming up to the 45–50mph bend at well over 100mph, he had found the brake pedal completely inoperative and the car finished upside down in the ditch. Poor Klenk had a badly fractured leg and would never race again.

Neubauer adjourned the test to the following day, when the three remaining drivers took several turns of three laps in the closed car. The final issue lay between Hans Herrmann and myself. I had been the faster in the open car, and now, with the closed car, we took a few seconds off our previous time on each lap. From the beginning of the tests there had never been more than a few seconds between us; no sooner had Hans achieved a best time than I beat it by a second or two, only to be beaten again by him. On my last set of three laps, I had again been improving and I was determined that the last lap would be my absolute best. But going into that last lap, due to lack of concentration I braked too early going into the first bend after the back straight behind the pits and I was so upset that I forgot to change up going into the Hatzenbach section – again, I had lost time. For the rest of the lap I took all risks, but once time is lost, it remains lost, and no *tour de force* can make up for it. I knew I had lost about 2 seconds and that was it. The stopwatch said 10min 51sec, the absolute best time of the test session. But Herrmann still had his three laps to do, and I knew that he was out to beat me; if he made no mistake, he would succeed. And he did, returning 10min 47sec.

Following this, I was invited to be part of the Mercedes-Benz team at Le Mans in 1954. About six weeks before the race, however, I got a letter from Neubauer saying that the cars would not be ready in time, and that I was freed from any engagement with his company. I immediately called John Wyer, whom I knew from previous encounters, as when he had managed St John Horsfall's pit at Spa in 1949, and he agreed to take me into his Aston Martin team to join forces with Carroll Shelby. We eventually retired, but apparently John Wyer had been pleased with my performance and said that he would like me to drive for him again at Le Mans the following year. But I still had Mercedes-Benz in mind. They had performed impressively right from the start of their involvement in Formula 1 in 1954, and the 300SLR was based on the same design. I therefore hoped that Neubauer would repeat his invitation in 1955, but when it came, at the end of October, I had visited the London Motor Show where John Wyer had repeated his offer, and, not having had news from Neubauer, I had signed up to drive for Aston Martin again. So I never raced for Mercedes-Benz.

The outcome was that my seat was offered to Pierre Levegh, who was killed in the race together with 88 other people in the worst racing accident of all time. Had I accepted Neubauer's offer, the accident would almost certainly not have happened, as it is most unlikely that I would have been exactly where Levegh was at exactly the same split second.

I have never regretted driving Astons at Le Mans. John certainly knew how to get things done and left nothing to chance. He could be quite sharp if someone under his control – driver or mechanic – did something wrong, but he was a very kind, intelligent and understanding person, and the atmosphere throughout the whole team was very friendly. The Aston headquarters were at the Hotel de France in La Chartre-sur-le-Loir, some 20 miles from busy Le Mans, a nice quiet place where excellent food was served.

Before Le Mans we went to the Mille Miglia where I drove a DB2/4, but unfortunately retired, then John sent a DB3S for me to drive in the Spa sports car race, which I won. At Le Mans, Peter Collins and I finished second in a disc-braked DB3S (the famous EMU 62), to the great joy of John Wyer and team owner David Brown, a result I repeated in 1959 with Maurice Trintignant in a DBR1, making it a 1–2 finish with Roy Salvadori and Carroll Shelby's identical car.

Chapter 5

The Mille Miglia and the British connection

WHEN MY FATHER was a student he spent a few weeks in Heidelberg to improve his German, and there he met an Italian student from Brescia following the same course. It started a friendship that continued into the next generation on both sides, and provided a good excuse to spend the occasional holiday in Brescia, and at the same time attend the Mille Miglia. I attended two before the war, in 1935 and 1936.

When I became a journalist after the war, I met Count Johnny Lurani whom I had known by name thanks to his racing exploits. He had founded a very popular magazine called *Auto Italiana* and, while still racing, also worked as a journalist. On one occasion, probably at the Geneva Motor Show of 1953, he suggested that I should take part in the Mille Miglia, for which I should try to get hold of a Jaguar Mk VII. 'You would be almost sure to win the big touring car class,' he said.

The Mille Miglia was the last of the big road races that had marked the beginning of car racing in Europe. It did not date back to the beginning of the century, however, but was unique of its kind when it was created in 1927 by three enthusiastic men: Count Aymo Maggi, at the time a successful gentleman racing driver who lived in a castle in Calino, near Brescia, and was quite influential in the area; Giovanni Canestrini, the most respected Italian motoring journalist of the period; and Franco Mazzotti, President of the Automobile Club di Brescia.

From the beginning the race ran from Brescia to Rome and back over public roads, many of which, in the early days, were still unmetalled, for a total of 1,000 miles (hence the title 'mille miglia'). The course varied slightly from year to year, but usually led from Brescia to the Adriatic coast and south to Pescara, from where it proceeded to Rome across the Abruzzo Mountains and north again to Florence, over the Apennines to Bologna and the north Italian plain back to Brescia.

Technically the roads were not closed to traffic, and in the 1950s, when I took part, the regulations still drew attention to the fact that 'the race takes place on public roads and the rules of the Highway Code must be followed'. In practice, the police were everywhere to stop all traffic in the direction opposite to the race, and only urgent traffic, such as doctors, ambulances and fire engines, was allowed to proceed carefully in the direction of the race if absolutely necessary.

The maiden race of 1927 was won by Rosa and Morandi, driving an OM made in Brescia, which made the race hugely popular in its home town. It was later dominated by Alfa Romeo up to the war, with a single interruption in 1931 when Rudolf Caracciola managed to beat the agile Alfas with his big supercharged 7-litre Mercedes-Benz SSK – a truly heroic drive. After this interlude the intense rivalry between Nuvolari and Varzi brought the country to its feet and the Mille Miglia weekend became a sort of national holiday, drawing all Italy along the 1,600km of the course. Even far from towns and villages people lined the roads, urging the competitors on, while in the towns through which the cars raced at unabated speed, the thickly packed streets hardly left room for the competitors to get through. It was all absolutely incredible.

Back in 1953, when Lurani encouraged me to take part in the legendary race, I still had to find a suitable car, preferably, as he had suggested, a Jaguar, which was undoubtedly the best car for the job. So I immediately wrote to 'Lofty' England, whom I knew well and who, in addition to being the company's service

André Milhoux and myself about to leave Brussels to participate in the 1953 Mille Miglia. Spare wheels on the roof rack were left on the practice lap in a garage near Rome to allow a quick tyre change at half distance in the race.

manager, had become responsible for motorsport. I asked him if he would make a Mk VII available for the Mille Miglia, but he was not interested. I then remembered that in the Spa Production Car Race of 1952, which I had won with an Oldsmobile 88, the Chrysler Saratoga had been the fastest car, but had been eliminated by a wheel failure. I therefore went to see Jo Beherman, the leading Chrysler dealer in Belgium at the time, and he immediately agreed to lend me a car. I opted for the 1952 model, because it was devoid of the latest model's power steering, which I found too vague. The result was that I not only won the class (Touring Cars over 2,000cc), but also beat a privately owned Jaguar Mk VII into second place by 2½ hours, which made me twice as happy as winning the class! Many years later the driver of the Jaguar became the publisher of the car magazine *AM* to which I used to contribute. So he had clearly forgiven me!

The Chrysler was virtually standard and put its 180 SAE gross horsepower down through the standard 'Torqueflite' semi-automatic three-speed transmission. The only preparation was to adjust the intake manifold to avoid steps where it met the cylinder head, to put a washer under the valve springs to be sure of avoiding bounce, and to remove the fan and one of the exhaust silencers – which we later found to be forbidden, but fortunately nobody noticed. I had driven the complete course only once before the race, with my navigator, André Milhoux, who later also enjoyed a short racing career after having been a motocross champion. He was to take a few notes, which he would read to me during the race.

Up to Rome we also carried four wheels and tyres, and left them in a garage on the Via Cassia, just beyond the city, which my brother had recommended. At the time he was with the Belgian Embassy in Rome and was to be in charge of a quick change of the four wheels before the gruelling mountain section leading through Viterbo, Siena and Florence to Bologna. In the event the plan worked beautifully: the pit stop, which included the wheel change and filling up with oil and water, took only 4 minutes and my brother remembers vividly burning his fingers on the almost red-hot wheel bolts!

Before departure from Belgium new brake linings were fitted and treated with an anti-fade compound, but novice that I still was, I did not realise that the linings of the poor American brakes would need changing after the practice lap. The result was that in the race itself, just after our self-organised 'pit stop', we found ourselves without brake linings. Braking was therefore steel-on-steel, and for the last 400 miles I could hardly use the brakes at all – and that was with the stiffest mountain stretch ahead of us. But we still managed, making the best of the car's understeering attitude to deliberately scrub off speed by winding on a lot of lock when going into corners.

Before the race, Mille Miglia competitors received a sticker reading 'Concorrente in Prova' ('competitor practising'), and cars with the sticker were usually treated kindly and with a certain respect by police out on the race route and were, of course, always a centre of public interest.

Despite losing its brakes, the big Chrysler finished the 1953 Mille Miglia in first place in the Touring Car Class over 2000cc.

Inevitably the race route included a number of railway crossings, and if there was a country where the gates remained closed longer than necessary, it was Italy. It was as if it were a deliberate move by the Italian State Railways to discourage travellers from using cars and other forms of road transport. Even the sticker 'Concorrente in Prova' did not help. On race day however, things changed; not only did the gates close later and open sooner after a train had passed, but in most cases there was also some enthusiastic person ready to open the gates just enough to let a car through if circumstances allowed.

In the course of the practice tour, somewhere between Viterbo and Siena, we had to stop at a railway crossing, and just ahead of us a C-type Jaguar, also practising for the race, was already waiting. Its two occupants each wore a helmet and, showing under one of them, I spotted some long, fair hair.

'Look, that's a girl there in the passenger seat,' I said to André.

I never thought that that girl would subsequently become a very important person in my life: 11 years later, Suzanne became my wife. That is why if someone asks me where I first met her, the answer is invariably, 'At a level crossing!', though in fact all I saw of her on that occasion was her helmet and some hair. I would later see a little more of her thanks to our friend Gilberte Thirion.

My next Mille Miglia was in 1955 when, being part of the Aston Martin team,

I was supposed to counter the works 300SL team with a DB2/4 in the big GT class – a hopeless task. With famous photographer Louis Klemantaski in the passenger seat, we retired in Ascona – less than 220 miles from Brescia – when the bonded clutch linings simply spun off the disc, but by that time a broken exhaust pipe had already put paid to our chances of finishing in any worthwhile position.

In 1956 I had two offers: Mercedes-Benz team manager Neubauer offered to take me into his team of 300SLs, and François Landon, the Renault sports chief, offered me a Dauphine 850cc saloon. I chose the Dauphine. In the previous year I had had a serious accident driving a Ferrari Monza in practice for the Swedish Grand Prix in Kristianstad, which, that year, was for sports cars, and I was not in an optimistic frame of mind. Racing a very fast car on almost unknown roads simply frightened me. I also had a contract to race for Jaguar in 1956; I thought that 'Lofty' would not be inclined to let me drive for the 'dreaded enemy', and it seemed more diplomatic not to ask to be released for the occasion.

So I finally drove a five-speed Dauphine, which was quite quick for such a little car; however, it retained its disastrous standard rear suspension with the result that I rolled it and ended up in a field. The car was not hopelessly damaged, though the front wheels toed slightly out; it was put back on to the road with the help of spectators and went on to finish the race. A passenger was no longer compulsory, so to save weight (important with less than 60bhp on tap), I had decided to go alone. Gilberte Thirion, the Belgian girl driver, then at the top of

Left *Practising for the 1955 Mille Miglia with a works Aston Martin DB2 similar to the car I drove in the race.*

Right *The five-speed works Renault Dauphines prepared for the 1957 Mille Miglia handled beautifully, in complete contrast to the 1956 cars. Here I am driving down the Raticosa pass towards Bologna.*

her form, had done the same and drove brilliantly to win the class, ahead of such famous Grand Prix drivers as Rosier (who also drove alone) and Trintignant.

In 1957, in the last of the 'real' Mille Miglia events, I again drove a Dauphine. The cars were now enormously improved and handled perfectly. They were great fun in the mountains, and so good that on the famous 60-mile stretch from Florence to Bologna over the Futa and Raticosa passes in the Apennines, I was 15 seconds faster than the fastest Porsche Carrera driven by the reputable Paul-Ernst Strähle. A slipping clutch caused by too tight an operating cable, which I had to adjust on the roadside, cost me victory in the 1,000cc class in which Touring and GT cars were mixed; after 1,000 miles of driving I was beaten into second place by a margin of only 3 seconds by a DB-Panhard two-seater coupé. That was the narrowest margin by which a class win was missed in the entire history of the Mille Miglia. But my race average with the 850cc Renault had been faster than with the 5.3-litre Chrysler in 1953.

Unfortunately, this was the race in which, due to a tyre blow-out, Alfonso de Portago's Ferrari crashed into the crowds lining the road near the village of Guidizzolo, only about 30 miles from the finish, killing 11 people, including the driver and his American navigator Ed Nelson. People had been killed in earlier Mille Miglia events, but this was the last straw and the race was banned by the Italian Government. Such an event would be unthinkable today, anyway.

For the winner, Piero Taruffi, it had been the last chance. A graduate mechanical engineer, he was a superb all-rounder. After a distinguished career

on motor cycles during which he also became a world speed record holder, later breaking international car records driving twin-fuselage cars of his own design, he had switched to cars, successfully driving for Bugatti, Alfa Romeo, Maserati, Cisitalia, Osca, Lancia and Ferrari in innumerable grands prix and sports car races. He was even invited to drive a Mercedes W196 in the Italian Grand Prix of 1955 on the Monza circuit, finishing second. But his speciality was real road races like the Mille Miglia, the Targa Florio, the Tour of Sicily and some lesser ones – when it came to improvisation on unknown roads, or at least those that could never be learned like a shorter grand prix circuit, he had no peer, except perhaps Olivier Gendebien.

Taruffi had driven in all Mille Miglia events since 1933 and had been in the lead in many of them, but fate had always intervened – always in the shape of mechanical problems – until in 1957, when at last he returned to Brescia victorious. At 50, Ferrari had again entrusted him with one of his cars, an open 4.1-litre V12, and he had done it, just beating 'Taffy' von Trips in a similar but 3.8-litre-engined car. This victory crowned a magnificent career. In later years, Piero became a personal friend and worked both as a journalist and as a consultant to the industry.

As related earlier, the British magazines *The Motor*, *The Autocar*, *Automobile Engineer* and *Motor Sport* had had a considerable influence on my taste for cars, and when I paid visits to the London Motor Show at Earls Court I met such important journalists as Laurence Pomeroy Jr, his colleague Joe Lowrey, Tommy Wisdom, 'Bunny' Tubbs, Dudley Noble (a founder of the Guild of Motoring Writers) and others, as well as industry people such as Roger Cra'ster of Rolls-Royce, who became a dear personal friend, Peter Wilks, Spen King, the gas turbine expert, and George Mackie, all of Rover, who together built the Rover Special single-seater that they drove in hill-climbs and sprint events, and together also built the short-lived but interesting Rover-based Marauder sports car.

In those days the staff of *The Motor* and *The Autocar* usually came to Belgium when they tried out fast cars and made all the performance tests on the so-called 'Jabbeke' motorway that later linked Ostend to Brussels, but at the time finished before Aalter, north-west of Ghent, and carried very little traffic. It was on this stretch, in this instance closed to normal traffic, that Col Goldie Gardner set up several speed records with a pre-war streamlined MG Magnette, and also with the same car fitted with a 2-litre Jaguar XK100 engine, the still-born unit originally intended to power a cheaper version of the XK120, which had been dropped.

The Motor's test crew usually consisted of its Technical Editor, Laurence Pomeroy Jr, the no longer so young son of the designer of the pre-First World War Prince Henry Vauxhall, of which he kept an immaculate example, and Joe Lowrey, a younger staff member who ran an HRG as his personal car. On some occasions the immensely witty 'Bunny' Tubbs also came along. Now and again they invited me to join them, and usually invited me to drive the test car to

Brussels where they stayed overnight. I remember being very impressed with a Bristol 400 that I drove back to Brussels, and an Aston Martin DB2 in which Pomeroy picked me up at my home.

Pomeroy was a strange personality, rather short, with little hair and a stiff leg. He always wore a waistcoat with golden motifs and usually a monocle. Visually he was a figure out of the past, but with an up-to-the-minute intellect. He was a very kind person, loyal to his friends and probably the best engineer among the journalists. He was also highly respected and influential, thanks to his clear judgements and his engineering background. Before switching to technical journalism, he had worked on superchargers with Jack McEvoy and was an expert on the subject. He was most interested in racing cars and his book *The Grand Prix Car* is a classic dealing with racing car technology and performance from the beginning of the century to the Second World War. I learned a lot from him and his writings.

In connection with the London Motor Show, the Goodwood Test Day, organised by the Guild of Motoring Writers, provided occasions not only to sample most of the latest British models, but also to meet many leading personalities from the industry. It was on these occasions that I met Bill (later Sir William) Lyons and Walter Hassan of pre-war Bentley fame, who contributed to the development of the Jaguar XK120 and later designed Jaguar's V12 engine with Harry Mundy. Other well-known personalities I met included Jaguar test driver Norman Dewis, Sydney Allard, Peter Morgan, Alec Issigonis (father of the Mini) and John Gordon.

There was a magnificently friendly atmosphere about those test days and they were also great fun. On one occasion Jaguar even brought a D-type along! The event provided a good occasion to compare cars of different makes and also to drive models we would never have had a chance of sampling on the Continent.

Of the cars I drove during the test days on the Goodwood circuit, a few stand out for their performance or exceptional handling. One was the original, Sampietro-designed Healey, the first real post-war high-performance British car, powered by a 2.5-litre four-cylinder Riley engine. Of course in those days 'very high performance' meant 100mph and a 0–60mph acceleration of 11–12 seconds, figures that even today's not-so-fast hatchbacks easily beat. Then, of course, there was the Jaguar XK120. Steering and handling were only so-so (today you would rank them as 'terrible'), but performance was just fabulous for the time, and not only did I enjoy it myself on the track, but I also enjoyed it no less as Wally Hassan's passenger on the way back to London.

I also remember being very impressed with the handling of the original Lotus Elite. Its monocoque fibreglass body – the very first of its kind – may have had its weaknesses, but the car's light weight combined with a clever and well-sorted suspension and hair-sharp rack-and-pinion steering made it an incredibly agile little car with an astonishing performance. In later years the original Elan, built around a steel backbone chassis, was just as impressive and far more reliable.

Another impressive car was the Gordon, built by John Gordon, later produced for a few years as the Gordon-Keeble. This was one of the Euro-American GT cars powered by a big American V8 (in this case from the Corvette), in the same vein as the Jensen Interceptor, the Italian Iso-Rivolta, the French Facel Vega and the Swiss Monteverdi, which were among the finest luxury GTs of their time. Not only did the Gordon perform in an impressive manner, but its handling also matched its performance.

Others impressed for different, and not always so positive, reasons. The Rolls-Royces of the 1950s, in which I was usually taken to Goodwood as a passenger, were the epitome of comfort and silence, but once on the track they were a complete disaster, assuming quite frightening roll and slip angles as soon as they were driven round bends at anything more than speeds of which my grandmother would have approved.

Most of the British touring cars of the early 1950s were designed to understeer strongly, in my opinion excessively. Examples were the Standard Vanguard, the first British mass-produced saloon of post-war design, and the Rover P4. They both wallowed their way through the bends of the circuit, and even Mk V and VII Jaguars were not quite immune to this fault. The best handling British cars of the period were the aforementioned Lotus, the Aston Martin DB2 and the Bristol 400 and later 401. The Bristols were virtually rebodied pre-war BMW 326s with a rigid rear axle controlled by longitudinal torsion bars, but the 326's conventional 50bhp, 1,971cc pushrod ohv engine was replaced with the hemispherical-head engine of the same capacity from the pre-war BMW 328 sports car, further developed to produce 100bhp.

There were other, less brilliant exceptions to grossly understeering cars: the interesting Triumph Herald, for instance, and the models derived from it, the Spitfire, the six-cylinder Vitesse and the GT6 coupé, looking like a diminutive E-type Jaguar. All had a steel backbone chassis and rear swing axles. They were very practical cars to work on, as opening the bonnet also lifted the front wheel arches, revealing the entire front suspension, steering and brakes in addition to the engine. At a later stage, the oversteer induced by the swing axles was much reduced by pivoting the transverse leaf spring at its centre, a modification implemented by a Cooper racing engineer, the South African Derek White.

Not all British manufacturers sent cars to Goodwood. Some, like Alvis, thought that a race track was not the right place to judge a road car, an opinion I tend to share. But some were very courageous, such as Jensen who, in the early 1960s, sent an FF, probably one of the two built at that time. A development of the Chrysler V8-engined Interceptor, the FF not only had permanent four-wheel drive by means of a clever Ferguson differential, splitting the front/rear torque about one-third/two-thirds, long before others had anything similar, but also had anti-lock brakes all-round, using the purely mechanical Dunlop Maxaret system, originally developed for aircraft.

This car gave me the biggest fright I had during the course of all the test days at Goodwood. I took this pretty fast car out on the circuit and when I braked for the chicane, at the end of the long Lavant straight, I thought I would never make it! In fact I did – just – but had been frightened stiff as the system not only effectively prevented the wheels from locking, but also from braking properly!

Many years later Ford also offered a purely mechanical ABS on the Escort, as a cheaper alternative to an electronic system, which proved just as disastrous. I had such a car on test for a regular series I did for a German TV network, and to make my point we rented a similar Escort, but without anti-lock brakes, from Hertz. We ran the two cars parallel at 75mph, myself driving the rented car and a professional driver at the wheel of the ABS car. At a given point I braked as well as I could, without locking the wheels, while the driver of the ABS car pushed the pedal as hard as he could. We did it several times with the TV cameras as witnesses. The result was that the car with the mechanical ABS needed about *17 metres* more to stop than the car without the device!

Needless to say, Ford was not very pleased when the test appeared on millions of TV screens, and it was not long before the mechanical ABS disappeared from the options list.

Chapter 6

Early cars owned and tested

EVEN BEFORE I became a full-time journalist, I began road testing for *Belgique Automobile*, the first magazine I worked for, immediately after the war. As at that time I was still working for the Jaguar importers, my test cars were necessarily confined to those of a different class.

A real eye-opener was the Peugeot 203, a nicely shaped four-door fastback. Its 1,300cc engine had pushrod-operated valves in hemispherical combustion chambers. Front suspension was independent by a transverse leaf spring and upper wishbones, rear by coil springs with a rigid axle, a torque tube and a Panhard rod. The body was monocoque, the rack-and-pinion steering was beautifully responsive and, in contrast to most contemporary cars, the then fashionable steering column gear-shift lever worked the four-speed box, of which fourth was an overdrive, with commendable precision.

Compared with this car, my 1939 SS-Jaguar, powerful and elegant as it was, seemed rather anachronistic with its rigid axles, cart springs, mechanical brakes, insufficient suspension travel, sloppy steering and fairly high weight, and I began to think of something more modern and agile. This came in 1953 in the form of a 103 series Fiat 1100, a complete departure from the previous 1100 model, of which it retained only the appropriately modernised power train incorporated into an entirely new compact four-door monocoque body. For its time it was quite lively, had a maximum speed of 120kmh (75mph) and was quite economical with fuel. This was the first car I bought new and I really enjoyed it, even though it understeered too much. Its worm-and-wheel steering was not as accurate as that of the Peugeot, but it was nevertheless a nice and enjoyable little car with very good braking by linered and finned aluminium drums.

Only a few months later Fiat announced the 1100 TV (Turismo Veloce), a faster and more lavishly equipped version of the 1100, with power raised from 36 to 50bhp thanks to a twin-choke carburettor, a higher compression ratio and probably a different camshaft. However, I had no regrets as the TV was considerably more expensive than the standard model, but I decided to modify my car's engine to go at least half way toward the TV's performance.

My Fiat 1100 during a reconnaissance tour for the 1954 Mille Miglia with Gilberte Thirion and Nadège Ferrier, at the time two of the fastest lady drivers. In the race Gilberte drove her 1100cc Gordini to 55th place overall.

After carefully consulting the spare parts catalogues of the two models, I skimmed 2.4mm off the cylinder head to raise the compression ratio from 6.7 to 7.6 (as on the TV). A 1mm washer was put under each rocker shaft support to retain a correct angle between rocker and valve stem, and 1mm washers were put under the valve springs to increase their force by 4kg. Finally the intake manifold was carefully adjusted to avoid any step with the ports, and the 32mm single-choke Solex carburettor was exchanged for a similar one, but with an accelerator pump.

Many stopwatch tests followed to achieve the best combination between the choke size and the various jets, and the results were pretty convincing as the following two-way figures indicate:

	Standard 1100	*Modified 1100*	*1100 TC*
Max speed (kmh)	120.5	131.0	133.5
0–100kmh (seconds)	28.5	22.3	21.0
80–100kmh in fourth gear (seconds)	31.5	17.3	19.5
0–400m (seconds)	22.8	21.2	20.9
0–1,000m (seconds)	–	42.0	–

I was very pleased with the results, but I had taken a risk: the TV model had lead bronze bearings that could not be fitted to my car because they required a hardened crankshaft. Some 15,000km later, after a long journey flat out on a German autobahn, a slight but ominous knock and low oil pressure indicated that the newly found power was more than the big end bearings could take. Fortunately a repair was quickly carried out in a Fiat garage before the crankshaft was damaged, but of necessity still with white metal bearings.

This happened when my wife and I were on the way to Kristianstad where I was to drive the Equipe Nationale Belge's Ferrari Monza in the Swedish Grand Prix, which, in 1955, was for sports cars. Being contracted to Aston Martin, I had been released by John Wyer for the occasion, as Astons had not entered; it was the first time I drove the Ferrari. There were two classes, one for production sports cars, for which the Monza qualified, and one for prototypes in which Mercedes-Benz competed with Fangio, Kling and Moss at the wheel of 300SLRs. They were faster than anything else, including Jean Behra's works Maserati 300S, which also ran in the prototype class.

Among the production sports cars, which included other Ferrari Monzas, I had easily done the fastest practice time, five seconds slower than Behra in the prototype class, but I felt that I could go still faster and beat his time – just for the glory. So I went out again, and going into the right-hand bend just after the pits I braked a little later than before. Unfortunately, just before the bend there was a hump, and braking later meant that I did so with the wheels off the ground – not a very good way of stopping a car. What is more, the Monza was a horribly understeering car. So there was nothing I could do except crash badly. The car overturned and fortunately I was thrown out and landed on grass, albeit dangerously near a solid telegraph pole. I was picked up with a broken left leg, which kept me in hospital for a couple of days with my leg in plaster. The doctors wanted me to fly back to Belgium, but I did not want to leave the Fiat behind, so we drove back without using the clutch, even including a few sightseeing detours. Fortunately, the Fiat had a hand throttle, so to start I operated the clutch with my right foot and accelerated the engine with the hand throttle, after which I just changed gear without declutching.

Though I loved my little 'Millecento' and was proud of my tuning efforts, I was a little unhappy about the bearing situation and was tempted by the Alfa Romeo Giulietta Sprint, which had just gone into production. Not only were its looks superb, but everything else seemed just right for someone who enjoyed fast driving, especially as its twin-cam, all-aluminium engine with wet liners and five main bearings promised to be indestructible. As for the rest – well, Alfa was a reputable make, wasn't it?

I have never been so wrong in my life! First of all, the handling was very disappointing. If you cornered fast, the car would hopelessly understeer and wallow – the last thing I would have expected from an Alfa. And reliability was a disaster. Even the engine gave trouble and blew a head gasket on a weekend in

In 1955 I won a touring car race at Spa with this Alfa, here demonstrating the perfect four-wheel drift. (Van Bever)

England. The bracket supporting the dynamo kept breaking. The front suspension rebound stroke was checked by a cable that broke regularly – a typical case of bad design. The front anti-roll bar broke, a front coil spring broke and the second-gear synchromesh was ineffective after only 3,700 miles. Worst of all, the telescopic shock absorbers tore their anchorage on the body shell to pieces, requiring welding and reinforcing – on two occasions in the course of long journeys across France. The rather vague steering column shift lever was only a minor fault.

I was so much in love with the car that, initially, I accepted the Giulietta's caprices, as you would forgive a beautiful woman her eccentricities. But the day arrives when you get fed up with them and slam the door shut. This is what I did with the Giulietta when its odometer turned 25,000km (15,000 miles). She was sold and I went straight to the dreaded rival make, Porsche, from whom I bought a 356A 1600 Super, which was a lot faster, handled much more to my liking and was a model of reliability.

In the Giulietta's defence, I must say that mine was a very early example, though that is not really an excuse, as endurance testing should have been done at factory level before the car was marketed, not by early customers. Not so long after I bought my car, Alfa Romeo produced the more highly tuned and lighter Giulietta Sprint Veloce with a central gear change. It was in one of these cars that I did the Tour of France, which at the time was France's most important road event in which the classification was obtained by the results of a large number of races and hill-climbs. It was a wonderful event in which the owner of the car, Adrien Scheid, was happy to let me do all the races and hill-climbs. The event was dominated by the Ferrari 250GT Berlinettas, and we finished seventh overall and second in class, just beaten by Harry Schell in a similar car, with whom I had wonderful dogfights. With power up from 65 to 80bhp, thanks to different cams and two twin-choke Weber carbs, less weight, an excellent gear shift and superb handling, the Sprint Veloce was an incomparably better car than mine.

Porsche reliability was guaranteed as long as the engine was not over-revved, a fact that I learned at my own expense. A French colleague had published a Porsche 1600 Super test showing a maximum speed figure at least 10kmh (6mph) slower than it should have been, timed on the Montlhéry oval. On a visit to Paris, I called him and we met at the track where I did a few laps of the oval with my own car, which he timed at around 178kmh (110.5mph). After that, he asked to take my car out on the road circuit for a lap or two. He never came back. On the downhill stretch called 'Côte de Lapize', which is followed by a rather sharp right-hander, he changed down to second gear (which was unnecessary anyway) much too early and bent all the valves, to the extent that the engine just could not be restarted. Fortunately Auguste, Sonauto's head mechanic in Paris, made a wonderful job of the rebuild, but my colleague never offered to pay for it!

When Porsche produced the 356B 'Super 90', I was tempted and changed my faithful 1600 Super for the new, more powerful model – and after some time

The Alfa Romeo Giulietta Sprint Veloce was a much better car than the regular Sprint. Here I am in 1956 with one at Rouen, one of the many circuits used for the Tour de France Auto.

In the 1970s the American V8 engines found in some European GT cars did not stand up to prolonged full-throttle driving: two maximum speed timed runs with Swiss-made Monteverdis ended in engine disasters.

regretted it. Performance was not significantly better and the maximum speed only about 3kmh higher than for the 75bhp model, because the high bumpers ruined the aerodynamics. The gearbox, now with a baulk ring added to the Porsche synchromesh, was pleasanter to handle, but had to be reconditioned after 20,000km apparently because some of the ball bearings were too small for the torque put through the box.

A special feature of the Super 90 was the centrally pivoted single leaf 'compensating spring' used in connection with slightly thinner rear torsion bars to reduce the rear roll stiffness and combat oversteer. I personally liked the 356A's handling (remember that this was still in the late 1950s) and did not think that the Super 90 was a significant improvement. But what is certain is that it made the car more uncomfortable. Road testing had shown that there were many cars as fast as the Porsche, more comfortable and less noisy. Add to this that my children were growing, and the result was that from 1962 onwards, for ten years, I had no Porsche in my garage.

This brings us to some interesting cars that passed through my hands for road testing. One thing that strikes me when I look into my test reports of the 1950s is that I was extremely courageous and did not hesitate to cover long distances in very much underpowered cars. For example, I drove from Brussels to Italy and back, covering a total of nearly 2,000 miles, in an early Fiat 600 that had a maximum speed of 60mph and took 30.5 seconds to reach 50mph!

In my life as a car tester, I experienced comparatively few complete breakdowns that left me stranded for good. But if I had to classify cars by the number of breakdowns in relation to the number of tests made, Rolls-Royce would probably come out as 'The Worst Car in the World'! In the 1950s a Wraith let me down completely when I timed its maximum speed because the heat resulted in a pressure build-up in the automatic gearbox (admittedly of GM manufacture), causing a seal failure and the oil to run out. I hitch-hiked back to Brussels and was picked up by an Englishman who could not believe that a Rolls had stranded me.

With a Bentley S1, which had been sent specially from England by air, exactly the same thing happened: when I drove it back to Ostend airport following a fast spell of autoroute, I just managed to crawl up to the runway, but the car could not manage the ramp into the plane and had to be pushed up by a group of strong freight handlers.

Complete blow-ups were rare. Probably the first I experienced was with an MG Magnette saloon of the BMC period, which broke its crankshaft, not in the course of performance testing, as you might expect, but on a quite normal drive on the road, in top gear.

Monteverdis, the Swiss Euro-American luxury GT cars, left me stranded twice when doing maximum speed tests. The first had a Chrysler engine, the second a Chevrolet. Those big American V8s of the 1970s were just not designed for sustained full-load and full-speed operation. Somewhere between Turin and Milan the Wankel engine of a first-series Mazda Rotary Coupé gave up the ghost when the cooling water got mixed with the engine oil, and the last of my victims was another American V8, albeit a tuned one powering a prototype Monica, which broke a valve almost exactly where the Mazda had stopped. This does not include breakdowns with my personal cars, which will be related later.

From a design point of view, Citroëns were probably the most outstanding cars to pass through my hands. The 2CV was a completely new concept. Pierre Boulanger, at the time Citroën's Managing Director, described the car as 'An Umbrella on Four Wheels'. His idea was for a car that would replace the horse-drawn carts in which peasants used to go out to their fields, and even into the fields without getting stuck. This and extreme fuel economy were more important than speed. The car should also require a minimum of servicing and lend itself to the carrying of any sort of goods as well as four passengers. To make it possible to carry large items, there was no metal roof, only a long canvas extending from the windscreen to the rear bumper, which could be rolled up partly or completely, down to the rear bumper. The steel tube seats had no casing, just cloth over rubber bands, and were instantly removable. One example of intelligent cost saving among many others was the windscreen wiper, which was operated by the speedometer cable, saving the cost of a motor. Nothing was spared to ensure that the car met its purpose. The suspension had enormous travel, the front and rear were interconnected (I believe for the first time in a car) to avoid pitching, and the longitudinal arms carried inertia dampers that kept the wheels firmly on the ground.

The air-cooled flat-twin engine overhung the front wheels, which it drove through a four-speed gearbox and Hooke-jointed (non-homokinetic) drive shafts. The engine had pushrod-operated overhead valves in hemispherical combustion chambers and developed 9bhp from its 375cc capacity. Its cooling fan provided some heating air for the passenger compartment. Originally the body came only in a dull grey colour on which dirt hardly showed, so that the car could be driven for a long time without being washed.

The original 2CV was the slowest real car I ever tested, but compared to the contemporary Renault 4CV it was much roomier, much more practical and infinitely more comfortable. Unfortunately, I have lost the performance figures I obtained when I tested one in 1951, but I well remember that, as part of the test, I took it from Brussels to Ostend and obtained a maximum speed of 66kmh (41mph), both in third and overdrive fourth gear, and that on the motorway I read the entire instruction manual while driving at full throttle back to Brussels!

In France the 2CV became really fashionable, a way of life. Designed for the country, it invaded the towns and in the 1950s I even saw a black example parked in the centre of Paris with a fully dressed chauffeur at the wheel, waiting for his employer; much later, the wife of France's first minister, Laurent Fabius, ran a 2CV.

My second Porsche 356 was this Super 90, which was louder and less civilised than my previous 75bhp 'Super' – and not as reliable. (Van Bever)

After a few years this unexpected success led to increases in engine capacity to 425cc (12bhp), 435cc (14bhp) and finally 602cc. When production ceased in 1990, 42 years after the model's introduction, the power was up to 29bhp and the maximum speed to around 120kmh (75mph).

I soon began to love 2CVs, and in the 1950s and early '60s I twice chose to borrow one to go on holiday for a whole month with the family – five in all – to Lake Garda in Italy with luggage in every space that could be found: in the rear locker, on the rear shelf, on the dash shelf, under the seats – it is incredible how much luggage that car could carry! With 12 or 14bhp to pull that load, progress was slow and relaxing. On mountain roads cars were never in the way – overtaking problems were left to others!

The only cost-saving measure I really objected to were the Hooke-jointed drive shafts, which caused strong reactions in the steering; on sharp bends alleviating this required slipping the clutch. Only in the 1960s did Citroën at last fit constant-velocity joints. Nevertheless, the 2CV was a genial concept.

No less outstanding was the DS19, a completely revolutionary car when it was announced in 1955. Its only link with the 'Traction' was its 1,911cc engine, though for the DS it acquired hemispherical combustion chambers and more power. Strangely, the monocoque construction was abandoned in favour of a pressed steel platform to which the excellently streamlined body was welded; in the interests of better streamlining, the rear track of 1,300mm was 200mm

The Citroën 2CV was a genial concept aimed primarily at farmers, but soon became a fashion. I had one as a second car and loved it. It was fun to drive and very comfortable.

narrower than the front. The car had an on-board high-pressure hydraulic system operating the automatic clutch, the power-operated four-speed gearbox, the power steering, the brakes and the automatic self-levelling system incorporated in the completely novel hydro-pneumatic suspension. The hydraulics also adjusted the front/rear brake pressure in accordance with the load distribution, and the front brakes were by large inboard discs. The suspension was extremely soft, frequencies being well below 1 Hz, and when passengers stepped out, people stopped to watch the car gently move back to its designed ride height some 10 seconds later, taking a deep breath in the process. Everything in the car was unconventional, from the superb face-level ventilation and the single-spoke safety steering wheel, to the 'button' operating the power brakes, with nothing on its left, and the finger-tip lever operating the power shift.

In the interests of straight-line stability, the car was designed to understeer, which was further helped by a cam locating the power steering in the straight-ahead direction. Shod with Michelin X radial tyres (also a novelty) and helped by its ultra-soft but well-damped suspension, the DS had – for the time – phenomenal grip, but drivers used to other cars had to forget all their former reactions and learn anew. The steering was extremely sensitive and the brakes very powerful, but the brake 'button', which had virtually no travel, took some learning before the driver could achieve the required progression. But once you had mastered its peculiarities, the DS was a really wonderful car to drive and, where comfort was concerned, it was miles ahead of any competition, with handling to match. The Citroën's comfort became the yardstick for all competitors, but which they tried to achieve by more conventional and less expensive means, while Citroën later retracted on some of its novelties, such as the 'button'-operated brakes and the power shift.

The Paris-Dakar Rally is nothing very new. Until 1960 a big international rally was staged, running from Algiers to Cape Town. But due to the civil war in the former Belgian Congo, later Zaire, it was changed in 1961 to Algiers-Bangui (capital of the Central African Republic) and back. Citroën entered four cars and I was asked to be one of the drivers. The cars were of the type ID19, a simplified version of the DS that retained the hydro-pneumatic suspension but had a conventionally operated gearbox and clutch and also relinquished the power steering. For the rally they were preferred to the DS for reasons of reliability. Except for the use of the station wagon's reinforced rear suspension and special wheels and tyres, the cars were almost standard.

As co-driver I chose Jean Vinatier, a young rally driver who had also raced small cars at Le Mans and whom I knew to be a good mechanic, his father having a garage in which he also worked. Six weeks before the rally, in December 1960, four of us went out to Africa to at least have a look at the most difficult parts of the route. We became stuck in soft sand a few times, but soon learned how to recognise those soft areas and avoid them, and were quite confident that on some of the very bad tracks in the more mountainous parts our hydro-pneumatic suspension, the ride height of which could be adjusted at will, would give us a serious advantage over the competition, among which were two Mercedes 220SEs driven by Karl Kling and Sergio Bettoia. Alas, a few days before the rally the local authorities went over the worst stretches with bulldozers, levelling the way for the faster Mercedes, which had no problems and won in the order Kling-Bettoia. We finished third, just ahead of another works Citroën driven by Gendebien and Bianchi. Whatever the result, it was a very interesting experience in countries so different from our old Europe.

Later in the year I joined Lucien Bianchi to drive a works, but very standard, Citroën DS19 in the Nürburgring 12 Hours race for touring cars in which, unfortunately, we did not finish, due to a faulty water pump.

Thanks to good aerodynamics, even early DSs were quite fast for their modest power of 65bhp; the first car I tested did 143kmh (89mph), but acceleration was nothing to write home about even in the late 1950s, the 0–100kmh (0–62mph) sprint being achieved in 20.8 seconds, with 39.9 seconds for the standing kilometre. However, thanks to their revolutionary hydro-pneumatic suspension and the effortlessness with which near top speeds could be held, surprisingly high average speeds could be achieved over long distances, even on quite bumpy roads, at a time when motorways were almost unknown in France and most of Continental Europe, except Italy and Germany.

With increasingly powerful engines, but few major changes, the DS remained in production for nearly 20 years, until 1974. It was designed under André Lefèvre, surely one of the most genial automobile engineers of the century. He had joined Gabriel Voisin at the end of the First World War when Voisin was still building his very successful aeroplanes. When Voisin turned to cars, Lefèvre stayed with him. He was one of the engineers responsible for the aluminium monocoque grand prix cars that competed (with a much underpowered 2-litre sleeve-valve six-cylinder engine) in the 1923 French and Italian Grands Prix, in which he was also one of the drivers (the only Voisin driver to finish in the French event). In 1932 he moved to Citroën, where he became the 'father' of the legendary 'Traction', before leading the teams that designed the 2CV and the DS and ID series. A truly ubiquitous engineer.

Chapter 7

Brussels to Bombay by car

IN THE LATE spring or early summer of 1953 a letter arrived from a gentleman I had never heard of, one Raymond Boschmans. He wrote that in earlier years he had explored Africa by car, mainly for cultural purposes, and that he was now planning to drive from Brussels to India, taking with him a film crew. The idea was not to drive to India as quickly as possible or break any records, but rather to take a route leading to historic and cultural sites and produce an interesting film. For this enterprise he would have four vehicles at his disposal, two Land Rovers and two Armstrong Siddeley Sapphire saloons. I would be in charge of one of the Sapphires, and during the trip I would be required to send articles to a Belgian newspaper relating our progress and, on my return to Europe, to write a book about the whole thing, in exchange for which I would keep the car, or what was left of it.

At first the whole thing seemed rather crazy, but worth some reflection, and after a few days I contacted Mr Boschmans. He was no longer a young man, I would guess over 60, and would make the journey with his wife. He had good contacts with the Royal Automobile Club of Belgium and Government officials, and every member of the crew would get a Diplomatic Passport to facilitate entry into the countries we were to visit. But why on earth Armstrong Siddeley Sapphires, for which we could never hope to get any service in the countries we would visit?

The reason was a certain Mr Mathieu Van Roggen, a Belgian industrialist who, back in 1922, had become Managing Director of Imperia, the car manufacturing company located in Nessonvaux, near Liège, which had been quite successful first with small and middle-range cars using slide-valve engines to the designs of his chief engineer, Arnold Couchard, as described in Chapter 2. Following the economic crisis of the early 1930s Imperia joined forces with the two other remaining Belgian manufacturers, Minerva and Excelsior, but finally had to give up its own production and built German front-drive Adlers under licence, but with different bodies.

After the war Van Roggen founded the 'Société Nouvelle Minerva', based in the old Minerva factory, near Antwerp, and capitalising on the famous old name. The company began making money building Land Rovers under licence, a large number of which went to the Belgian Army and police forces under the name of Land Rover-Minerva. Van Roggen's ultimate ambition, however, was to revive the Minerva luxury cars, but as he did not have the money required to design and produce a completely new model, his idea was to assemble the Armstrong Siddeley in Belgium, giving it a radiator grille masquerading as the typical old Minerva example. Our trip to India, documented by the film and my writings, was to introduce the new Minerva to the Belgian market, and was called 'La Croisière Minerva' ('The Minerva Cruise').

The party was made up of nine members, none of whom I knew before our preliminary meetings. They were Raymond Boschmans and his wife, two cameramen, one of whom was also the film producer and came with his wife and 10-year-old son, two camera assistants, one of whom was my regular passenger, a law student who had been enrolled as a mechanic, and myself. Our law student mechanic, Guy de Pierpont, in fact proved to be first class and seemed never to be as happy as when he could report a major catastrophe likely to keep him busy for several days and nights. He later became a fairly well known Triumph TR3 driver in Belgian rallies.

The two Land Rovers, one short-wheelbase, the other long-wheelbase, both with closed bodies, need no further introduction. The Armstrong Siddeley, however, is much less widely known. With its elegant, typically British six-light saloon body, separate chassis frame and 3.5-litre, straight-six engine with pushrod overhead valves in a 'V' formation in hemispherical combustion chambers, the Sapphire was a direct competitor to the Jaguar Mk VII. Front suspension was by transverse wishbones and coil springs, rear by leaf springs and

The Armstrong Siddeley Sapphire attracts villagers somewhere in Yugoslavia (left), and encountered this sort of transport in Iraq and Iran (below).

a rigid axle. With 150bhp on tap, the Sapphire easily reached 100mph. In view of the abominable conditions of the roads and tracks encountered, the cars proved surprisingly reliable, though both windscreen pillars cracked on the Boschmans' car, which carried a rather heavy load on its roof rack.

We usually did not drive in convoy, deciding instead on a place where we would regroup, either for the night or where there was an item of interest, though usually the two faster Armstrongs and the two slower Land Rovers were never far from one other when the going became difficult. And difficulties abounded.

Not all the cars did exactly the same route, as sometimes the two camera teams separated to shoot different sites. Such separations were, however, not numerous and did not happen before we reached the Middle East. In short, my route was as follows. From Brussels we drove through Germany and Austria to Belgrade, the Yugoslav capital, then through Greece to Istanbul, where we put the car on a ferry to cross the Bosphorus and reach Asia. From Turkey we proceeded to Aleppo in Syria, Beirut in Lebanon and through Jordan to the Arab part of Jerusalem. The Israeli part of the city could not be visited because at the time the frontier was closed to any traffic coming from an Arab country.

From Jerusalem we drove to Amman, the capital of Jordan, thence on muleback to the magnificent rock-cut necropolis of Petra. Back at the wheel, we proceeded to Baghdad, the Iraqi capital, then on to Tehran in Iran, where we also visited Persepolis, the ruins of Persian Emperor Darius's castle, and Shiraz, with its famous gardens. From Iran the route led via Zahedan into Pakistan and through Quetta and Lahore to India where I spent a day in Delhi before driving on to Bombay where I was to ship the car (and myself) back to Europe.

Altogether the trip was to take me just two months, of which the slightly larger part was devoted to sightseeing rather than driving. The rest of the party would take a week longer, as I would have to hurry to catch a ship in Bombay for the car to be back in Belgium in time for the motor show.

We left Brussels in early October, which was supposed to be the best season for such a trip, but as soon as we reached the south of Yugoslavia we were faced not only with abominable roads, but also with disastrous floods, which caused us to lose a day and which prompted Raymond Boschmans and his wife to put their car on a train. After visiting Istanbul for two days, we proceeded to the Asian part of Turkey and the Arab countries, visiting the superb ruins of the Roman temples of Baalbek in Lebanon.

In Tehran Boschmans, who knew that the Shah of Iran was interested in fine cars, had arranged a meeting and we were all introduced to him, after which he examined our cars.

At Petra, which can be reached only by mules, so narrow is the access to it, we spent the night in a large tent and it was well worthwhile. Daylight disclosed the gigantic façades sculpted in the rocks. Petra is among the most impressive sights I have ever seen. Neither can the sculpted walls of the ruins of Darius's castle at Persepolis be forgotten. Here we spent the night in a guest house, and another thing I will always remember is the delicious variety of pancake the locals ate as their bread – especially if you ate it with honey … In Iraq and its capital Baghdad a hostile atmosphere could be felt, but it was worth enduring in order to visit the historic site of Babylon.

By the time we had gone no further than Greece, the driving conditions changed. At night, for instance, oncoming drivers never used dipped headlights. The technique was to switch off completely while the car in the opposite direction kept its main beam on. Then the first car would switch its main beam on again and the other switch off completely, and so forth. The driver who switched off was supposed to have seen enough to proceed for a while in darkness, while the other had his main beam on. I was forced to adopt the same method, otherwise oncoming cars would keep their main beam on.

From the Asian side of the Bosphorus onwards, the biggest hazard was lorries carrying huge quantities of small wood that overhung at least 4–5 feet on either side of the vehicle, which, at night, could be seen only at the last moment. It cost me a damaged windscreen, fortunately of laminated glass.

Everywhere in Asia most roads were just earth tracks producing a huge amount of dust on which the traffic created high frequency waves, known as 'corrugated iron'. If a car was not to be shaken to pieces, the speed had be kept above the resonance period, which created another risk, that of driving too fast into a big hole or over a hump concealed by another car's dust. Asphalt roads were usually even worse, full of enormous potholes. The most terrible was the main road leading to Tehran, some 95 miles of which we covered at night in pouring rain, having to stop at least once every 12 miles or so to clean the headlights.

In Tehran I noticed that the front ride height of my car had dropped somewhat, but the worst was to come. For once we were on a fairly good, apparently newly made straight road, to the left and right the Iranian desert with now and again a well contoured mirage. For once I was able to enjoy the Sapphire's performance, though still with some restraint, and was driving at around 80mph when suddenly we struck a quite unexpected hump. The car took off and landed with a bang. This time there was no doubt that the front wheels were much deeper inside the wheel arches than they should be, and a look under the car disclosed that the shape of the wishbones was decidedly non-standard, while the wheels had acquired considerable negative camber and a lot of toe-out. Even the front transverse member of the chassis and the bumper overriders had obviously hit the ground.

On the spot we roughly adjusted the front track, and in the evening, with the help of our law student mechanic and a tyre repairer, we put a thick rubber washer under each spring as a provisional repair, but the springs were not properly located and on the following night, in Kerman, famous for its hand-made carpets, we found a blacksmith, removed the rubber washers and straightened the wishbones. To our great surprise the blacksmith also had an electric welding apparatus, so we added a welded reinforcement and the car was back in good shape.

In Baghdad we had been told by the Ambassador of Pakistan that it was impossible to cross from Pakistan to India without going through Afghanistan, for which we did not have a visa. But when we reached the Pakistani town of Quetta, we were informed that it *was* possible, though it meant taking a difficult and dangerous road over the mountains.

A booking had been made for a P&O liner sailing from Bombay on 10 December so that the car could be back in Belgium in time to be exhibited at the Brussels Motor Show. We had reached Quetta on 2 December, and the only way to reach Bombay in time was for me to leave the group and proceed alone. A room had been booked for me by telephone in a guest house in Dera-Ghazi-Khan, about 300 miles away on the other side of the mountains, and unfortunately I could not leave Quetta before early in the afternoon.

The Sapphire is dwarfed by the Agarkof Tower in Iraq; this 3,500-year-old monument is made entirely of sun-dried bricks.

After only about 25 miles the road narrowed, changed from asphalt to earth with scattered stones, and began to wind its way into the mountains. After filling up in Loralai, the sun soon disappeared below the horizon with 175 miles still to be covered. Traffic was virtually non-existent and in the darkness the road constantly changed from firm with lots of stones to soft, to the point where great concentration was needed to avoid getting stuck. Suddenly the road went down steeply towards a ford where it crossed a torrent full of big stones. In the light of the headlights it looked quite impressive, but I managed to avoid the biggest rocks. Now and again, along the lonely track, there was a milestone with the letters 'DGK' confirming that I was heading towards Dera-Ghazi-Khan where I would find a meal and a bed.

Shortly before 9pm, with another 60 miles to go, I found the road blocked by a barrier attended by a soldier. 'During the night the road is closed,' he said.

'Why?'

'Too dangerous. You must wait here until tomorrow morning.'

'Why is it dangerous? Bandits?'

'No, it's the road itself. It's a difficult, dangerous road.'

'Well, I have come from Europe with this car,' I said. 'Surely I can manage. I am in a great hurry.'

'OK, at your own risk,' said the soldier, and let me go.

The road really was very narrow and full of stones, and I could not dismiss the idea that I would be an easy victim for robbers, so I felt rather relieved when I saw a milestone 'DGK 2 miles'. But after a few hundred yards the road was closed and half an hour went by before I found a small path leading across fields to the town and the guest house – firmly closed! No food, no bed! That is a drive I will never forget.

Next day the guest house attendant sincerely apologised and served me an excellent breakfast before I again took to the road, crossing the Indus river on a huge wooden bridge. The mountains were now behind me and at last the scenery was trees and fields. The road to Lahore was a narrow asphalt strip with dusty dirt recesses that had to be used for passing other vehicles, and traffic – cars, buses, cyclists and animals – was quite dense. Nevertheless, I noticed that I had covered 57 miles in an hour's drive – a record. But soon after this there was a bang and the clutch pedal hit the floor. A ball joint in the clutch linkage had broken and I drove the remaining 185 miles to Lahore without being able to use the clutch.

At 5.00pm in Lahore all garages were closed and nobody seemed to be prepared to work overtime. So I parked the car and dismantled the linkage to have the broken part welded the next morning. An English gentleman (what was he doing in Lahore?) watched me, we struck up a conversation and finally he offered me a bed for the night. Next day the car was back on the road, but as I reached the Indian border another setback awaited me. Apparently the Indians did not recognise the Royal Automobile Club of Belgium, and the carnet issued

Crossing the Indus river on a 'boat bridge'.

in Brussels meant nothing to them. For hours we discussed it to no avail until the customs officer suggested that I should go and see the Director of Customs in Amritsar. But it was now 8pm and, getting no answer to his telephone call, the officer finally signed the carnet and let me go.

Delhi was still 280 miles away, but the road was good. Six hours later, at 2.30am, I finally reached the Indian capital. I could hardly believe my eyes. The barely illuminated streets were full of rubbish, cows, buffaloes, donkeys and other animals scattered all over the place, half asleep, mixed with people sleeping on the footpath or sheltering under the balconies of miserable houses falling apart. It was all beyond the imagination even of the producers of the most morbid movies!

Fortunately, my hotel was in New Delhi, a complete contrast with the old town. I was able to spend only one day in the modern part of the capital, which was designed by British architects, and into which the historic monuments had been cleverly integrated. Avenues were wider than anywhere else in the world and important buildings far apart from each other. The Indians said that New Delhi was obviously designed by people who had cars, and except for a happy few, the Indians could not afford them. It has hardly changed today.

The reason why I could spend only one day in Delhi was that I had been informed that the P&O liner that was to take me and the car back to Europe would sail later than scheduled, but that on 9 December, the day before the original sailing date, I could catch the *Victoria*, a beautiful Italian liner of Lloyd Triestino, sailing for Naples. That meant hurrying even more to reach Bombay in time and, passing through Agra, I didn't even take the time to stop at the nearby famous Taj Mahal (which fortunately I had a chance to visit with my wife Suzanne 16 years later). But I did stop for a short time when, in a village after dusk, I saw a crowd looking at a brightly illuminated park with a large and well-kept house in the background. They were watching a ceremony in which lavishly dressed people rode on the backs of elephants; onlookers informed me that it was a wedding ceremony.

Finally I reached Bombay, a modern city in the American style, in time to catch the *Victoria*. The passage to Naples took about ten days in mostly beautiful weather, and it was funny to observe how around the open-air swimming pool the Europeans tried to catch as much sun as possible to get a nice tan, while the Indians preferred to sit in the shade and look on, amused. In Suez the shipping company had arranged buses to take interested passengers to Cairo for a night and a day and catch the ship again in Port Said. This gave me a chance to visit the magnificent Cairo Museum and, on a camel's back, the Pyramids and the Sphinx.

My brother, who at the time lived in Rome, came to meet me in Naples, from where we drove to Rome in pouring rain, listening to a Benjamino Gigli recital on the car's radio, which had miraculously survived the Indian adventure.

As scheduled, the car was back in Brussels in time for the 1954 motor show, after which it was dismantled for inspection. It had survived the adventure surprisingly well and, as previously agreed, I wrote the book, which was duly published. In exchange for it I should have kept the car; however, it was never put back together again, Minerva went broke and that was the end of the matter.

In those days, from Turkey westward the vast majority of motor vehicles were lorries, mostly Swedish Scania and German Mercedes-Benz or, when it came to slightly smaller units, ex-US Army Dodge and GM. Private cars varied according to the zones of influence. In Turkey Ford and General Motors models (mainly Chevrolet) were quite prominent, but in Syria and Lebanon many French and Italian cars – mainly Peugeot and Fiat – could be seen on the roads. In Iran and Iraq the majority were old American models, but as Pakistan and India were reached British cars – mainly Hillman Minx – and Jeeps dominated, though in India the fashionable car was the Hindustan, a locally built Morris Oxford that was then fairly modern. But believe me, it is still in production today, virtually unchanged from the Morris Oxford's 1950 specification, except for a modernised engine.

Chapter 8

To East Germany, and racing for Gordini

FOLLOWING THE WAR, many German car factories found themselves in the Russian-controlled eastern zone of Germany. These included the production sites of the four Auto Union makes of Horch, Audi, Wanderer and DKW, which were all in Saxony and were now grouped under the banner of 'Sachsenring', as well as BMW's former Eisenach factory, where the Munich-based company made its cars before the war. Some of these factories had apparently not been too badly damaged and the Communist authorities, which were desperately in need of foreign currency, decided to resume production of BMW and DKW cars, mainly for export.

The first BMW model to resume post-war production was the type 321, a two-door saloon on the lines of the better-known 326, but shorter (4.50m), lighter and with rear half-elliptic springs rather than torsion bars. It was powered by the well-known 1,971cc six-cylinder ohv engine, which, in this single-carburettor version, produced 45bhp. Early cars were marketed with a BMW badge, but legal action by Munich forced a change to EMW (for Eisenacher Motoren Werke), though the shape of the BMW badge was retained with the blue parts changed to red, as befits a Communist country. The type 321 was soon followed by the EMW versions of the type 326 and the sporting 327 drophead, but only with the 55bhp engine. The hemi-head 328 engine never reappeared.

The pre-war twin-cylinder two-stroke DKW also came back to some West European countries, also from Eisenach, as the factories in Saxony had been destroyed. In this case, too, legal action by Auto Union, which had been re-established in West German Düsseldorf, later moving to Ingolstadt, forced a change of name to IFA. A short time later, IFA marketed its type F9, a well-styled two-door sedan powered by a 900cc three-cylinder two-stroke engine developing 30bhp. This model had been fully developed when the war broke out and had been scheduled to go into production early in 1940. All the drawings and some material were still to hand in Saxony and the now state-owned company only had to organise the model's production in the Eisenach factory, next to the EMWs. One or two years later, an almost identical model was produced by the new Auto

Union in Düsseldorf, but launching the production had taken a lot of time because most of the drawings had been left in the East. Some could be retrieved through underground channels, some were re-made from unfinished tools that had rusted away in the open during the war, and the rest were draughted anew. The Western model, called F91, had a different front grille from the IFA, was more expensive, but was also of much better quality. Its engine, though essentially similar to the Eastern one, had also been further developed and produced 40bhp DIN.

On the occasion of the Brussels Motor Show in January 1954, the IFA importer suggested that I should visit the Eisenach factory, together with two journalist colleagues, on the occasion of the International Fair in Leipzig, which would make it easier for him to obtain the necessary visas for us. For the trip he would provide an IFA F9. As hotel accommodation was unobtainable at the time of the fair, he had arranged for us to stay in a private house, Leipzig citizens being only too happy to make some money by renting a bedroom and a bathroom if they had one.

In Belgium, due to the proximity of the sea, winter temperatures seldom fall below –4 or –5°C, but as we proceeded into Germany, especially into the Eastern

In 1954 I drove an East German IFA, powered by a two-stroke three-cylinder engine, to the Leipzig Fair with two journalist colleagues. The state of the compressed air distributor is typical of the decay found everywhere in East Germany.

zone, the temperature fell to around −15 or −20°C, which was a lot colder than the IFA's heating system could cope with. Though our visas were perfectly in order, going through the checkpoint into East Germany took more than an hour – every single coin we possessed had to be meticulously declared and it was compulsory to change a certain amount of Western money for Eastern marks at the official rate. All the Eastern marks obtained had to be spent in the country because whatever was left could not be exported and would have to be left with the customs against a receipt that was obviously useless!

Our visa only allowed us to drive to Leipzig and to Eisenach, from where it was obligatory to return via Berlin, staying on the *autobahn* that included a stretch near Dessau on which, before the war, many speed records had been established. From the checkpoint into East Germany we had to follow a compulsory route from which we could not deviate. This was regrettable, as we would have liked to visit villages and small towns that had not been specially trimmed to impress foreign visitors, but what we saw was depressing enough anyway. In addition, the preset route that visitors to the Leipzig International Fair were compelled to follow had one advantage: it was kept fairly free from snow and was gravelled and sanded wherever necessary.

The IFA F9 gave us a fairly trouble-free run, but we found it essential to largely shield the air intake grille, not only to get any sort of heat out of the interior heating system, but also to prevent the engine from seizing up. Fortunately, a freewheel was incorporated in the gearbox, so whenever the engine seized it just stopped without suffering serious damage and could be restarted almost immediately. I have known light alloy pistons to seize up as a result of running too hot, but in this case the seizure occurred every time the engine ran too cold. Maybe the cylinder bores were so cold on the side opposite the hot exhaust ports that they suffered a large deformation that caused the seizure?

Leipzig was rather gloomy, but the people who had provided accommodation for me were very kind, though they did not seem too happy and were obviously afraid to speak about their lot. The machine tool section of the fair was rather interesting. The car section included only Eastern models, the military vehicles being Russian copies of Ford Model A trucks and GM or Dodge all-wheel-drive vehicles.

After spending an evening at the opera house, we proceeded to Eisenach where we met the Managing Director of the factory producing the IFA F9, who mentioned future developments that in the event never happened. Surprisingly, we were allowed to visit the EMW racing department, which I was very keen to see. The 1.5-litre EMW sports racing cars had come several times to the Nürburgring and had given the Porsches a good run for their money, driven by Rosenhammer and Edgar Barth, the latter obviously a very fast driver.

The people in the racing department were extremely enthusiastic and keen to show us what they had achieved with obviously rather limited means. Except for the cylinder block, the cars had inherited almost nothing from the pre-war BMW

328. The chassis was a completely new design and the front-mounted engine had overhead cams. This is where I first met Edgar Barth who, only a few months later, left everything he had in the East and fled to West Germany with his family, where he obtained a contract to race for Porsche. In 1958 he was my co-driver at Le Mans when we finished fourth overall with a 1,500cc Spider RSK. He later became a European hill-climbing champion with Porsche. Sadly, he died from cancer in the mid-1960s, but later his son Jürgen not only won Le Mans in 1977, but is also known world-wide for his involvement with Porsche and as one of the three founders of the now defunct BPR GT series, the initial 'B' standing for Barth. Unfortunately, Edgar Barth's move to the West put an end to EMW's racing activities.

In Berlin, where we stayed in the Eastern sector, we made a short incursion into the Western part of the city, which again entailed a complete check of our car by Communist Government officials and a declaration of every coin of foreign and East German money we had, this being repeated when we drove back to East Berlin. In apparently deliberate contrast, the Western officials just had a quick look at our passports and waved us through.

Before we could leave Berlin, where I found that the school I had attended and two of the three buildings in which I had lived with my parents had been completely destroyed in the war, we had to go through more formalities. A permit was necessary to drive on the 185-mile *autobahn* separating Berlin from the interzone checkpoint in Marienborn, on the way to Hanover in West Germany, where we were happy to be in a civilised country again!

At last the IFA F9 brought us safely back home. It had performed decently, without any problems, except for the occasional engine seizure that we were able to avoid once we had found out that it was essential to keep the engine warm enough. Comfort was not the car's strong point, and neither was the heater! However, the three-cylinder two-stroke engine ran smoothly, if noisily, and was a strong middle-range puller.

In later years the car was renamed 'Wartburg', after the fortress dominating Eisenach where Martin Luther worked for several years (a black mark on a wall is said to have been made by an ink bottle thrown by Luther at the Devil who had appeared to him).

Together with its new name, the IFA also acquired a completely new – in my opinion less elegant – body together with a trailing-link rear suspension, but the rest of the specification, including the three-cylinder two-stroke engine, remained in production until 1990, when Germany was reunited and the whole of East German car production was stopped. On the site of the old Eisenach factory, Opel built a new, highly modern building where Astras and Vectras are now manufactured.

Back in the West, the time had come for me to think of the forthcoming 1954 racing season. In 1953 HWM had had a disastrous season and lack of money ruled out any chance of success in 1954, when Formula 1 was changed from 2 to

The East German EMW gave the Porsches a surprisingly good run for their money on rare outings to the West, particularly when driven by Edgar Barth.

2^1/$_2$ litres. My past results were surely not sufficient to think of Ferrari, so I decided to turn to Gordini, whose six-cylinder single-seaters had been quite competitive. For 1954 the engine's capacity had been increased to 2.5 litres (its original design target) and, driving one of these cars, Jean Behra had beaten the works Ferraris and Maseratis at Pau.

Amédée Gordini was an Italian who had emigrated to France before the war and had adopted French nationality, also Frenchifying his first name, originally Amadeo. When, in 1935, the Simca company was founded by Henry Pigozzi – also of Italian origin – to build Fiat cars under licence, Gordini obtained financial help from Simca to tune and race Simca cars, which he did with great success. He obtained his best results with cars based on the Simca 8, the perfect equivalent of the Fiat 1100 for which he designed aerodynamically optimised racing two-seater bodies. He became very popular in patriotic France, as Simca ranked as a French make.

After the war he added single-seaters to his programmes, based on a tubular ladder frame to which he grafted Simca mechanical units. These small and light 1,100cc cars soon became the strongest competition for the Cisitalia of the same Fiat origin and were successfully driven by such top drivers as Wimille, Fangio, Manzon and Bira.

Up to 1952 Gordini had been financially supported by Simca, enabling him to develop new cylinder heads and aluminium cylinder blocks, but from 1953 Simca stopped its support and Gordini, now sponsored mainly by Shell and Messier, who supplied shock absorbers and, later, disc brakes, decided to build complete cars under his own name. The six-cylinder engine that powered his new single-seater in 1953 was completely his own design, and so was the car itself, which was very simple, almost crude, compared with contemporary Ferraris and Maseratis. It was based on a simple tubular ladder frame, the four-speed (later five-speed) gearbox was in unit with the engine, and the rear suspension was by a Simca run-of-the-mill rigid axle and longitudinal torsion bars. In 2.5-litre form the engine produced no more than 200–210 horsepower, but the simplicity of the design resulted in a very light car, which explains why it was reasonably competitive, especially on winding courses, even though it was no real match for the Italian cars, not to mention the Mercedes.

I had known Gordini for many years. My first encounter with him had been as a journalist, in 1950. At the time the only event in which I had competed at the wheel of a car was the 1948 Spa 24 Hours with the old MG, so driving for the great Gordini could only be a dream and was not even suggested.

I had made an appointment with him to report on his activities and drove from Brussels to his premises at 69 Boulevard Victor in Paris in the 1939 SS-Jaguar saloon I had recently bought from my father. His welcome was not very encouraging. After shaking hands, the first thing he said was that too many journalists came to see him, taking much of his time that he would rather dedicate to his work. He then invited me to his study and the conversation was rather uneasy until I mentioned the performance put up by his cars in the previous year's Spa 24 Hours race, where they had been surprisingly fast, but had failed to finish. This brought us to discussing index of performance formulae, on which we hardly agreed. But at last the ice was broken and we finally spent an hour and half in his workshop, discussing engines, suspensions and many other items while looking at his partly dismantled cars.

In the end he seemed to have enjoyed my company and as I was about to leave and drive back to Brussels he invited me for a drink. I asked, 'Where shall we go?'

'I don't know – leave it to me, just follow,' was his answer.

He jumped into his Simca 8 (alias Fiat 1100) saloon and drove like a scalded cat. Following with my big and unwieldy Jaguar was not an easy task, but I did my best not to lose sight of the agile Simca in the dense Paris traffic. After a hectic drive of about 5 or 6 kilometres the Simca stopped in the Avenue de Iena, in front of the famous 'Bar de L'Action Automobile', the traditional meeting point of Paris car enthusiasts. I stopped just behind (in those times the parking problems in Paris were not yet so acute), we both stepped out and the only thing he said was, 'You've got quite a good car there!' We had our drinks and talked for another half hour, but I never found out whether he had actually tried to shake me off or not.

Thereafter we had many contacts and Gordini had many opportunities to watch me racing, so when I went to see him about a place in his team, the conditions were very different and it did not take him long to agree. In fact I think he was quite happy as, with the loss of Maurice Trintignant and Robert Manzon, who had both moved to Ferrari, only Jean Behra and the relative novice Jacky Pollet made up his regular team.

My first race for Gordini was the 1954 Belgian Grand Prix, and it was a disaster. Due to a porous cylinder head (for which no spare was at hand), the engine misfired continuously and finally the differential broke. Next came the 'Supercortemaggiore' 12 hours sports car race at Monza, for which I teamed up with Jean Behra in the team's only 3-litre car, powered by a straight-eight engine based on the six-cylinder of the single-seater. The car was quite competitive against the horde of Ferraris (mostly Monzas) and Maseratis driven by such people as Mike Hawthorn, Froilan Gonzalez, Juan Manuel Fangio and the like, and for some time we even led the race. But then the inevitable happened: a sleeve lever in the valve gear broke when we were still in third place. It was

Watching Amédée Gordini check my car's plugs before the Belgian Grand Prix in 1954. (Van Bever)

changed, but soon another broke and the car was retired. I had nevertheless really enjoyed the drive as the car handled really well and was superb in the very fast 'Curva Grande'.

The biggest problems with the Gordini team were lack of money and lack of organisation. The latter reached a climax on the occasion of the French Grand Prix at Reims, which, for Gordini, was probably the most important race of the whole season. Three cars had been entered for Behra, Pollet and myself. Arriving in Reims for the first of the three practice sessions, all scheduled for the late afternoon, I was told in the garage where the cars were supposed to be that they would not arrive before the following day – which they failed to do. Neither did they arrive for the last session. While waiting for them I was out on the track watching the Mercedes team prepare for their first post-war grand prix appearance, the cars wearing a full-width streamlined body. They were highly impressive and created a panic among the Italian teams.

Then, quite unexpectedly, about 30 minutes before the end of the final practice a Gordini appeared on the track, driven by Jean Behra. His car had only been finished in the afternoon, much too late for Gordini's old Lancia transporter to reach Reims in time, and he had driven the single-seater all the way from the centre of Paris – about 125 miles. On arrival the officials let him on to the circuit for a few practice laps!

Jacky Pollet's car and mine arrived late that night by transporter. Fortunately,

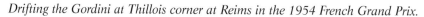

Drifting the Gordini at Thillois corner at Reims in the 1954 French Grand Prix.

the organisers allowed us to start without previous practice, but we had to do so from the last row of the grid.

Luckily I knew the circuit, having taken part in the previous year's 12 Hours sports car race at the wheel of the Jaguar-engined HWM that I had shared with George Abecassis, and I finally had my hour of glory, which brought the spectators to their feet. At some time in the middle of the 500km race, after a quick stop for oil while in sixth position, and with the two other Gordinis already out of the race, I was lapped by the two Mercedes driven by Fangio and Kling. They were obviously taking it very easy, running to team orders after the Italian challenge had faded. Just after they overtook me, a short rain shower dampened the track and soon I was back on Kling's tail. No wonder – I was still racing and he was touring. After a few laps he let me through, and for 12 laps the little Gordini, looking fairly prehistoric compared with the impressive streamlined German cars, remained sandwiched between them. I was the last French hope and, even though I was two laps behind, the episode created enormous excitement. It was, however, my car's swan song: soon after this, much to the crowd's dismay, the differential broke while I was in fifth place.

It had now become a habit for Gordinis not to finish races, but what happened in the German Grand Prix at the Nürburgring made me decide to resign from the team. This time the cars had arrived in time for practice and were to be driven by Jean Behra, the Argentinian driver Clemar Bucci, who probably had bought himself into the team, and myself. Practice went extremely well for me as I was consistently faster than Jean Behra. To save the car I did only five laps, my fourth being in 10min 9.0sec and my fifth in 10min 5.9sec, while Jean did no better than 10min 11.9sec. Poor Bucci, who did not know the 'Ring, was some 35 seconds slower. Pole position went to Fangio's Mercedes in 9min 50.1sec, but only five cars had achieved a better time than my Gordini. After Fangio came Hawthorn (Ferrari), Moss (Maserati), Herrman (Mercedes) and Gonzalez (Ferrari).

What put me out of the race was something I could not forgive. After rounding Bergwerk corner, before reaching Kesselchen, I saw my right-hand front wheel fly high into the air, complete with the brake drum – a stub axle had broken and, as the car had only a single braking circuit, I was not only on three wheels, but also without brakes. Fortunately, that particular stretch of the 'Ring is fairly straight and slightly uphill, so I managed to park the car and walk away. But had it happened, for example, 2 kilometres earlier, on the winding downhill stretch to Breitscheid, I would not be here to tell the story.

After the race I told Gordini that I would not drive for him any more, and I established contacts with Ferrari team chief Nello Ugolini, which eventually led to a test drive for Ferrari on the Imola circuit and to racing in the team in 1955.

Especially since Simca had stopped supporting him, the French press kept emphasising how remarkable Gordini's achievements were, considering the limited budgets available, suggesting that with more support his cars would surely be a match for any comer. While there is no doubt that a larger budget

My performance with the Gordini in practice for the German Grand Prix earned me an invitation to Maranello. (Van Bever)

would have helped in reducing fatigue failures such as those that had caused my four retirements in four races, I do not think that more money could have made his cars noticeably more competitive.

Gordini was one of four children of a very modest family living in the Bologna area. His father worked on a farm and died when Amedeo was eight. At 11 he had to leave school to go to work, first on a farm and later repairing horse-drawn vehicles and bicycles. That he emigrated to Paris, alone, and achieved what he did proves that he was both courageous and intelligent. He was obviously a genial mechanic, but his knowledge of automotive technology was purely empirical. He did not have a scientific approach to technical problems and was diffident with – maybe jealous of – people with a scientific background. Experience had taught him how to make fairly reliable engines, but their specific power was low compared to the opposition. This was partly compensated for by the fact that his cars were unsophisticated and consequently light. But if those that I drove handled reasonably well, it was more thanks to luck than to a scientific approach.

As an example, in French an anti-roll bar is usually called a 'stabilising bar'. In 1958 Gordini prepared a team of Renault Dauphines for the Tour of Corsica Rally, which included a large number of long timed special stages. The Dauphine had an overhung rear engine and swing axle rear suspension and was consequently a pronounced oversteerer, which could have been tamed by fitting a strong front anti-roll bar. But Gordini's solution, probably because the rear end was 'unstable', was to add the 'stabilising bar' to the *rear* suspension.

When he designed his last Formula 1 model, which had independent suspension all round, he explained to me the reasons for using a suspension where the hub carrier was pivoted on a leading and a trailing arm forming a Watt linkage. But even then it was known that much better results could be achieved with suspensions allowing controlled camber variations than with parallel wheel motion.

After the failure of his last attempt at Formula 1 with cars that had grown and lost their lightness, the earlier Gordinis' major asset, Gordini gave up being independent. He went into partnership with Renault to develop sporting versions of production engines (Dauphine Gordini, Renault 12 Gordini) and a racing 3-litre V8 for an Alpine-Renault Berlinetta with which Renault hoped to become a challenger in the larger-capacity classes at Le Mans and elsewhere. But again the engine failed to produce the required power and Gordini was pushed more and more into the background.

That marked the end of his professional career and even his name disappeared from the factory Renault had built for him in Viry-Chatillon, near Paris. That is where later the formidable Renault Formula 1 engines were developed and built, but by that time the factory's name had been changed from 'Renault-Gordini' to 'Renault Sport'. *Sic transit gloria …*

Chapter 9

Enzo Ferrari: the man, the company and the cars

I FIRST MET Enzo Ferrari in the summer of 1948, when I drove to Italy with my newly acquired 1925 Ballot 2LTS. This was just a year after Ferrari No 1 had won its first race, the Rome Grand Prix with Franco Cortese at the wheel.

Ferrari had earlier been known as a racing driver, and, after retiring in 1929, he founded his own team, the Scuderia Ferrari, which had its headquarters in Modena, and to which, from 1933 onwards, Alfa Romeo entrusted the management of its racing activities. It was in Ferrari's Modena workshop that the Alfa Romeo 'Bimotore' was built under Luigi Bazzi's leadership in an attempt to beat the German cars in Formule Libre races, and where the famous Gioacchino Colombo-designed Alfa Romeo 158s, better known as 'Alfettas', were made. But after a disagreement, Ferrari severed his links with Alfa Romeo to found his own company to build racing cars, having its base in Viale Trento Trieste, Modena.

As racing cars were hardly useful during wartime, Ferrari specialised in the manufacture of machine tools, which were made in Maranello where today all Ferraris are made. In those days Ferrari's racing activities were still concentrated in Viale Trento Trieste, in the building where, until not so long ago, Ferrari's Service Department, headed by the late Gaetano Florini, was located.

At that time Ferrari had not adopted the habit of shutting himself away in an inaccessible ivory tower, and when I went to see him, as a young and unknown motoring journalist introduced only by a letter from the obscure *Belgique Automobile* magazine, he was immediately available. Ferrari's road car production was then virtually nil, and the cars in the workshop were Type 166 racing two-seaters. I well remember Ferrari himself explaining that his cars could run as well in Formula 2 as in sports car events, the latter with headlights and cycle-type wings added. I also remember a real single-seater with a Roots-supercharged 1½-litre single-cam engine in the course of being built, with which Ferrari intended to compete for Formula 1 honours, a car that was to be successful only when the Alfas were absent. In the course of 1949 the engine acquired twin camshafts per bank and a two-stage supercharger and won the Italian Grand Prix in which the Alfas did not participate. But when in 1950 Alfa Romeo came back with two-stage-supercharged cars and more power than ever, Ferrari changed his mind and ordered his young chief engineer, Aurelio Lampredi, to design a new, bigger V12 to try his luck with a 4.5-litre atmospheric engine, the alternative to the supercharged 1.5-litre allowed by the Formula 1 regulations of the period. The historic British Grand Prix of 1951 in which a Ferrari driven by José Froilan Gonzalez beat the Alfas for the first time, is one of the highlights of motorsport history. Thanks to Juan Manuel Fangio, Alfa Romeo retained its world championship title, but decided to retire, which led to the abandonment of Formula 1 for two years, when the world championship was based on Formula 2.

Enzo Ferrari remained a fairly enigmatic but still accessible man until the death in June 1956 of his son Dino, who, he had hoped, would some day succeed him. Dino's death obviously moved him considerably and many things changed. He became less accessible and his study took on the air of a sanctuary that the sun never penetrated directly. What you saw when you were introduced into the study, usually after having been kept waiting for sometimes several hours, was a man hidden behind large dark glasses, sitting behind an enormous empty desk and, behind him, a large photo of his son Dino with, at the bottom of the frame,

With Enzo Ferrari at the factory in 1963. This photo is always kept with the car papers when driving in Italy – it might help if stopped by the police! (Van Bever)

an artificial rose and a dim light. Not exactly an atmosphere to immediately put one at ease.

I went to see him many times before and after Dino's death and I remember him showing me the engine of the projected 'Ferrarina' (small Ferrari) which was virtually a group of four cylinders from a 3-litre V12. It eventually never bore the Ferrari badge – Ferrari sold all the rights and the beautiful little 'Berlinetta' became the ASA 1000, a mechanical marvel but a commercial disaster.

I always found it difficult to start a conversation with Ferrari, especially after the death of his son. He was obsessed by women and, whatever the subject discussed, he always found a way to come back to beautiful women who, as often as not, made him digress from the real subject. Neither was he ever short of an answer to any question, even if his reply did not answer the question at all, and his annual press conferences, when he discussed the past season and announced his plans for the following year, were a supreme example of a one-man show.

At table with a glass of Lambrusco, things became much more relaxed. One of his favourite places was the Gatto Verde, on the Abetone road, where he took me once, personally demonstrating a Pininfarina-bodied 250 GT. I remember one occasion when he was particularly relaxed. I had organised an Italian tour for a group of Belgian journalists belonging to the Belgian Motor Journalists Association of which, at the time, I was the president. I accompanied them with my wife Suzanne in an Alfa Spider Duetto. The tour comprised visits to Fiat, Alfa Romeo and Ferrari. It was something like 5.00pm when we arrived at Maranello, where we were welcomed by Franco Gozzi, responsible for public relations (and about everything else!), and after we had visited the factory, including the racing department (which, in those times, was hardly secret), Ferrari met the journalists and answered their questions.

According to the schedule, this was to be the last item on the programme, but after he had answered all questions he suddenly suggested that we all go and have dinner at the Cavallino, the little restaurant just across the road which, in those days, was not yet as famous and as well appointed as it is today. Ferrari was in brilliant form, apparently happy to talk to us all, and made a lot of jokes. It was a memorable occasion that is fondly remembered to this day by all those who were present and are still with us.

Two typical examples of Ferrari's ability to answer any question to his advantage were provided when I went to Maranello shortly after Olivier Gendebien and I had won the Le Mans 24 Hours race in 1960, driving one of his 3-litre Testa Rossas. The race regulations required a 25cm-high windscreen and Ferrari had made not the slightest effort to integrate it in such a way that it would not work as an air brake. The result was that the car hardly reached 260kmh (160mph) down the Mulsanne straight (I timed it at 259kmh during the race!). So when I went to see him to thank him personally for taking me into his team, I asked why he had not made a greater effort towards an aerodynamically better shape, adding that, in earlier races at Le Mans, I had driven D-type Jaguars that, with less power, were noticeably faster. For a moment he looked at me, then said, 'You know, Frère, aerodynamics are good for those who can't make good engines!'

And to my question why, in 1960, he still used carburettors in his racing engines, when most others had gone over to fuel injection, his answer was, 'Well, listen – if from the early years everyone had used fuel injection, and someone now came with a device as simple and efficient as a carburettor, everyone would switch over to carburettors immediately.'

What I had said about the Testa Rossa's speed (or lack of it) at Le Mans must nevertheless have given him something to think about, for a few days later he sent Giotto Bizzarrini, the engineer responsible for GT cars, who was supposed to be an unbiased person, to check the Le Mans car's maximum speed on the Bologna *autostrada*. As the result (258kmh) confirmed my claim, Ferrari immediately entrusted him with improving the Testa Rossa's aerodynamics. Needless to say, two years later all Ferrari Formula 1 cars also had fuel injection.

The Testa Rossa with which Olivier Gendebien and I won Le Mans in 1960 required a windscreen of regulation height, but Ferrari made no effort to make it aerodynamically efficient. When I inquired about this, Ferrari answered, '… aerodynamics are good for those who can't make good engines.'

Many of the drivers who drove for Ferrari have said or written that Ferrari deliberately created rivalries among his drivers to incite them to go faster. Personally I was definitely never put under pressure by him and I always thought that the reason might have been that I was never one of his employees; I never had a contract with him or with the Scuderia. He asked me to drive whenever he thought fit or if the Royal Automobile Club of Belgium or the Equipe Nationale Belge asked him, on my behalf and on specific occasions, if he would take me into his team, which he usually did. But quite recently Phil Hill, who was a full member of the Scuderia for four years, told me that he had never felt any pressure from Ferrari either. That said, I think that pressure in such circumstances is completely unnecessary; a racing driver is necessarily a competition-minded person, and being on equal terms with his team-mates, who drive identical cars, his first priority is automatically to better their performances.

What dominated Ferrari's policies during the 1950s was the rivalry with Maserati. Here you had two small companies essentially making racing cars, only about 12 miles from each other, who fought for supremacy not only on all the European circuits, but also as far afield as Sebring in Florida, Watkins Glen in the heart of the United States or Buenos Aires in Argentina, apparently without paying much attention to the other competitors. I will always remember team manager Nello Ugolini briefing us – Farina, Trintignant and myself – on the morning of the 1955 Belgian Grand Prix and making his recommendation: 'We know that the Mercedes will be very difficult to beat, but our main target is to beat the Maseratis.' On that occasion we did, Farina taking third place and myself fourth … but behind the two Mercedes of Fangio and Moss.

The following year Mercedes retired from the grand prix scene, and I finished second in the Belgian Grand Prix, behind my former HWM team-mate Peter Collins, who had never beaten me before. For many reasons I had decided to concentrate on sports car racing (in that year I was in the Jaguar team) and had not driven a Formula 1 car for exactly one year. It was a complete surprise to me when Ferrari asked me to take over the car (a type D50 Lancia-Ferrari), which Luigi Musso should have driven but was unable to because he had broken a wrist in the Nürburgring 1,000km race the previous weekend. My performance apparently impressed Ferrari and he invited me to Maranello to make an attractive proposal. He offered me the opportunity to become the Scuderia's test driver, responsible for the preparation of the cars prior to the races and, at the same time, to be a full member of his sports car team. It was certainly tempting!

But in 1956 I was already 38, living in Brussels and with three daughters who were at school, and I was much in demand as a motoring journalist. Accepting Ferrari's offer would inevitably have implied moving to Modena with the entire family and seriously disturbing my daughters' studies and social life. If I had felt that it could have been a long-term post, I might have accepted. Maybe my daughters would have lost a year in their studies, but they would have learned Italian (which they did anyway, as we spent many holidays in Italy). But at 38 I was not sure that I had the ambition to continue to race for many more years. I had proved to myself that I could successfully mix with the 'greats', which had been my objective. I also knew that Ferrari had fallen out after a short time with many people who had worked for his company. In his offer I could see a fascinating short-term job, but no future, and I reluctantly declined.

Left *Rounding La Source hairpin in the 1955 Belgian Grand Prix.* (Van Bever)

Right *Although I only finished fourth in the 1955 Belgian Grand Prix, I was invited to the podium, next to winner Fangio, as 'first Belgian finisher'.*

One person whose departure from Ferrari shocked me was Aurelio Lampredi, who did not leave on his own initiative. He had been enrolled by Ferrari as a development engineer for the racing cars when the links with Gioacchino Colombo, who had designed the original Ferrari V12 as a consultant, were severed. Lampredi not only designed the bigger V12 with which Ferrari beat the Alfettas in 1951, won Le Mans in 1954 and which was also used in some production models such as the 'Superfast' and the 'Superamerica', to name only the best known, but he was also the man who persuaded Ferrari to replace the V12 in his 2-litre single-seaters with a four-cylinder engine. Because of the valve gear and other limitations, the revving potential of a V12 with a stroke of only 58mm could not be exploited. A four-cylinder could be revved just as fast and would have the advantage of much lower friction and heat losses, resulting in a higher power output, lower fuel consumption and a better torque curve.

The four-cylinder was said to develop 180bhp, some 20 more than the V12 of equal capacity, and gave Ferrari and Alberto Ascari the 1952 and 1953 world championships, against strong competition from the six-cylinder Maseratis. For

King Leopold of Belgium visits the Ferrari team before the 1955 Belgian Grand Prix. From the right are René Baken (clerk of the course), King Leopold, Nino Farina, Maurice Trintignant (partly hidden by Farina), chief engineer Aurelio Lampredi, myself, Harry Schell and team manager Nello Ugolini (partly hidden by Schell). (Van Bever)

1954 it was uprated to 2.5 litres, the limit of the new Formula 1, but Mercedes-Benz's return to racing put an end to its supremacy, and Lampredi's career with Ferrari neared its end. After Ferrari took over the entire Lancia team of V8-engined D50s, designed by Vittorio Jano, Lampredi was joined by Jano who acted as consultant, but he finally left, to be replaced by Carlo Chiti for 1958. After leaving Maranello Lampredi joined Fiat as head of the engine department where he was responsible for some brilliant engines.

With some hindsight, I have never really regretted not having accepted Ferrari's interesting offer. In the 1950s and early '60s there were many who, for one reason or another, did not survive for more than a few years with Ferrari, beginning with the team managers Nello Ugolini, Eraldo Sculati, Eugenio Dragoni, Romolo Tavoni, Franco Lini and Peter Schetty, who followed each other in quick succession. Carlo Chiti, who succeeded Lampredi, left Maranello in 1961 with another key engineer, Giotto Bizzarrini, following disagreements with Ferrari. If I had accepted Ferrari's offer, it would have been at the expense of test driver Martino Severi, who soon left anyway.

However, a few members of the Ferrari staff managed to resist: among them were Enzo Ferrari's secretary Valerio, and Franco Gozzi, technically responsible for public relations, but the person in the company who knew Ferrari best and knew absolutely everything that was going on in the factory. He was probably one of the few people able to make Ferrari change his mind – at least on non-technical matters. He could have made a brilliant career in diplomacy, and if anyone is in a position to write an inside story about the Ferrari 'establishment', it is Gozzi. But he is probably too loyal to Ferrari to do it.

Another faithful member of Ferrari's staff, entirely devoted to the boss, was Luigi Bazzi. Originally a racing mechanic with Alfa Romeo from 1924, he joined Ferrari in 1933 when the Milan company entrusted its racing activities to the Scuderia Ferrari. He was responsible for the construction of the Alfa Romeo 'Bimotore', featuring one supercharged Alfa Romeo 8C engine in front and one behind the driver. The car was designed to beat the Germans in Formule Libre events, where the 750kg maximum weight was not enforced. Unfortunately, contemporary tyres were not up to the car's weight and its 320kmh (200mph) maximum speed. In the 1950s and '60s Bazzi was Ferrari's engine expert and as loyal to his boss as anyone could be. I will always remember his distress when, due to a miscalculation, two of the four works cars entered for Le Mans in 1960 ran out of fuel before the first refuelling stop. Fortunately one of the two cars left won the race, driven by Olivier Gendebien and myself – I will never forget his thanks, with tears of relief in his eyes, for saving the day for him.

When I first knew him, Enzo Ferrari was known as the 'Commendatore', an honorary title given by the Italian Government for meritorious achievement. In later years he was made an Engineer Honoris Causa by, I believe, the University of Bologna, and from then on he liked to be called 'Ingegnere', even though he considered himself more a great organiser and promoter than an engineer. But his honorary title was not an empty one – he certainly had a very good flair for engineering, even though, in his later years, he became rather conservative. No decision was taken without his approval, and it was not easy for him to 'digest' the racing car revolution that took place between 1957 and 1962 – rear engines, disc brakes, fuel injection and welded tubular suspension parts, all things that saved weight and improved performance. However, whenever I raced a Ferrari I was confident that no vital part would break and no wheel would be lost.

The racing cars were really Ferrari's only serious interest in his company. His only reason for making road cars was to make money to keep the racing

With Olivier Gendebien on the Le Mans podium – winning the 24-hour race is an unforgettable experience. (LAT)

department going. And he was too proud of his racing cars to accept sponsorship that would force him to turn his beautiful red cars into racing advertisement panels. Tobacco companies tried hard, but Ferrari proudly said, 'My cars don't smoke'! The only stickers he accepted on his cars were those of the companies concerned with the actual racing: suppliers of brakes, tyres, ignition systems, fuel, oil, etc.

As long as he retained control over all his company's activities, no engine was ever designed specifically for a road car; production engines were always more or less detuned racing engines. Unfortunately, in the 1960s the profits made by the production cars were no longer sufficient to cover the ever-increasing costs of racing, and some outside help became necessary. Ford was very interested in acquiring Ferrari and all the terms of an agreement that would have made Ferrari a very rich man had been agreed. Only the signatures needed to be added when Ferrari woke up to the fact that if he signed, he would not be the boss any more, and he sent the Ford delegation back to Detroit.

At this point Gianni Agnelli realised how important Ferrari was for the prestige of the Italian automobile industry, and Fiat acquired 50 per cent of the company's assets. Enzo Ferrari retained 50 per cent of the shares and remained the sole manager of the racing department, while Fiat took over all the responsibilities for the road car department, even though Ferrari always remained a sort of honorary consultant.

After Enzo Ferrari's death, Fiat took over 90 per cent of the Ferrari shares and also controls the racing department, while Enzo Ferrari's other son, Piero, now the company's Vice-President, retains the remaining 10 per cent.

Chapter 10

Driving
for Ferrari

THE MOMENT MY Gordini lost its right-hand front wheel in the German Grand Prix of 1954, leaving me driving a brakeless three-wheeler (see Chapter 8), my mind was made up: that was going to be my last race for Gordini. A few weeks later the Nürburgring 1000km race for sports cars would take place, and since before the German Grand Prix I had achieved a very good practice time, which Ferrari team manager Nello Ugolini could not have failed to notice, I went straight to him and asked whether he would have a place for me in his team for that race. He promised nothing, but seemed rather interested.

Unfortunately, the race was cancelled, but obviously Ugolini had not forgotten my request and in the spring of 1955 I received a letter from Ferrari himself inviting me to a practice session at Imola. The appointment was at Modena, from where I was taken to Imola, together with team manager Nello Ugolini, in the

The start of the 1955 Belgian Grand Prix: my Ferrari is on the third row at the extreme right.
(Van Bever)

Scuderia's Fiat 1100 TV driven by Mimmo Amorotti, a friend of Ferrari always in attendance in the pits to take any decision on technical matters. The car I was to drive at Imola was a Type 625 four-cylinder Formula 1, the weather was fine, and Maurice Trintignant and Harry Schell were also to drive the car, while Nino Farina was there to set the bogey time. As usual, Ferrari had remained in Maranello. Today I have no idea of the times we achieved, but we must all have done fairly well, as we all drove for the Scuderia on various occasions in 1955.

Back at the factory Ferrari called me into his office and we began to talk. He never went straight to the point and used to start talking about things that had nothing to do with the real issue. When that part of the discussion was over, he said that he would like me to drive for him on some occasions, while I made it clear that, though I was very keen to drive for the Scuderia, I was now a fairly reputable journalist (partly thanks to my racing activities, which gave me credibility), that I had family responsibilities and that, at 37, I was not going to abandon everything to start a professional racing career.

That, apparently, he fully understood and said that he would call on me whenever he thought I could be of use to him. I thanked him for his understanding, adding that I would be grateful if the imminent Monaco Grand Prix would not be such an occasion. I had many reasons for that: I thought that Monaco was a rather difficult race, I also knew that I was a better driver on a circuit with fast bends than slow corners, and I was anxious to put up a decent performance in my first race for Ferrari. Upon this we shook hands and parted.

The inevitable result – typically Ferrari – was that two weeks later a letter came asking me to drive for the Scuderia in the Monaco Grand Prix …

In the Principality the Ferrari team was in a garage only a few yards away from

At full speed in the Ferrari Super Squalo up the rise to Les Combes at Spa during the Belgian Grand Prix of 1955. (Van Bever)

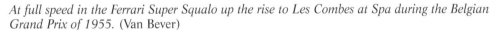

the Boulevard Albert 1er, the longest 'straight' of the circuit, which is really a long curve on which our hotel, the Bristol (which no longer exists), was located. When, on the following morning, I went to the garage, Ugolini told me that I had been asked to come as a relief driver to Piero Taruffi, which made me feel rather relieved, as I would not have liked to take the start. This really gave me more confidence. I no longer remember what my practice times were, but they did not compare too badly with those of the other team drivers, Taruffi, Trintignant, Farina and Schell. In fact, the Ferraris were completely outclassed by the Mercedes and the Lancias. Knowing that I would not have to take the start, I was now completely relaxed, and on race day I had lunch with Maurice Trintignant and his 18-year-old nephew Jean-Louis, who later became a very popular movie actor and occasional 'gentleman' racing driver.

At that stage nobody could have suspected that Maurice, who had always been very good on short, winding circuits, would miraculously win the race. But on that day the unbelievable happened: all three Mercedes, which in 1955 won all the other Grands Prix, retired, all with an identical valve gear problem, and Ascari, who had taken the lead, dived into the waters of Monaco harbour with his Lancia, handing an unlikely victory to Trintignant and his Type 625 Ferrari.

Practice had been an eye-opener on how little knowledge the Italian racing car manufacturers had about the basics of car dynamics; 20 years after Maurice Olley had published his famous papers on the subject, they relied almost exclusively on power to win races. The car I was to drive was a Type 555 'Super Squalo' ('Super Shark'), so called because of its shape. It had a very short wheelbase of 2.16m and most of the fuel was carried in the bodysides within the wheelbase. After practising for a few laps, it was obvious that it was not at all suitable for the 'round-the-houses' circuit, understeering horribly. So I stopped and asked 'track engineer' Amorotti if I could try the car with the front anti-roll bar disconnected to reduce the understeer. He looked at me as if I had insulted him and said, 'M Frère, the anti-roll bar is part of the car's concept, we can't touch it!' So the only thing we could do was to play around with the tyre pressures, which hardly had any effect.

The Ferrari also had only four speeds, which was usual at that time, but the gearbox pinions were integral with the output shaft, so the gear ratios could not be chosen individually and were much too widely spaced for Monaco – only three gears could be used on the circuit. The only choice we had was between a 'tall' final drive, which gave us the choice of the three lower gears, or a 'short' final drive, giving the use of the three upper ratios. Both combinations were tried and we finally opted for the tall final ratio and the three lower gears, which gave a better spread of ratios, though first was too high for a good start and the shift from first to second was slow. First was also too high for the slowest corners of the circuit (Station corner, now known as Loews Corner), and Gasworks Corner (subsequently modified), which left the engine, spluttering through its two twin-choke 58mm Weber carburettors.

Even so, we had to shift 12 times per lap, which meant that in the course of the race, which in those days was over 100 laps, we had to shift 1,200 times. Compare that with later years, when the cars had six-speed 'boxes, and today's semi-automatic systems!

My next race with Ferrari was the Belgian Grand Prix on the Spa-Francorchamps circuit where, two months earlier, I had won the sports car race in an Aston Martin DB3S. In practice I drove both a Super Squalo and the earlier Type 625, and found the former, which had been improved since Monaco, better suited to the fast circuit. I drove it in the race to finish fourth behind the unbeatable Mercedes of Fangio and Moss and behind my team-mate, Nino Farina. I was quite happy with my fourth place, but Farina was certainly not pleased with a car that obviously had no chance against the German opposition. After the race he threw his helmet furiously into the pit and yelled to Amorotti and Lampredi that he would never drive their ridiculous cars again. And after one of the best races he had ever driven, that was, in fact, the end of Farina's racing career.

In the team everyone was pleased with my performance. Trintignant, the third driver in the team, had only finished sixth. What I did not know was that this was going to be my last race for the Scuderia in 1955.

In that year the Swedish Grand Prix was for sports cars and was dominated by the Mercedes-Benz 300SLR. Before the main race, in which were also entered works teams from Ferrari and Maserati, there was another, shorter race for so-called 'production sports cars' for which the Ferrari Monza entered for me by the Equipe Nationale Belgique qualified. Practice was separate for the two races.

My accident during practice for the 1955 Swedish Grand Prix at Kristianstad: I was thrown out uncomfortably close to a telegraph pole but suffered nothing worse than a damaged knee.

Apart from another Monza I had virtually no real opposition in the production sports car class, and after eight or nine practice laps I was easily ahead of the field, 6 seconds quicker than the other Monza. Ferrari team manager Ugolini, who had kindly decided to take care of me, even though I was a private entry, suggested that I should therefore call it a day; the race was only 100km, and it looked as though it would be a walk-over for me.

However, I was looking for a challenge. I was sure that I could do better than the 2min 34sec with which I had been credited, as I never had a lap when I was not slowed by traffic. In practice for the main race my old rival Jean Behra had lapped in 2min 29sec in his 3-litre Maserati, and I felt sure that I could challenge that time. Ugolini therefore allowed me another four laps as soon as there were fewer cars on the circuit. I will never know how fast I went. At the end of the pit straight there was a brow followed by a right-hand bend, and as everybody knows brakes are of little use when a car is airborne. I was therefore still much too fast when I entered the right-hander. I tried to fight the car, but in vain. It understeered off the road and rolled, and the next thing I knew I was lying in a field with a broken leg. Fortunately the rolling car stopped before it caught up with me.

Following that accident, and even though it had happened in a sports car, I decided to concentrate on sports car racing, which for some obscure reason I found less stressful. For 1955/56 I was included in the Jaguar team, which fielded its D-types. Thus for one full year I had not driven a Formula 1 car when, as briefly related in the previous chapter, Ferrari sent his team of Lancia-Ferrari D50s to the 1956 Belgian Grand Prix with one driver missing, Luigi Musso, who had broken a wrist in an accident during the Nürburgring 1,000km race a week

earlier. Ferrari had instructed his new team manager, Eraldo Sculati, to 'call Frère and make him drive the car'!

Having decided that I would no longer drive in Formula 1, I at first refused. I was so determined that, despite having to report on the race for several publications, I deliberately did not attend the first of the three practice sessions, hoping that some other solution would meanwhile present itself. But when I arrived next day there was still an empty car in the Ferrari pit and Sculati insisted that I should accept Ferrari's offer. I was, of course, very interested in trying the car, which was then the best Grand Prix car around, and a track test would make

Left *The crumpled Equipe Nationale Belge Ferrari Monza back on its wheels again at Kristianstad.*

Above *After finishing second in the 1956 Belgian Grand Prix, driving this beautiful Lancia-Ferrari D50, I never regretted having changed my mind and finally accepted Ferrari's offer to be an impromptu stand-in for the injured Luigi Musso.* (LAT)

Right *Plugs being changed after the V8 engine has been warmed up before the start of the 1956 Belgian Grand Prix.* (Van Bever)

a good article. While still insisting that I would not race, as Friday's practice was nearing its end, I asked to be allowed to do two or three laps, a request enthusiastically granted. After those laps nobody, including myself, had any doubt that I would not miss this unique opportunity.

My hesitation meant that I only took part in Saturday's practice sessions, which was not enough in a car completely new to me and whose steering was so sensitive that initially I had some difficulties holding it in a straight line down the very fast Masta straight. My practice time was consequently rather mediocre and I started from the third row of the 3–2–3–2 grid.

While practice had taken place in glorious weather, it rained at the start. The rain fell in showers and only the last stages of the race were run on a drying track. Thirty-six laps (508km or 316 miles) were to be covered and it took me about ten laps to really feel at ease in the car.

The showers permitting, my lap times rapidly began to improve and I picked up several places. My greatest pleasure came when I passed Jean Behra into second place, exactly at the bend where, the day before, he had told me that he was a match for Fangio! And for me to finish second in a world championship Grand Prix in which I was never supposed to take part, and after a full year's absence from a Formula 1 cockpit, was fantastically satisfying, a wonderful day in my life with cars.

The car I drove was one of the nine Vittorio Jano-designed Lancias that Gianni Lancia had handed over to Ferrari at the end of 1955, when his company was facing serious financial problems. They had been modified by Ferrari, who discarded the side fuel tanks in favour of a rear tank. I am not sure whether this was a good idea, but the car was certainly the best front-engined grand prix car I ever raced. Its 2.5-litre V8 engine was brilliant and the test bed figures Amorotti showed me indicated that the cars taken to Belgium all developed between 268 and 272bhp. It also handled better than any racing car of the period I have driven, and its five-speed gearbox, of which first was used only for starting, was a delight to handle.

For the next three years I never drove a Scuderia car, though I did race the Equipe Nationale Belge's 2-litre TR 500 and later its V12 TR on a few occasions and partnered Olivier Gendebien in 1957 and 1958 to win the Reims 12 Hours race in his works-maintained 250GT LWB Berlinetta. So Ferrari had not completely lost sight of me when I decided that, having twice finished second at Le Mans driving Aston Martins, I should really try to win the race. And the only tool with which to achieve this ambition was a Ferrari V12 Testa Rossa.

So Ferrari was asked by Pierre Stasse, manager of the Shell-sponsored Equipe Nationale Belge, whether he would team me with Olivier Gendebien, who was a regular Ferrari team driver, and he accepted. But even before Le Mans, he

Right My Ferrari Testa Rossa leads the Wagstaff Marsh Lotus Elite through the Esses at Le Mans in 1960. Here, Oliver is at the Helm (LAT)

offered me a drive in the Targa Florio, where I was supposed to share a 2-litre front-engined Dino V6 with Willy Mairesse.

Official practice took place only on the Saturday morning before the race, but most teams were on the spot long before to practise on the 72km circuit on unguarded roads. For practising Ferrari had a terrible, four-year-old Monza and … a hired Fiat 1100! Before taking the Dino round for one lap on the Saturday before the race, I had done about 15 laps at the wheel of the 1100 and with the Monza, with which I went off the road twice, though with little damage. I was still at the stage where I was *almost* sure the next corner could be taken 'flat', but not *quite* sure and brave enough to do it, only to find I had things mixed up and was in trouble.

Finally it was all to no avail as, during the official practice session, Cliff Allison had an accident on the only fast stretch of the course, caused by a tyre failure, and damaged his Testa Rossa beyond repair. He was fortunately not hurt, but suddenly there were too many drivers and, being the one who knew the course least well, I had to step out – rather to my relief, I must confess. To be both fast and reliable, I would have needed at least ten more practice laps.

As is now well known, my career with Ferrari was rounded off in the best possible way by achieving my ambition of winning Le Mans, sharing a V12-

Ambition achieved: winning Le Mans in 1960 with the Testa Rossa I shared with fellow Belgian Olivier Gendebien. (Van Bever)

Jumping out of the Testa Rossa at a refuelling stop – no time to be lost with victory in prospect at Le Mans! (Van Bever)

engined TR59/60 with Olivier Gendebien in 1960. That year Ferrari had entered four cars, two of which, for Phil Hill-von Trips and Gendebien and myself, were TR59/60 models, updated 1959 cars with de Dion rear suspension. The other two were TR60s with independent rear suspension that had a 65kg weight advantage over the TR59/60, but their handling was said to be more tricky on the fast Le Mans course. They were to be driven by Willy Mairesse/Richie Ginther and Lodovico Scarfiotti/Ricardo Rodriguez.

It is now a matter of history that even before the first refuelling stop, the two cars then being driven by von Trips and Scarfiotti ran out of fuel on the track and had to be retired, while Gendebien just managed to get our car spluttering back to the pit for me to take over. At that time we were running second to Masten Gregory's 'Birdcage' Tipo 61 Maserati, which was very fast thanks to its clever streamlining and its exceptionally low weight (nearly 200kg less than our Ferrari), but which nobody expected to finish. In fact, after its first pit stop, the starter motor refused to do its work and we led for 22½ hours all the way to the finish, gaining a lap on our team-mates Mairesse and Ginther during the 8 hours of rain that poured down mainly during the night, before they retired with transmission problems.

Olivier had been a magnificent partner. He was certainly the best endurance driver of his time, able to go very fast while nursing his car and making very few

Nobody is perfect! I drive back from the escape road at Mulsanne Corner. (Van Bever)

mistakes. No wonder he won Le Mans four times, and I consider it a pity that Ferrari never gave him a fair chance in Formula 1. So did Olivier, who sadly left us, a very sick man, in January 1999.

As far as I am concerned, I was more than happy with our victory. I felt that it was the best achievement an amateur like myself, whose primary occupation was not motor racing, could hope for, and I am still the only other motoring journalist apart from the immortal Sammy Davis (who won Le Mans in a Bentley in 1927) to have had the honour of winning the most famous of all endurance races.

For me 1960 had been a very good season. Not only had I achieved my main ambition, but I had also won the first post-war South African Grand Prix (a non-championship race), driving a Formula 2 Cooper-Climax owned by Equipe Nationale Belge, beating Stirling Moss, who admittedly had an engine problem in the last stages of the race. I had also won the Grand Prix de Spa for sports cars in pouring rain at the wheel of a Porsche RS60. So I felt that I had proved to myself that I could hold my own among the 'greats', and decided that it was now time for me to hang up my helmet.

In fact, I nearly stuck to my decision, and when, in later years, I track-tested various racing cars, I always wore a better, more modern helmet!

Chapter 11

An undeserved win and an undeserved failure!

FOLLOWING MY ACCIDENT in the Equipe Nationale Belge's Ferrari Monza in Sweden, I rather lost confidence in my ability. For some time I had seriously contemplated retiring from racing, but on the other hand I hated the idea of doing so following a setback. Due to the accident I had done only three races with Aston Martin in 1955, but I had won at Spa and finished second at Le Mans – not too bad a score.

Mercedes-Benz had packed up after a fantastically successful season, marred by the tragic accident at Le Mans, so I could no longer expect anything from that source. But when I went to discuss the future with John Wyer, Aston Martin's team manager, who had meanwhile been promoted to Technical Director, and told him that 1956 would probably be my last season, he bluntly answered that, in that case, he would rather sign up an ambitious up-and-coming young driver. So I turned to the arch rival, Jaguar, but before we came to an agreement 'Lofty' England wanted to see me at work and be sure that the accident had not had any detrimental effect on my confidence in terms of speed. We therefore made an appointment at the Silverstone circuit, where he organised a test session to find out.

The car was a prototype D-type with a de Dion rear axle, which I thought was not really an advantage – at least on Silverstone's smooth surface – but the upshot was that he took me into his team. A few months later he must have regretted it … In the five races I did for the team, I destroyed two cars and threw away an almost certain Le Mans victory.

My first assignment for the team was to drive a Mark VII in the Touring Car race at the *Daily Express* meeting at Silverstone. I was extremely nervous and two bad accidents in the races before the touring car event certainly did nothing for my morale; neither did the fact that in the race I was passed by Duncan Hamilton's 2.4-litre Jaguar and, of all things, Ken Wharton's astonishingly quick Austin Westminster. I was not too pleased with myself, but at least I had not made any mistakes and my confidence was returning. 'Lofty' was probably not too impressed either, but he nevertheless agreed to enter a Jaguar 2.4 for the

Touring Car race that was to take place a few weeks later on the Spa-Francorchamps circuit.

There were three races on the programme. The first was for small touring cars, the second for touring cars up to 2,600cc and GT cars up to 2 litres, with separate classifications, and the third for sports cars, with a separate classification for those up to 2 litres. In addition to driving the Jaguar in the touring and GT race, I had also agreed to drive the Equipe Nationale Belge's 2-litre Ferrari 500TR in the third race. The second race is the one I should never have won. The biggest competition for the Jaguar came from Joakim Bonnier's Alfa Romeo 1900 TI and two Mercedes-Benz 220SEs, which were works cars driven by Erwin Bauer and 1952 Le Mans winner Fritz Riess. These cars had just done extremely well in the Mille Miglia, finishing sixth and seventh overall, and were managed by Karl Kling.

As the race was for modified touring cars, the Jaguar that works test driver Norman Dewis had driven from Coventry was one of the Silverstone cars. It had a C-type cylinder head, two big SU carburettors and a close-ratio gearbox, which made it much faster than the standard car, its maximum speed being not far off 125mph. Its suspension had also been tweaked and it handled very well, so I had every reason to be confident. 'Lofty' was probably equally so; the race being of one hour's duration and with no pitwork required, he had not seen any reason to send a mechanic along. The only Jaguar man around was Norman Dewis.

Two practice sessions were programmed, but after setting the fastest time for the touring cars I had to stop because the bodyside bracket of the Panhard rod had broken – a familiar problem with Mk 1 and Mk 2 Jaguars. Investigating the damage Norman also noticed that the oil seal at the rear of the gearbox was

leaking. Overnight the bracket was welded, the gearbox filled up and the seal left to be attended to later.

After the second practice session, which took place on a partly wet surface and during which nobody improved on the times set the previous day, Norman decided to investigate the oil leak and found that it was due to the seizure of the splines allowing the propeller shaft to move axially. Unfortunately, when he tried to remove the defective part the entire gearbox secondary shaft came with it, and all the gears, washers, etc fell to the bottom of the casing! Having removed the top of the box, poor Norman tried all night to put the parts back on the shaft with a deadline of 9.00am looming, when the car had to be in the parc fermé. Fortunately for him, Ecurie Ecosse had entered two D-types for the sports car race, and at 5.30am on Sunday he decided to wake up one of the Scottish mechanics to give him a hand.

There was no solution but to remove the gearbox and reassemble it on the bench, but the gearbox of a Mk 1 can only be removed together with the engine, and no winch was available. So the two decided to cut a large piece out of the bulkhead to remove the box while leaving the engine in place. It was by now unthinkable that by 9.00am the car could be in the parc fermé where it was to be filled up with the fuel provided by the organisers and the tank sealed. Fortunately, Léon Sven, the clerk of the course, was a friend of mine, and said, 'OK, 12 o'clock will do, but no later!'

Having obtained this concession, I drove back to the garage in Stavelot at 10.45, only to find two completely exhausted fellows with bloodshot eyes staring at a heap of gears next to an almost empty gearbox casing. Poor Norman hardly knew where he was and every time he threaded a gear on its shaft, it seemed to

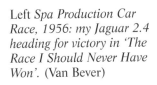

Left *Spa Production Car Race, 1956: my Jaguar 2.4 heading for victory in 'The Race I Should Never Have Won'.* (Van Bever)

Right *'Lofty' England in typical pose at Le Mans; he later became Jaguar's Managing Director.*

be the wrong way round, while washers and needles from bearings seemed to mysteriously disappear. But work was nevertheless proceeding and 40 minutes later the box was reassembled – only to find that fourth gear could not be selected! Norman was finished and even the impassive Scot began to get nervous. I could no longer stand it, and drove back to the paddock to try and get a further concession from Sven, who finally agreed that, if by chance the car was finished in time, it could be filled up at the garage at Stavelot and driven to the course after the first race of the day was finished.

At 12.15, a quarter of an hour before the start of the first race, I phoned Sven's instructions to Norman who said that the gearbox was now nearly reassembled and would hopefully work. But if it did, I thought, he would still have to put it back on the engine, connect all the tubing and wiring, put the floor and the seats back in place and fill up, all within the next hour and a quarter – a seemingly impossible task.

While watching the race for small touring cars, I felt very frustrated that I would be a non-starter in a race that I felt I could have won. But then the miracle happened: 15 minutes before the start of the second race, Norman drove up in front of the pits in a filthy, untidy but working Jaguar! I just had time to don my helmet, adjust the seat and drive to the starting grid.

Having witnessed the pandemonium of the last 18 hours, I was rather anxious: a gearbox seizing or locking is the last thing you want in a race, as there is nothing the driver can do to prevent the car from skidding off the road. I therefore took the first lap fairly easily, but nothing undesirable happened so I quickly decided to get on with the race. Even taking it rather easy I had been leading all my direct competitors and was already ahead of most of the Porsche Carreras that made up the bulk of the GT group. Only those of Sailer and Nathan, two of the best Porsche exponents of the period, were ahead of me, and not very far, fighting it out between themselves, so hard that Sailer eventually crashed out. Two laps later I noticed that I was making up ground on Nathan and realised that I could win not only the Touring Car class, but the race outright. Now fully confident of my car, I made an ultimate effort and overtook Nathan on the last lap, which also happened to be my fastest, 15 seconds faster than my best with a 5.3-litre Chrysler Hemi two years earlier. I later learned that the Porsche had lost third gear.

I was happy and did not have too much time to think about all the protests that could have been filed against me for not having been to the parc fermé, for not having respected the time schedule, for not having filled up at the official filling station, and for having raced with an unsealed tank. I just had time to appear on the podium and jump into the Ferrari for the next race, in which I eventually finished in third place overall behind Sanderson's D-type and Parnell's Aston Martin DB3S, winning the 2-litre class.

But nobody protested, not even Bonnier, who finished second with his quick Alfa and who would have become a sure winner, nor the Mercedes boys, who had the responsibility of works cars. They all knew that protesting against the 'local hero' would have created an uproar in the crowd and made them for ever extremely unpopular. Or should I believe that there was a finer sporting spirit in those days? Whatever the answer, that was the race I should *never* have won.

I had now completely regained my confidence and looked forward to the rest of the season at the wheel of a D-type, a car I really liked. It looked wonderful and efficient, had a nicely flexible engine – by racing standards – and had few of the unpleasant failings of the racing cars of the time; the pedals did not require a Herculean force, the rack-and-pinion steering was nicely sensitive and accurate, the gearbox had excellent synchromesh (strange because it was basically the same as the contemporary production unit of which the synchromesh was definitely weak), the well-shaped windscreen offered good protection, and it was not outrageously noisy. Because of its rather heavy rigid rear axle, it was not too good on rough surfaces, but for Le Mans it was perfect. Victory there was Jaguar's main objective and the car had been designed for that particular race.

In 1956 it was again Jaguar's main objective, and in order to prepare for it 'Lofty' had organised a two-day testing session on the very fast Reims circuit, a venue comparable to Le Mans from a racing point of view. To try and keep the speeds down after the frightful accident of 1955, the 1956 Le Mans regulations limited the engine capacity to 2.5 litres for 'sports prototypes' and 3.5 litres for 'production sports cars' with a minimum production of 100 units, which Jaguar actually built, only for the minimum to be reduced to 50, probably to help Aston Martin. In addition the fuel consumption was limited to approximately 26 litres per 100km (10.9mpg imperial).

Testing with Jaguar on the Reims circuit to prepare for Le Mans in 1956.

This was really a gift for Jaguar, but 'Lofty' decided to make sure that the D-Type would fulfil the fuel consumption requirements and organised a testing session on the Reims circuit with two cars for Ivor Bueb and myself, one 'normal' car fitted with three Weber twin-choke carburettors and one with Lucas fuel injection. We also tested brake pads and new Dunlop racing tyres, probably the first radials designed for racing. These were two very pleasant and interesting days in which I broke the sports car lap record for the circuit.

Unfortunately, it was to be the last time my membership of the Jaguar team gave me cause to rejoice. Practising for the Nürburgring 1,000km race, in which I was to share a D-type with Duncan Hamilton, I left the road at the fast Wippermann section in pouring rain. The car somersaulted down a ravine, broke several small trees and finished up on its wheels about 15 yards below the circuit with me still in the cockpit, without a scratch. I could just as easily have been killed. This was Friday, and on Saturday afternoon Norman Dewis turned up with another D-type that he had driven all the way from Coventry. Unfortunately it broke its gearbox after I had moved up to sixth position, having started from the last row in a field of over 80 cars.

The Reims 12 Hours race, which traditionally started at zero hour on Sunday, was a dress rehearsal for the all-important Le Mans event. Jaguar entered three cars and 'Lofty' decided that I would team up with Mike Hawthorn, which indicated that he had not lost confidence in me. But there was a problem: Mike had been entered to drive a Vanwall in the French Grand Prix and the rule was that any driver who took part in both races should not be driving in the 12 Hours after 7.00am. The Jaguars could run for $2^{1}/_{2}$ hours between refuelling stops and it was Mike who took the start in our car. This meant that after I handed it over to him at 5.00am, he would have to stop less than 2 hours later, and we would have had one stop more than the other two cars.

Up to 6.00am we were all allowed to do battle with our team-mates, but for the last 6 hours we would have to keep our positions. By that time our car was leading and it was still in the lead when Mike handed it back to me before 7.00am to drive to the finish. Following 'Lofty's' instructions, I started lapping 3–4 seconds slower than the car's potential and assumed that the other drivers were doing the same. But suddenly I saw Duncan Hamilton coming up and, as I continued to lap at the agreed pace, he soon caught and passed me. This meant that we had lost the race as, due to Mike's early stop, I would have to refuel once more than the Hamilton-Bueb car before the finish. Mike and I had been robbed of victory and the fact that 'Lofty' immediately fired Hamilton did not give it back to us.

This episode was still in my mind when Le Mans came up. Practice had shown that the race would be a gift to Jaguar. The works had entered three cars, one with fuel injection for Hawthorn/Bueb and two with three twin-choke Webers for myself and Titterington and Fairman/Wharton. To improve safety after the previous year's disaster, the pits had been moved and the pit straight widened and completely resurfaced. Unfortunately, after a gloriously sunny week rain began to fall 10 minutes before the traditional Le Mans start. And what happened then shows how, in certain circumstances, one can be fuddled by nervousness and the importance of the occasion.

As the legendary Charles Faroux dropped the national flag, I ran across the road and jumped into the car, but it seemed ages before the engine would fire. Hawthorn had gone and Fairman's car also fired before my engine would respond. Driving up the rise under the Dunlop bridge, it was immediately obvious that the new surface, which had never seen a drop of rain before, was

Le Mans, 1956: disaster in 'The Race I Should Have Won'. My Jaguar D-type has just hit the barrier in the Esses, Jack Fairman's Jaguar spins without damage, but de Portago's Ferrari also comes along spinning and is about to hit Fairman's car. All three cars had to retire.

In vain I try to drive back to the pit. On seeing this photo, team manager 'Lofty' England said, "Ah, this is our new short-chassis job!"

extremely slippery. But stupidly, what really mattered to me was that the other two team cars were ahead of me and that, at some stage, 'Lofty' would give instructions to keep our positions; however, I completely dismissed the fact that, should that happen, it would certainly not occur before we were well ahead of the opposition and that he would surely not issue such an order before at least half distance. For Jaguar and for me, this was the most important race of the season and I had a car capable of winning. I was determined to take my chance and certainly did not want to stay behind Jack Fairman.

I passed him before we reached White House corner, heading for the second lap. Driving under the Dunlop bridge, I remembered that the track was very slippery and started to brake well ahead of my normal braking point before going into the 'Esses' at Tertre Rouge. But I immediately knew that it was too late. I knew that I would not be able to take the first left-hander. When I came to the bend I was still going much too fast, and spun halfway round, the car's tail hitting the protective wall bordering the track. Fairman, who was coming up behind, went broadside while trying to avoid me and was hit by de Portago who, as he later told me, had also lost control of his Ferrari. We all tried to get the cars back to the pits, some 8 miles away, but I soon realised that the damage was too serious and ruefully walked back in the rain to face 'Lofty'.

All three cars were out, and to cap the Jaguar disaster the fuel injection car driven by Mike Hawthorn was in serious trouble with an engine running on five cylinders. He lad lost 17 laps before the origin of the trouble – a cracked injection pipe – was diagnosed and the pipe replaced. But he had lost all chances of winning the race. You can imagine 'Lofty's' state of mind when I walked into the pit to apologise for my stupidity. But he just shrugged his shoulders and said, 'Well, that's motor racing.' What a wonderful man!

Everyone was very kind to me, including Pat Appleyard, the daughter of Jaguar founder Bill Lyons, but thinking of all the work and money that had gone into the cars, the preparations for so all-important a race and of the impact the Le Mans victories had on Jaguar's sales, I felt terribly bad. Jaguar's only hope now rested on the Ecurie Ecosse car driven by Ron Flockhart and Ninian Sanderson, who were battling neck-and-neck in the rain with the Aston Martin of Stirling Moss and Peter Collins. I spent the night and the rest of the race in agony, praying for the Scots to stay on the road and resist the Aston's assaults. Fortunately they did indeed save the day for Jaguar and for my peace of mind. But what a day!

Thinking back on it, with the Hawthorn/Bueb car way behind since the early stages and driving a works car marginally faster than the Scottish entry, this disastrous Le Mans for me and co-driver Desmond Titterington was a race we *should* have won …

Chapter 12

1957–58:
driving 'à la carte'

WHEN 1957 ARRIVED I had not made any arrangements for racing. I was very busy reporting races and road testing for the Belgian paper *Les Sports* and writing for various magazines, had a family to look after and wanted to be free to pick the races I wanted to do as it suited me, having decided to concentrate on sports car racing. I knew that it would never be difficult to get a drive in a good car in a long-distance race and that, if I could not get a works drive, the Equipe Nationale Belge, of which I was a member and which was managed by Pierre Stasse (who was also the Managing Director of *Les Sports*), would be only too pleased to lend me one from its stable. This, in 1957, comprised a D-type Jaguar, two 3-litre Ferrari Testa Rossas, a 2-litre Testa Rossa and a Porsche 550 Spyder.

My first race in 1957 was to be the Sebring 12 Hours in Florida, for which Renault had entered three little 850cc Dauphines to support their efforts to get a foothold in the American market. The team consisted of a blue, a white and a red car – the French colours. They were driven, respectively, by Maurice Michy and Maurice Foulgoc, Gilberte Thirion and Nadège Ferrier (two very quick girls), and Jean Lucas and myself. All three cars finished, but after the race I swore that I would never again agree to drive a mobile chicane in a big race, especially on a short circuit where the Jaguars and Ferraris passed you almost twice in a lap! It was the race to which Zora Arkus-Duntov brought the famous Corvette SS, which was very fast but unfortunately not sufficiently developed to last the distance. It is a pity that GM decided to shelve it.

The main reason why I had accepted to drive a Dauphine at Sebring was that I had made a deal with Renault: in return for the drive, they agreed to lend me a Dauphine with which I could drive from the East Coast to the West Coast and back. Nadège Ferrier came with me on the westward journey along the Gulf of Mexico, when we visited New Orleans, the Petrified Forests National Park, the Grand Canyon, the Yosemite National Park and Las Vegas before we reached Los Angeles and proceeded from there to San Francisco, where Nadège left me to stay with a friend. Until then everything had been fine, except for a violent sandstorm in Nevada, the headwind being so strong that the poor little Dauphine was hardly able to exceed 50mph.

For the return journey I followed Route 66 and all was fine until there was an ominous noise from the engine, which made me instantly switch off. There I was, in the middle of the desert, with a dead engine, and there was nothing I could do. Fortunately the Americans are very helpful and the first car that rolled along, a big Pontiac, stopped and immediately the driver offered to push me into the next small city, Craig, Colorado, where the Dauphine was rolled into a service station that fortunately had a pit. The attendant kindly lent me his tools – all imperial, whereas the Dauphine's nuts and bolts were, of course, all metric. I nevertheless managed to get the head and the sump off, but it proved impossible to undo the connecting rod bolts with the imperial spanners. So I had to call Renault in New York and ask them to send me a 12mm ring spanner. In the meantime a kind gentleman driving a big Ford Fairlane agreed to take me to Denver, some 125 miles away, where I had called the Renault dealer to make sure he had the parts – a piston, a valve and sundry gaskets.

Back in Craig I had to wait two or three days before the spanner arrived, which gave me time to write an article about the Dauphine and listen to the radio, which was about three-quarters commercials, mainly for car dealers, and one-quarter Elvis Presley. Once the all-important 12mm spanner arrived, I was soon on the road again, only to have another valve drop! Fortunately, this time it was in a built-up area, near a garage. I walked in and asked if they would help me.

'Not now,' was the answer. 'We're too busy. Maybe in the afternoon'.

'Could I please borrow some of your tools?' I asked.

'Yes, sure'.

Fifteen minutes later the cylinder head was on the garage bench and the garage people were so amazed that they left their work, pushed the Dauphine into the garage and did everything they could to help me. The only thing to do, however, was to find out when the next train to Denver, now much nearer, was due to leave. In the evening I was back with the parts and the garage owner invited me to have dinner at his home and stay there overnight.

Next day I was on the road again, with a spare valve in my bag, but from then on the Dauphine behaved and when we reached Salt Lake City I could not resist the temptation to drive on to the Great Salt Lake, but without any intention of breaking John Cobb's land speed record! Then, through Chicago and Detroit, I was finally back in New York, about 12 days after departing from San Francisco.

Fortunately I returned to Europe in time for the Mille Miglia, where I drove a Dauphine again, which was much more fun than driving one on a circuit. The nimble car, which now handled beautifully and had a superb five-speed gearbox, was a pure joy to drive, especially on the mountain stretches. But that has been dealt with in the earlier chapter devoted to the Mille Miglia.

In Sebring I had asked Olivier Gendebien, who raced a Ferrari there, if I could be his co-driver in the forthcoming Reims 12 Hours race, the first long-distance event open exclusively to GT cars. Olivier had a long-wheelbase 250GT Berlinetta and, though it was privately owned, because he was a Ferrari works driver his car was always serviced by the factory and always had the latest modifications.

The race ran from midnight on Saturday to midday on Sunday and the start in the darkness was quite impressive. Olivier made a bad start as the engine was slow to fire, but after 2 hours he was in second place, led only by Phil Hill's Ferrari. I knew that Hill's co-driver, Wolfgang Seidel, was not nearly as fast as the American, and when I took over it did not take me long to get our car into the lead, where we stayed for the rest of the race.

The following year, 1958, with the same car, we gave a repeat performance, though not without problems, as after 4 hours racing the dynamo packed up, fortunately just before sunrise, and we had to change the battery at every pit stop. And to cap it all, nearly 2 hours before the end the toughened glass windshield suddenly broke when I was doing 250kmh (155mph) on the straight. This meant

Left *Two hours before the finish of the Reims 12 Hours in 1958, the windscreen shattered on the Ferrari Tour de France I was sharing with Olivier Gendebien. To avoid wind pressure pushing out the rear window, the mechanics removed it and I drove the last two hours in a gale. Olivier and I stand where the rear window should be!* (Van Bever)

Right *At Le Mans in 1957, Freddy Rousselle and I shared an Equipe Nationale Belge Jaguar D-type. We finished fourth after an electrical problem dropped us from second place with five hours to go.* (Van Bever)

a pit stop to remove all the splinters from inside the car and another to allow the mechanics to remove the rear window which, they thought, might be blown out by the air pressure. I was thus condemned to drive to the end in a rather stormy wind tunnel, which slowed the car quite a lot on the straight, but we still managed to finish one lap ahead of the similar Ferrari of 'Beurlys'/Mairesse.

I remember that in 1957 or '58 a Ferrari driver – I think it was Jo Schlesser – came to the race desperately looking for a competent co-driver, his having been taken ill. He was put in touch with a tall American who, for some reason, had no drive. The American's name meant nothing to him, but as there was no other solution, he agreed to try him and ended up delighted – his name was Dan Gurney! At that time Europe had never heard of him.

When Le Mans came round again in 1957, I really wanted to make up for my stupid performance of the year before, when I had crashed my D-type going into the second lap. I decided that I would drive the Equipe Nationale Belge's Jaguar and chose Freddy Rousselle as my co-driver. With Gendebien driving a works Ferrari, I thought that this little-known driver, a garage owner in Verviers in southern Belgium, was the fastest and most reliable partner I could find, and this he proved to be. To our great surprise we found ourselves in second place on the Sunday morning, led only by the winning Ecurie Ecosse 3.8-litre D-type, driven by Ron Flockhart and Ivor Bueb. Then, just after 10.00am, Rousselle stopped at Mulsanne with a dead engine. Most drivers would just have left the car there, unable to locate the problem, but not so Rousselle, who diagnosed that one of the points of the contact breaker in the ignition distributor had come adrift. He managed to make a provisional repair and get the car back to the pits to have a

Rounding Mulsanne Corner in the D-type, which was a joy to drive at Le Mans. Note the aerodynamically optimised windscreen and tonneau cover over the passenger seat. (Van Bever)

new part fitted. Unfortunately, when the car rejoined the race we had fallen back to sixth place, but we had a magnificent time driving as fast as we could for the last 4 or 5 hours to move up to a final fourth. Jaguars finished first, second, third, fourth and sixth, a splendid swansong the for D-type!

Even though, with Edgar Barth as partner, we finished fourth at Le Mans in 1958 with a 1,500cc Porsche Spyder RSK – not bad for a 1,500 – I felt frustrated by the two races I did that year for the Porsche team, the other being the Nürburgring 1,000km earlier in the year. In that race I was partnered in a 1,500 RSK by Harry Schell, the American notable for speaking perfect French and bad English, having been brought up almost entirely in France. Porsche had three identical works cars in that race, the others being driven by Giorgio Scarlatti/Richard von Frankenberg and Jean Behra/Edgar Barth. Behra was not happy with his car, with which he was unable to equal the lap times he had achieved in a private testing session, so he asked to try ours and immediately lapped much faster, getting down to 9min 54sec, the first time a 1,500cc car lapped the 'Ring in less than 10 minutes. As he was the number one driver, he kept the car and we had to make do with his, with which I could do no better than 10min 17sec, while Schell was even slower. In the race we eventually finished seventh overall and second in the 1,500cc class, behind the private RSK of de

Beaufort-Frankenberg, after the Behra/Barth car retired with a broken valve spring cup.

Later, when the cars were back in the factory, it was found that, following an earlier accident, the chassis of our car was completely out of shape, the explanation for its poor performance.

Six weeks later, at Le Mans, after a freezing cold and rainy night, Barth and I were running fourth with a 1,500cc RSK behind two Ferraris and the Behra-Bonnier 1,600 RSK. For some laps the latter car slowed because its front brakes were finished, and Barth, who was driving at the time, was only one lap behind our team-mates. Before I took over for the last stint, team manager Huschke von Hanstein approached me, saying that the brakes of the Behra-Bonnier car would have to be changed and asked me if I would agree to drive slowly so that, with new brakes, the sick car could catch up, and we should try to make it a dead heat at the finish. We would get the signals to make sure the scheme worked. Making a dead heat is virtually impossible anyway, but I was stupid enough to agree, and so did Barth when he came in.

I tried my best to achieve the dead heat, but when the flag fell I turned out to be exactly one lap behind. As I had always scrupulously followed the pit signals, I have always felt that the one lap difference had been well organised. Had we

At Le Mans in 1958 I shared a Porsche RSK 1500 with Edgar Barth. We were running third overall two hours from the finish when team orders required us to let the Behra/Herrmann RSK 1600 through. (Van Bever)

said 'No' to Hanstein, Behra would never have caught us; and whatever the order, Porsches would have finished third and fourth anyway, a magnificent performance for the little Spyders. So why insist on reshuffling what would have been the logical order? Did Huschke fear Behra's wrath? He could have had many reasons.

At the end of 1957 I was seriously thinking of retiring from active motor sport and, in fact, raced very little. But with the 1958 Spa sports car race coming up, for which Aston Martin had entered two 3.9-litre DBR2s, I had second thoughts. As the regular team drivers, Tony Brooks and Roy Salvadori, were due to race at Monaco on the same day, I sent a telegram to Reg Parnell, who had taken over as team manager from John Wyer (who was promoted to Managing Director): 'Retired racing driver would be delighted to drive Aston Martin at Spa. Regards.'

Parnell immediately agreed, and the second car was driven by Carroll Shelby. The D-type Jaguars were now ageing, but I had not reckoned with the two Lister-Jaguars, which were much lighter than the DBR2 and very competently driven by Masten Gregory and that fantastic disabled driver Archie Scott-Brown, who had only one hand and very short legs, but had many times given Stirling Moss something to think about. After practice Masten, who knew the course well, had achieved the fastest time, with me second, Archie third and Shelby

The start of the 1958 Spa Sports Car Race: driving one of the DBR1 Astons (number 1), I finished second to Masten Gregory's Lister-Jaguar in a race marred by Archie Scott-Brown's fatal accident. (Van Bever)

fourth. I did not like the handling of the DBR2, which I found rather erratic, and I was sure that I would not be able to hold the Listers.

Practice took place on the Friday and Saturday before the race. In those days the 'bus stop' chicane did not exist, and the 'Seaman curve' preceding La Source hairpin was very fast. This was where, in 1939, Dick Seaman had been killed when leading the Grand Prix in a Mercedes in pouring rain. On the Friday it struck me that at the exit of that curve a road sign was exactly in the way, should a car run off the road. I therefore went to see my friend Léon Sven, the clerk of the course, and suggested that the sign be removed. When Saturday's practice came, the sign was still there and I again insisted that it was very dangerous and should be removed. But still nothing was done.

In the race, after half a lap, on the long, fast rise from Stavelot to Francorchamps, the two Listers simply drew away from the Astons. It had begun to rain, but only locally, and one could never be sure whether, around a corner, the road would be dry or wet. Out in front, Masten and Archie had a fantastic dogfight, but after six or seven laps, when I came out of the 'Seaman curve', a huge column of black smoke was rising high into the sky. Archie had gone off and hit the signpost, which made the car unsteerable; he was trapped in his burning car. I am sure that, had the signpost been removed, he would have had a good chance of rejoining the road and might have got away with it.

In the end Masten won, I was second and Shelby third, but we were all less than happy when Archie died only two days later in hospital.

This tragic episode emphasises how much safety in racing has progressed since what many people call 'the golden years of motor racing', when it was 'normal' for three or four well-known drivers to be killed in a year in Europe alone. Where, on modern circuits, enormous run-off areas, strategically placed guard rails and heaps of tyres are arranged to make running off the road as harmless as possible, in the 1950s and '60s the racing circuits were lined with trees, ditches, banks, brick walls, houses, and even barbed wire fences, which cut off more than one driver's head. Deformable safety tanks did not exist, and fire was a much more serious menace than today. The cars themselves were fragile when they hit an obstacle, and very often the best chance of survival was to be thrown out and hope to land in a field or other not too hard a surface. There were also no safety belts – but in the absence of roll-over bars, they would have made things even worse.

Enthusiasm must have made us blind to the risks we took every time we started a race. Credit must be given to Jackie Stewart who, after a frightening accident at the Spa-Francorchamps circuit, when he sat wounded in a bath of petrol for 20 minutes before he could be extracted from his BRM, began to make drivers aware of the risks they took and created the Grand Prix Drivers' Association, where car and circuit safety was discussed and more safety was demanded from the FIA, race organisers and car manufacturers.

To achieve the degree of safety reached today, it was absolutely necessary that

My ambition before retiring was to win at Le Mans. I had twice finished second – here with Maurice Trintignant in an Aston Martin DBR1 in 1959 – but that was not good enough. (E. Richartz)

the FIA, working in close co-operation with the racing car manufacturers, should impose strict safety regulations that manufacturers could not be expected to implement on their own initiative if, as is so often the case, they affected performance in any way. New technology has also contributed to better car safety, a clear example being the carbon-fibre composites of which the monocoques of top-class racing cars are made, and which form a very light but immensely strong survival shell.

More safety, however, has also had negative effects. In the 1950s and '60s a driver knew that an unfair manoeuvre involving another could cost not only his own but also the other driver's life, and none of them would have risked pushing anyone else off the road, voluntarily or not.

Safety also means many more marshals, firemen and doctors around the circuit, a resuscitation facility, and helicopters to fly injured drivers to hospital. The cost involved is one reason why long circuits like the old Nürburgring have disappeared in favour of circuits of 5–6km (3–4 miles) in length, Spa-Francorchamps and Suzuka being the longest at 6.9km (4.3 miles) and 5.9km (3.7 miles) respectively.

Chapter 13

African adventure

As I was not contracted to any particular team in 1958, I was able to accept an invitation from the Belgian Congo to take part in the 'Kivu Rally', based in Bukavu, on the shores of Lake Kivu. Three weeks after the rally a so-called Grand Prix for sports cars was to take place in Leopoldville, today's Kinshasa, for which the Equipe Nationale Belge had entered two cars, its 'customer' Ferrari Testa Rossa V12, which I had been invited to drive, and an old 4.1-litre 'America' Touring Superleggera Berlinetta lent by 'Blary', brother of the better-known 'Beurlys' (in reality Jean Blaton), who hoped that the car would be sold locally after the race. It was to be driven by Alain de Changy.

Jet passenger planes were very rare in those days, and I left Brussels in a Sabena DC-7 via Rome and Cairo to Stanleyville, from where two further connections were supposed to land me within 24 hours in Bukavu on Lake Tanganyika. However, even before starting from Brussels we had to wait for an hour in an unbearably hot plane for some unexplained reason. Then the Rome stop, which was supposed to last $1^1/_2$ hours, took 5 hours because, it was announced, of a defective radio. In Cairo the stop should have lasted 2 hours, but 15 minutes before we landed at 5.30am we were informed that we would not depart before 2.30am the next morning because the crew would otherwise exceed their allowed working time. OK, I thought, that gives us the opportunity to visit Cairo and its wonderful museum. When we finally landed in Stanleyville, over 24 hours behind schedule, the DC-4 on the connecting flight to Usumbura (now Busumbura) was full and I had to wait for another 24 hours for the next plane, spending the night in the Sabena Guest House. Meanwhile, some kind officials who had met me at the airport took me for a wonderful drive in the equatorial forests.

In Usumbura I was met by Pierre Slosse, a former racing manager for the BP oil company whom I knew well, so the wait before departing in a DC-3 in Bukavu seemed short. However, after I had embarked there was a problem with one of the engines and all the passengers were sent back to the terminal. Yes, flying in the 1950s was still an adventure and a reasonable level of reliability only came

The Ferrari Testa Rossa

The Ferrari Testa Rossa belonging to the Belgian National Team was a 'Customer's Version' differing in many points from the works car I drove at Le Mans two years later, though both were powered by basically similar 3-litre V12 engines.

The V12 Testa Rossa was first officially entered by Ferrari for the 1957 Le Mans 24 Hours race and was driven by Olivier Gendebien and Maurice Trintignant. It was a development of the earlier 2-litre, four-cylinder TR500, of which the tubular chassis frame had been lengthened by 10cm to accommodate the V12. It had a four-speed gearbox in unit with the engine and retained the four-cylinder model's live rear axle and coil springs, while the brakes were Ferrari's usual drums with two leading shoes. This easily serviced model became the 'customer model', of which 19 units are said to have been made for 1958. Most of them were left-hand drive and are easily recognisable by their front fenders leaving a large gap between their front part and the front cowling, designed to increase the air flow to the brakes.

The factory cars for 1958 were largely similar, but had a differently shaped body and a de Dion rear end. For 1959 the cars were considerably lightened by the use of a small-tube spaceframe and widespread use of magnesium. A new five-speed gearbox was used with the primary shaft higher and to the left of the output shaft, and while the propeller shaft was in the centreline of the chassis, the engine was moved 10cm to the left, so compensating for the driver's weight. During the racing season, dry sump lubrication was adopted and disc brakes replaced the drum brakes. All cars had right-hand steering.

For 1960 the wheelbase was shortened by 100mm to 2.25m at the front end and the car we had at Le Mans had a five-speed rear-mounted gearbox for better weight distribution, which made it in fact a very different car from the 'customer model' I drove in the Congo.

with the jet planes. Fortunately, Slosse had waited to see the plane off, and rather than let me wait for hours, he drove me to Bukavu, my final destination, 90 miles away, in his Studebaker over a fairly good tarmac road. On arrival I was welcomed like a hero, long before the DC-3 arrived.

In Bukavu I met my car, a well-kept 60bhp Porsche 1600, and my navigator, a Belgian named Roger Beerten, who had finished second in the previous year's rally. On this occasion the rally was over 1,130 miles in four loops of the same course, including two timed sections, one of 63 miles, during which the imposed 70kmh (43.5mph) average speed would take some energetic driving, and one of 17 miles on a narrow dirt road in the mountains, with stones all over the place, which would surely decide the issue because the required 75kmh (46.6mph) average was obviously impossible to achieve by any of the cars entered, the main contenders being four Porsche 1600s, an 85bhp Volvo 544 and a quick but fragile Fiat-Abarth 750.

My car had been well prepared with an undershield coming straight from Stuttgart, and off I went with my co-driver to have a look at the two special stages. However, as it turned out they were not the worst – some of the roads on which an average speed of only 50kmh (31mph) was required were so bad that even that pace would be difficult without breaking the car.

Local papers gave me tremendous advance publicity, but five hours after the start (with cars departing at five-minute intervals because of the dust) 'The Crew to Beat' was already beaten; a stone had apparently cracked an oil pipe and, after finishing the first loop within schedule, except for the 'impossible' special stage, 2 litres of oil were missing from the sump and I drove the car back to the garage with the engine making unpleasant noises. The rally was won by another Porsche, with the quick little Abarth second.

Such was the enthusiasm of those colonial Belgians that the VW and Porsche dealerships in Bukavu and Usumbura not only prepared four Porsches (including mine, which was their demonstration car) and three Beetles free of charge, they also gave every crew five new tyres and promised to give their car a complete service, including repairs, after the rally, also free of charge.

With the rally over, I had over two weeks to spend before flying to Leopoldville for the Grand Prix. This gave local friends an opportunity to take me for a most

Preparing for the start of the Rallye du Kivu, Central Africa, in 1958. My locally prepared Porsche 356A did not last the distance. Organiser Jean Wathelet is seen behind the camera.

interesting tour through Rwanda-Burundi and Uganda to the Albert National Park, where we spent the night surrounded by lions, elephants, antelopes, etc. I was also taken to a party on the shores of Lake Kivu where I learned water skiing and – I am proud to say – succeeded at my first attempt. I liked it so much that the following year I bought a pair of skis and a boat to go skiing in Italy on Lake Garda, while on holiday with the family. My three daughters were also soon quite proficient, and all of us became good water skiers on mono-skis; I even went so far as to buy 'figure-skis' and make 360-degree turns.

From the Albert Park I was taken to Safari Lodge in Uganda, at the heart of Park Elizabeth, and to the channel linking Lake George and Lake Elizabeth, full of hippopotamuses mixing with bathing elephants and superb birds. This brought us to Usumbura, from where I finally flew to Leopoldville where I was met by Pierre Stasse, manager of Equipe Nationale Belge, his wife Colette and Mauro Bianchi, the team's mechanic.

There were still a few days before the race, so we were taken to many interesting sites by members of the local automobile club and the Shell company, the team's sponsors. The local press was full of articles about the race and the 'famous drivers from Europe' who were competing. This was obviously to be one of the year's major events.

The circuit of only 1.5 miles was in the town centre, leading through a park and Leopoldville's main avenue, lined by modern buildings. The race was over 120 laps for a total of 181 miles, and the heat was such that I was really wondering whether I would be able to bear it in the hot cockpit of the Ferrari. After all, I was faced with 1,440 gear shifts and 480 applications of the brakes!

The entry list was really a joke. I knew that de Changy had no chance whatever with his old Berlinetta, and the rest of the entry were all local drivers in run-of-the-mill Austin-Healeys, Triumph TR2s and 3s, Porsche 1600s and even one flat-twin 850cc Panhard Dyna Junior, together with a standard Fiat 600 fitted with a 750cc Abarth engine!

There was just one practice session, on the eve of race day after sunset, the streets being illuminated only by the public lighting system and the cars' headlights. My pole position was a foregone conclusion, even though practice indicated that I would have to seriously nurse the brakes. But against such opposition, I could have won even without brakes! Those of the other Ferrari lasted even less time. Fortunately during the evening the news came through that Pierre Berchem, a Belgian driver, had arrived by air in the afternoon with his twin-cam Lotus Eleven and that he would be welcome to start even without having taken part in the official practice and would be allowed to do a few laps before the race began.

This promised to make things a little more interesting as I was sure that, given a good driver, a Lotus Eleven, thanks to its agility and light weight, might be a match for the Testa Rossa on such a short and winding circuit. So I asked Mauro

Bianchi, our mechanic, to give me signs about Berchem's progress during the early stages.

The Lotus started from the rear of the grid and, not knowing how fast it would be, I did my first few laps at a fairly fast gait, already overtaking back markers early in the third lap, but I soon eased back as Bianchi indicated that the Lotus was quickly losing ground, while the travel of the Ferrari's brake pedal was increasing quickly. When, after 70 laps, I pitted for fuel for the car and a bottle of water for the driver, I was five laps ahead of the Lotus, and still four laps to the good when I restarted. However, after 106 of the 120 laps, when I was six laps ahead, without any warning there was a horrible noise in the rear axle and the car came to a full stop, letting the Lotus through to win.

From the sporting point of view my African campaign had been a complete flop, but I had a wonderful time. I was nevertheless sorry for all those people who had extended so much kindness and help and for the disappointment of the public, black and white, who quite obviously had come to see me win.

Around midnight on the eve of the race, while I was having a drink with friends

Equipe Nationale Belge sent its Ferrari Testa Rossa to the Léopoldville (today Kinshasa) Grand Prix in 1958 at the request of Shell, the team's sponsor, and I was asked to drive it. Whatever the antics of the Dyna Panhard Junior behind me, the Ferrari stayed in front – until its differential broke.

in the black part of the city, a local came up to me, asking for an autograph. On the next day, after the race, I has having dinner with Bianchi and two friends in a Portuguese restaurant, and the owner invited us all for lunch on the following day, prior to our departure.

On the morning after the race, the black hotel valet knocked at my door and came in with a vase with six small red carnations.

'Who sent these?' I asked.

'It's me,' came the shy answer.

If I had not asked, he would have been too shy to say so.

A few minutes later a 10-year-old black boy came in with a large bunch of flowers and presented them blushingly to me. 'You must be sad not to have won,' he said, 'and I am so sad for you.'

Flowers never made me so happy as those.

Chapter 14

The von Döry brothers, and Armando and Orlando

COMING BACK HOME after the London Motor Show of 1959, I found a telegram from Arthur Westrup, NSU's PR Manager: 'Would you like to drive an NSU Prinz 30 in the Argentinian Gran Premio de Carretera [literally 'Road Grand Prix]?' This was a race over 2,500 miles of mixed roads and desert tracks, climbing up to 10,000 feet in the Cordillera de las Andes, with the start and finish in Buenos Aires. To such a question there could be only one answer, 'Yes, with great pleasure', whatever the car and whatever the roads.

The suggestion had come from the NSU importers in Argentina, the brothers Anton and Peter von Döry, two very enthusiastic Hungarian emigrants. They both raced Porsche Spyders in South America and elsewhere, and I had actually met Anton, the elder of the two, at the Nürburgring on an earlier occasion.

Now you may not know what sort of car an NSU 'Prinz 30' was. It was the first post-war model from the Neckarsulm factory, near Heilbronn (now owned by Audi), the sports version of a rather inelegant, diminutive and cramped two-door, four-passenger saloon, powered by a single-ohc air-cooled parallel twin engine; the engine and four-speed gearbox unit were mounted transversely on the rear. The '30' stood for the more sporting version developing 30bhp, compared with the normal version's 20bhp. The fuel tank was at the front and suspension was by coil springs all round, with double wishbones at the front and swing axles at the rear.

Taking part in a real race over sometimes incredibly bad and mostly dirt roads with a fully standard 600cc car (modification was forbidden, except to the shock absorbers) seemed completely crazy, but probably the NSU management did not realise the task lying ahead, and the enthusiasm of the von Döry brothers had overcome any reluctance. Four cars were entered, for Fangio's protégé Juan Manuel Bordeu, Peter von Döry, Porsche works driver Edgar Barth, and myself.

So, early in November 1959, Barth, NSU mechanic Wilhelm Schrack and myself disembarked from an Aerolineas Argentinas Lockheed Constellation at Buenos Aires airport where we were met by the von Döry brothers, who took us to our hotel where we arrived late at night.

Of the four drivers, only Bordeu had any experience of this sort of race. So, after spending a few days in Buenos Aires sightseeing, attending receptions but mostly just filling time, we – that is Peter von Döry, Edy Barth and myself – took a DC-3 heading for San Juan where we were to hire a car to have a look at the most difficult part of the course, in the Cordillera. As a guide we had with us Miguel Galuzzi, a former Argentinian motor cycle champion. In a country where distances are enormous and at a time when roads were both rare and primitive, aircraft took the place of buses and trains. Safety measures as we then knew them in Europe, when piston aero engines and propellers were still the rule, were completely ignored. The old DC-3s flew from small town to small town where they landed on grass airfields and restarted after a 10–15-minute stop, without any testing of engines, flaps, rudder, etc, as was compulsory in Europe. Just as you might start the engine of your car and drive off, so the DC-3's two engines were started and the plane took to the air. But even 40 years ago, the accident record in Argentina was said to be not much worse than in Europe.

With no services on board, the plane stopped for one hour in Mendoza to give us time for a quick lunch, and we finally landed in San Juan, a horrible little town that had been completely destroyed by an earthquake in 1944 and had been hastily rebuilt, apparently without any thought to planning. A blazing sun kept the 65,000 inhabitants in their homes and all the shops were closed.

As the heat was unbearable, we asked a taxi driver to take us to a place where we could have a swim. He took us 12 miles away to a large pool, well sheltered from the winds by the nearby mountains, but when we looked at the water we decided that, after all, the heat was not such that we so urgently needed to have a bath!

As we drove back to town, a policeman stopped us because suddenly a motor cycle race was going on! In fact the riders were only practising for the following day's race. The course was in the streets and park of the town and was closed to traffic, but not to pedestrians who crossed the roads as they chose. I am quite convinced that at least half of the participants in the practice had nothing to do with the following day's race and had just joined the fray to have fun; I just can't imagine that anyone would run an NSU or HMW moped against a 175 Ducati! Police made great efforts to force the riders to wear helmets, but apparently there were twice as many riders as there were helmets, so as soon as the police turned away, off they went again … without a helmet!

But we had not come to San Juan to watch a motor cycle race. We wanted to find a car to go over the two most difficult stages of the Gran Premio de Carretera. Galuzzi tentatively asked the taxi driver who had taken us to the swimming pool if he would be prepared to take us to Catamarca, over the mountains. Fortunately he argued that the tyres of his car, a 1940 Ford V8, glistening with all the most useless chrome-plated junk you could imagine, were not good enough. I was relieved, as I had noted that the direction his car took had little to do with how he turned the steering wheel, which had about a quarter-turn play. Later I noted that this was not at all unusual: many other taxis had at least a *third* of a turn play!

We finally made a deal with two gentlemen called Armando and Orlando. Armando was the owner of an IKA 'Estanciera', a Jeep Station Wagon made under licence by IKA (Industrias Kaiser Argentinas), in fairly good order, and Orlando was supposed to be his mechanic. At 6.00am the next morning the three of us, Barth, von Döry and myself, were on our way to Catamarca, 435 miles away, with Armando at the wheel, Orlando next to him and, as we were soon to find out, a pistol and a high-class FN shotgun on board! The journey was obviously not going to be easy. During the night a big thunderstorm had swollen innumerable small torrents that had already dried up, but not before having removed the road surface, creating deep drains across the road, 200 to 300 yards apart. Such were the hazards the drivers would have to face in the Gran Premio de Carretera.

Suddenly, Orlando shouted 'Una martinetta!' ('A partridge!'), a bird the Argentinians like to eat. Armando stopped all square without even a look in the mirror, Orlando jumped out with his pistol and … of course missed the bird.

Peter von Döry waiting for the start of the Gran Premio de Carretera. Bela, the team's chief mechanic, is in the back of the NSU receiving final instructions before transferring to the team's aircraft, which will fly ahead to the various checkpoints.

'Next time I will use the shotgun,' he said, taking it out from under the front bench seat. I never found out whether the two carried the weapons for hunting or because the mountain roads were unsafe.

Some time later we had our own back. After Orlando had had his picnic with two or three glasses of the red wine the two had taken with them, he fell deeply asleep. Suddenly we yelled, 'Una martinetta, una martinetta!' Orlando immediately woke up, grasped his gun and vainly searched for the precious bird, which only existed in our imagination, while we took great pains not to laugh and to appear sorry for his vain search.

In the Andes mountains the inhabitants of all the villages are mostly descendants of the Incas. They live in small houses made of branches and clay, usually wear bright clothes of European influence and cover large distances riding horses or mules. They all speak Spanish, but among themselves they speak a very strange language that nobody else can understand. As the heat is quite intense in the region, most of them spend the night in a pergola, outside the house, which shelters them from the wind and, in daytime, from the sun. Every house has its own bread oven made of clay.

It was 11pm when we reached Catamarca after driving over unending roads bordered by high mountains – beautiful scenery that reminded me of Iran. It had taken us 17 hours to cover the 435 miles, but a good bed in a decent hotel awaited us.

Compared with the following day that had been a good speed. To reach Tucuman, the town in which the Independence of the Republic of Argentina was proclaimed, the road went up to 6,500 feet, then down to 2,600 feet to Santa Maria, then up to a pass at 11,500 feet followed by 125 miles at 10,000 feet before starting the descent to Tucuman. The distance was 323 miles, so the departure was scheduled for 6.45 next morning.

In the morning, driving through some superb scenery, we reached Santa Maria in time for lunch. But Armando was beginning to calculate that the deal we had made with him before the start was less profitable than he had thought. Up to this point the Estanciera had done only about 11mpg; he would have to adopt a more economical driving style. His method in the mountains was to stick to top (third) gear until the speed was down to 15mph, and *never* to go higher than 22mph in second gear. This was not going to get us to Tucuman very early, but never mind, it was not every day that we got a chance to drive through the superb scenery the Andes could offer. But down the mountains his fuel-saving methods began to worry us; at the top of the pass between Catamarca and Santa Maria, he switched the engine off and descended 4,000 feet using only the Estanciera's primitive drum brakes! As the scenery was so beautiful, we had very good reason to ask Armando to stop several times during the descent to take photos, without suggesting that the photos were not the main reason for the halt …

We left Santa Maria after a short reception at the Automobile Club, which gave

I was the first starter in the Gran Premio, leaving Buenos Aires at midnight.

Armando and Orlando time to 'retune' the Estanciera's side-valve engine for more economy. Included in the operation was the removal of the air filter, an accessory he probably judged perfectly useless (especially on the dusty dirt roads we were on) and invented only to increase cost and fuel consumption. Apparently some jets were also changed.

The day was very hot and we still had 200 miles ahead of us. A couple of miles after leaving the town the road began to rise. At 12mph in top, the poor Estanciera almost pinked its head off, but Orlando, who had now taken the wheel, still did not change down. He was saving fuel! Soon the thermometer showed 100°C. Orlando stopped and put the original jets back into the carburettor while Armando removed the radiator cap from which a boiling geyser emerged. He topped up with fresh water that, fortunately, he had taken on board and waited for everything to cool down. What worried us was that we had covered only a few miles from Santa Maria, the altitude was 2,750 feet and the summit of the pass was at nearly 11,500 feet!

Finally we restarted, now with Armando at the wheel. We tried to explain that if he allowed the engine to rev a little higher than 12mph in top and 10mph in second, it would overheat less, but to no avail. We stopped again after less than a mile. Armando put back the air filter and … we waited. We restarted once more and stopped again as soon as the thermometer showed 100°C. In fact, thanks to the pressurisation, the water did not boil, and even after stopping the engine it could not be heard to be boiling. But Armando did not believe it and, to prove his point, he removed the radiator cap again; of course, as soon the cooling system was depressurised, up came the geyser.

Fortunately, as we drove higher the air got cooler, Armando was relieved and returned to his natural good spirits. Every time we rounded a blind corner, he laughed at the sight of the road climbing higher and higher into the mountains.

It was night when we tackled the last mountainous section before descending towards Tucuman. The mountain peaks around us were covered with dark clouds, and we were soon in the middle of a heavy thunderstorm and thick clouds, which the Estanciera's tired headlights, one directed towards the sky, the other a few yards ahead of the front bumper, were unable to penetrate. We were surrounded by lightning, the wind was blowing forcefully and within a few minutes we had changed from almost unbearable heat to bitter cold. Armando stopped his car. 'I can't see anything,' he said. 'We must wait for the clouds to disappear!'

This did not suit us at all and we suggested that he adjusted the headlights and did something about the screen wiper, which naturally did not work. All his half-hearted attempts failed, but courageously he opened his door window and leaned out in the rain, trying at walking pace to pierce the wall of darkness and fog, but still giving us the frights of our lives. We could not see the deep precipices bordering the narrow road, but we knew they were there!

I was the first who tentatively offered to take his place at the wheel, and he enthusiastically accepted. I was probably even more relieved than he was, for if we managed to get out of that thick fog I am sure that he would have descended the 10,000 feet to Tucuman in neutral with the engine switched off, a prospect that did not make me happy at all. Barth then swapped places with Orlando to sit next to me, and so we proceeded, peering out of the open window with Barth occasionally shouting 'rechts' or 'links' ('right' or 'left') if I came too near the precipice or the rocks. We finally left the clouds behind, losing a minimum of time, and reached Tucuman late that night. Armando and Orlando still sat in the back and, far from claiming back the driver's seat, they were fascinated by being driven by racing drivers who had come all the way from Europe to participate in the great race. They became so interested that, having driven us to the plane that was to take us back to Buenos Aires, they decided that rather than drive straight back to San Juan, they would make a large detour to follow the race route, and they soon disappeared, heading for Cordoba.

Chapter 15

Grand Prix in the Argentinian pampas

AFTER COVERING ABOUT 800 miles of the 2,500-mile course, Edy Barth and myself came to the conclusion that if the managers of the NSU company had seen for themselves what their little cars would have to face, they would surely not even have contemplated taking part in this gruelling event. Even though it was divided into several stages to avoid night driving, except when leaving Buenos Aires, it was a sort of triple Mille Miglia, with at least half the course on earth tracks over the mountains or through deserts where the cars sent up clouds of dust, on roads fording innumerable torrents, where those that had dried up were usually even more uncomfortable than those with running water, and on ridged tracks with humps sending the cars flying for several yards. Add the intense heat and altitudes up to 13,000 feet and you will begin to have a vague idea of what the Gran Premio de Carretera was like. In fact, we were the first Europeans ever to take part in it.

The race had two classes: Gran Premio and Standard. The latter was for strictly standard four-passenger cars, except for a free exhaust and uprated shock absorbers. But even the choke size of the carburettor(s) had to be standard. For the Gran Premio cars, the regulations were much looser. Chassis and engine had to be of the same make, and the wheelbase and track had to be retained, though the chassis could be reinforced and modified. For the engine, only the cylinder block and crankshaft had to be standard, and the valve gear had to remain of the original type. Any non-standard parts had to be of Argentinian origin.

Practically all the cars running in the Gran Premio class were highly modified pre-war or immediately post-war side-valve Ford V8 or ohv Chevrolet straight-six dickey-seat coupés from which the local tuners managed to extract some 200bhp – about twice the original power. Pre-war cars were generally preferred because they were smaller and lighter. The Fords had a rigid front axle anyway, and for the Chevys a rigid front axle was preferred to the more fragile wishbone independent system. Radiator shells were ruthlessly discarded in favour of much larger than standard units and any non-essential sheet metal part was deleted, bonnet sides included. For many participants, cost was no object.

In Buenos Aires I got a ride in a Ford V8 fed by a huge quadruple-choke Weber carburettor originally designed for the 4.5-litre Maserati, and Fangio's workshop in Balcarce took three twin-choke Webers that had come straight from a Maserati 250F and adapted them to a Chevrolet straight-six! All leaf springs had at least twice the original number of leaves, huge anti-roll bars were added and all cars had eight shock absorbers, usually truck-size Houdaille examples. The discarded rear seats were replaced by a 300-litre fuel tank, plus a water and an oil tank with appropriate hand pumps to be operated by the riding mechanic. Most of the Fords were fitted with more modern Lincoln brakes, while the Chevys used Chevy truck brakes. When ready to race, with driver and mechanic on board and the three spare wheels carried by most competitors, the cars weighed about 1,900kg, but they were still good for 125mph! They were real hot-rods!

The touring cars were grouped in four classes. Our four 600cc NSU works entries and a fifth car entered by a courageous owner made up the 0–750cc class; the 750–1,200cc class included several Auto-Union (DKW) 1000s and Fiat 1100s and a sole Lancia Appia, which eventually won the class; the 1,200–1,500 class included a Peugeot 403, a Borgward Isabella and a Volvo PV444, and several pre-1952 American cars up to 4,100cc were also included in that class. The large car class was dominated by American cars, Ford, Mercury and even a Cadillac, but also included smaller cars considered to be sports versions of lesser models, such as an Alfa Romeo 1900, an 85bhp-engined Volvo and a 1,200cc Simca Aronde Montlhéry.

Fangio, who before he came to Europe had been a hero of the Gran Premio de Carretera and other cross-country races, was now five-times world champion and had retired, and the big names were now the brothers Juan and Oscar Galvez, Rodolfo de Alzaga (who eventually won), Oscar Cabalén, Peduzzi, Risatti and others we had never heard of in Europe.

The race started at midnight in front of the Automobile Club of Argentina, in the centre of Buenos Aires. Several hours before, the streets leading to the main road to Mendoza had been cleared of any traffic and were lined with huge crowds, while the grandstand facing the Automobile Club was also packed with people. They would have to wait for another three hours before they could acclaim their heroes, Juan Galvez, five times winner of the event and three times second, and his brother Oscar.

First came the Turismos, starting with the smallest-capacity cars, and fate decided that I should be the first competitor away. I drove up on to the starting podium and a huge clamour arose as Fangio came to my window to wish me good luck. I was blinded by the spotlights, but not enough to miss the starting flag, and off we went, heading for San Juan via Mendoza, 797 miles away, powered by a mere 600cc.

Although with the help of Jo, my German-speaking mechanic, I had rehearsed the route out of Buenos Aires several times, the huge crowds lining the streets and the absence of traffic completely changed the scene, and I felt that I was losing time. Indeed, even before we left the city my team-mate Manuel Bordeu, Fangio's protégé who started 30 seconds after me, in second position, had caught up with me. No wonder – he was in his home town and knew the route perfectly, so well in fact that I could hardly follow his tail lights as they disappeared around corners. But the public cheered and waved, and some even threw lumps of earth against our car – I was told that it was their way of encouraging us!

We had hardly covered 15 miles when it began to rain and suddenly I saw headlights facing me: they were Bordeu's, who had been over-confident and spun into a field. He was soon back on the road, however, and for the rest of the night I was content to follow him on those unfamiliar roads.

Jo switched on the radio and we got some news of the race. Peter von Döry and Barth seemed to have been delayed and Bordeu and I were still heading the race. Only around 3am did a pair of headlights loom up behind, those of Marcolongo's very fast Borgward Isabella.

The NSU organisation was very efficient. At intervals of around 125 miles a service crew awaited us with fuel and help. While it was dark I took great care to keep my young team-mate in sight, as he knew the road better and probably had better night vision. But I noted that my car was slightly faster than his and worked out a plan: as soon as the sun rose, I would overtake him and try to leave him behind. The scheme worked and we reached Mendoza three minutes before Bordeu.

Bordeu's NSU in spectacular scenery between Catamarca and Tucuman.

In Mendoza the race was suspended for an hour to allow the racers to cross the town at a reasonable speed. Von Döry and Barth soon joined us; the former had been slightly delayed by a choke that would not close properly, and in Buenos Aires Barth had hit a kerb with the two right-hand wheels, blowing the tyres, and had to fit the two spare wheels we fortunately carried.

When the race resumed, a few Turismos and some of the hot-rods overtook us, but the rain, which had made the roads very slippery, took its toll. Several potential winners went off, among them Oscar Galvez and the highly popular all-round sportsman Carlos Menditeguy, who excelled in polo, horse-riding, tennis and swimming, and even shone at the wheel of Formula 1 Maseratis on the occasion of the Argentinian Temporada. He nevertheless continued with a bent front axle, after his Ford had led the race in the early stages.

From Mendoza a magnificent, almost completely straight road led us to San Juan, the end of the first stage, 101 miles away, which the little NSU covered at an average speed of 74.4mph, our overall average for the 797 miles covered since Buenos Aires being 69.3mph, which made us first in our class. Other Turismo class winners were a two-stroke, three-cylinder Auto Union 1000, Marcolongo's Borgward Isabella and a Mercury, the Borgward being fastest. The Ford V8 hot-rod with four-choke Webers had averaged 118mph on the 101-mile stretch between Mendoza and San Juan!

Our arrival in San Juan will forever remain engraved on my memory. For the last 6 miles to the finish of the stage, the road, lined by magnificent trees, was invaded by a dense, waving crowd that parted at the last second to let the racing cars through; the density and temerity of the crowds by far surpassed anything I had experienced in the Mille Miglia when it was still a real race. I was told that every year several people were killed, but that nobody cared because everyone was supposed to look after his own safety.

Racing days alternated with days of rest, during which the cars were kept in a parc fermé. During the rest-day the Turismos were allowed to leave the parc for $1^3/4$ hours for service and repairs, and again on the following race day for $1^1/2$ hours, which, for our team, was never necessary. The hot-rods, however, were not allowed to leave the parc on rest days, which left precious little time for repairs and service. However, the competitors were well organised, and many of them took advantage of the 1-hour suspension of the race in Mendoza to quickly swap the rear axle for another with a shorter gear ratio in view of the slower roads lying ahead. Others did the same after the following stage in Catamarca, where the real mountain section began.

The second stage being mostly over unmade roads, the hot-rods were sent off first to avoid eating the dust raised by the Turismos. In each group the cars were sent off in the order of the general classification and I felt pretty proud, with my 600cc car, to be 17th out of the 80 Turismos that had left Buenos Aires two days earlier. Before us lay 30 miles of asphalt, then we would have to tackle the earth roads with their dust, stones and 'badenos', fords that were dry most of the time, but which could just about destroy the road when heavy rain turned them into a swollen torrent, leaving just a heap of rocks.

This was the first part of the road that we had rehearsed with Armando and Orlando. Danger spots were usually well signposted, but when we had gone over the course the week before Armando had drawn our attention to a particularly dangerous bend, invisible just over a brow. One of the Gran Premio drivers had fallen victim to it; his car lay upside down in a nearby field, but apparently the crew were unhurt. Other hot-rods were stopped by the wayside with their crews working feverishly.

About 155 miles after our departure from San Juan, we reached the Miranda Pass. The little NSU climbed valiantly, unperturbed by the rough dirt road on which the Estanciera's radiator had turned into a tea kettle. Reaching the top, we got a magnificent view of the surrounding mountains and of the plain to which we were now heading, where the contrast with the road over the pass was total. It was completely straight as far as the eye could see, but full of badenos and severe humps over which, careful as I was, the car made impressive jumps, taking off altogether to crash heavily back on to the road. Near the small town of Villa Union, things at last became less monotonous, and the road crossed a large sandy area in which a Volvo had become stuck. We only just managed to get through, then to my great surprise Bordeu appeared in my mirror! I thought we had both decided to take it easy to save the cars on that murderous stretch!

The course had already taken its toll on my car. First a leak appeared in the exhaust system and later, fording a dried-up torrent, the silencer was ripped off and suddenly we had a free exhaust making the car unbearably noisy. We pressed on, but after a few minutes a smell of burning rubber invaded the cockpit – the exhaust system had broken away at the cylinder head flange and the hot gases were hitting the plug wires and the two coils directly. We wondered whether they would last for the 375 miles still ahead of us before we reached Catamarca, the end of the stage.

We would never find out. A little further on, driving through a desert on a track marked by sand banks, a big Mercury that we had seen stuck in the sand a little earlier, caught up with us. I moved over to let it through and was completely blinded by the impenetrable cloud of dust raised by the American car. About 500 yards further on the track made a right turn that I could not see, and suddenly we found ourselves on top of the bank. Jo and I both got out to investigate, but just as we stepped out there was a big crash – the driver of a Borgward had been in the same situation as us, had not seen the bend and hit the tail of our hitherto undamaged car square on. I was in the process of getting out, and the NSU's central pillar hit my right shoulder so hard that it was dislocated and Jo was shocked to the point that he was about to faint. The car was too badly damaged to continue: its rear engine had moved and the suspension was badly bent. We were also too badly damaged to continue, with 1,550 miles of gruelling roads still ahead of us.

Two minutes after the accident, Bordeu arrived and stopped. He was now leading the class and I tried to persuade him to proceed, but he refused. He would not drive on until Jo and I had been taken care of by himself and von Döry who, meanwhile, had also arrived. We had no alternative, and placed ourselves in their care. Barth, who had also stopped, drove on but waited for his team-mates at the next checkpoint, refusing to take advantage of the help they gave us.

Being driven in Bordeu's NSU for nearly 20 miles to the nearest checkpoint with a dislocated shoulder was not a particularly comfortable ride, but there Jo and I were transferred to an official car that took us the 125 miles to Rioja. There we changed cars again, this time to be taken to Catamarca, the end of the stage, in Juan Galvez's 'Auxilio', as the Argentinians call the service cars.

The road to Catamarca was a long one and I was really grateful to Juan Galvez's crew for taking Jo and me there in their van in which there was hardly enough space for themselves and all their equipment. We were all pretty well squeezed, but nobody complained, and everyone did their best to make us comfortable, which, on those bad, rutted roads, was not easy, as my shoulder was very painful and the Estanciera's suspension had not been designed with invalids in mind! But squeezed or not, Juan Galvez's service crew were in excellent spirits: the radio had just announced that their boss had won the Catamarca stage and was now only 7 minutes behind the leader, Rodolfo de Alzaga.

Radio played a very important role in the race and several stations in Buenos Aires dedicated their entire programming to it, as did all the local stations along the course. This was a great help for the competitors, who all had a radio on board. Radio stations also transmitted private messages; any competitor needing help gave the message to a radio reporter when driving through a village. The message soon went on the air and the required shock absorber, spring or windscreen would be ready to pick up wherever it was required.

Most of the competitors had emergency pits along the route, where mechanics were ready with the most likely spare parts and provided information about the race and the most important competitors. A popular way of passing on messages was to insert them into a bicycle tyre held up within easy reach of the co-driver as the car passed.

In Catamarca my shoulder had become very painful and, together with Jo, my navigator, I went to see a doctor who diagnosed torn ligaments and a displaced left clavicle. I was tightly bandaged to keep everything in place and while Jo decided to fly back home to Buenos Aires, I decided to continue to follow the race in the twin-engined Bonansa plane hired by the NSU importers.

The difficult stage from San Juan to Catamarca had completely reshuffled the classification. Rodolfo de Alzaga was leading with Juan Galvez 7 minutes behind, both driving Fords. The third and fourth-placed competitors were already 40 and 45 minutes behind. Galvez, a hero with the crowds, decided that he would play safe. In view of the enormous amount of dust his engine had swallowed, he would change all the pistons, connecting rods and bearings of his Ford's V8 engine in the 90 minutes allowed between the opening of the parc fermé and the start of the next stage. With the help of two mechanics, he did it in 42 minutes! Unfortunately it was to be to no avail as, later in the race, he lost over an hour due to a broken gearbox and de Alzaga went on to win.

In those days sponsorship was unknown in European motorsport, but in Argentina it was the rule and although radio broadcasts about the race seldom mentioned the make of the cars driven by the local heroes, the sponsors' names were never omitted. Our NSU team was sponsored by Suixtil, a big company specialising in menswear in which Fangio had interests. On rest days between stages the big sponsors organised parties and, as we were the first Europeans ever to take part in the Gran Premio, we were very much in demand. In San Juan Barth and myself had been virtually kidnapped by two employees of Camart, a shirt-maker, who had apparently been instructed to drag us, alive or dead, to a Camart party. This was attended by an excited local crowd cheering any driver who spoke even a few words into the microphone of the local radio, even if they did not understand a word of what they said. We did our part, and in recognition were both presented with a Camart T-shirt.

Four days later, in Tucuman, it happened again. I was having a drink with Barth and Bordeu on the terrace of a café when another Camart man spotted us and again dragged us to a room full of people where we were asked to say a few words for the radio. 'It's worthwhile,' he said. 'You will receive a wonderful T-shirt.'

As we wanted to be friendly we went. Bordeu spoke for about a minute to an

Back in Buenos Aires for the finish, the three NSUs make a triumphant arrival.

enthusiastic crowd. Next came Barth, who was asked to speak English as nobody would understand German in the Argentinian province. He tried his best, but once faced with a microphone he forgot what little English he knew.

'Is that all?' asked the Camart man.

'Ja,' was his short and shy answer.

We all felt a little embarrassed and I tried to save the day by making an enthusiastic speech in Italian, a language most of the Argentinians understand. But I missed my reward. I had come to the studio wearing the shirt I had been given in San Juan. After our performance Bordeu received his 'wonderful Camart T-shirt'. Barth also received one, even though his performance had been limited to a 'Ja' of relief.

'And what about me'? I asked.

'You,' the man said, 'you are already wearing one!' And that was it!

Though nearly half the field had been left by the wayside, the other three NSUs were still in good shape and even the well-worn, privately entered NSU Prinz, driven by two intrepid and enthusiastic Argentinians, was still there, albeit several hours behind the team cars. On the next stage, from Catamarca to Tucuman, the NSUs were completely at ease on the dirt roads with their humps and loose stones, and at the top of the highest pass of the course, at nearly 2,200 feet, Peter von Döry was a fantastic second overall in the standard car class, headed by an unassailable Peugeot 403.

We were already having dinner in Tucuman when Nico and Pancho, the two privateers with the well-worn NSU, appeared in the dining room. As usual they had been in dire trouble. Suddenly, at 1,900 feet, they had noticed that the oil pressure had vanished. They stopped and found that the sump's drain plug had been lost. They walked back along the trail left by the oil on the dirt road and, after about half a mile, miraculously found the plug in the middle of the desert! But they still had no oil. They stopped several competitors, but none of them could help until one arrived who was only too glad to exchange 2 litres of oil for 2 litres of petrol. The engine had obviously suffered, but they had reached Tucuman, the end of the stage.

The next morning it proved almost impossible to unscrew one of the spark plugs: its thread had been damaged by the piston rising higher than its normal stroke because the big-end bearing material had melted and the bearing had developed enormous play. It was also discovered that one of the shock absorbers had torn the sheet metal to which it was anchored, requiring a difficult welding operation.

'But why bother?' asked Bela, the NSU chief mechanic. 'That car will never finish the race. If it does, I'll retire and open a hairdresser's shop! It can't be done within the time schedule anyway.' And he left them with their problem.

The miracle was that with their sick engine and three shock absorbers, Nico and Pancho managed to reach Santa Fé, the end of the following stage … with a second shock absorber through the sheet metal. To our team of mechanics the

At relay stations organised by the competitors, information about the race gathered by crew members is passed on in bicycle tyres, so that the car does not have to stop!

required repair seemed impossible within the time available, but Nico and Pancho had made an expensive bet and they were determined to finish at all cost. After all, from here there were only 300 miles to the finish in Buenos Aires and the roads were fairly good. They had a friend in the racing category who was a competent welder, and he fixed *both* shock absorbers within the time allowance.

The standard car group had shrunk to 35 and only three cars had survived unscathed: Laredo's Peugeot 403, which had built up a commanding lead, an old Ford V8 and Peter von Döry's little NSU, our team being still complete except for my car. All the other cars were more or less battered, some almost beyond recognition, as was the case with the Lancia Appia, which had rolled several times and was hiding its wounds under yards of adhesive tape. But it was still leading its class!

As we flew over the route leading to Buenos Aires, we could see the huge crowds lining the roads and, overtaking the cars that remained in the race, we noted that Juan Galvez, who had again been delayed, this time by punctures, was quickly gaining on Risatti and would finally manage to finish second to the unassailable de Alzaga.

As we approached Buenos Aires the crowds became thicker and thicker, hundreds of cars and even many small planes lining the road. The finish was at the 'Autodromo', and we pressed on to land there before the cars arrived, a Volkswagen minibus rushing us to the finishing line. We hardly had the time to sit down when the huge crowd stood up to cheer their idol: car No 1, driven by Juan Galvez, was first back in Buenos Aires, though in terms of time he was only second since, after his problems in the early stages, he had never been in a position to catch de Alzaga, the elegant businessman who spoke perfect French and English in addition to Spanish and who raced for the fun of it.

A few minutes later a car of the Standard class was announced, but in fact there were three, which, in their class-winning order of Bordeu, Barth and von Döry, entered the gates for their lap of honour. I was the only missing member of the team. But the NSUs were soon forgotten as the overall winner arrived, greeted by deafening cheers.

After the winner's arrival the crowds slowly dispersed and we were taken back to our hotel, but Anton von Döry, the President of the NSU importers, and the mechanics remained at the track. A week earlier they had hardly taken any notice of Nico and Pancho and their well-worn little NSU. But after all that they had overcome, they were anxious to see if they managed those last 300 miles on fast roads. It seemed impossible that with an engine that had run without oil, with run bearings and a car falling to pieces, that joyful pair had any chance of reaching the finish. But their enthusiasm and courage had overcome so many seemingly hopeless situations in the past few days that now nothing seemed impossible. That three of the four works cars had brilliantly reached the finish was a superb success, but the von Döry brothers felt that the exploit of two pure amateurs finishing the gruelling event with a car that already had over 30,000 miles on its odometer before the start would make NSU's success even more credible and popular.

It was 3.30pm when the three team cars crossed the finishing line, and to be classified as finishers Pancho and Nico would have to cross it before 8.00pm. But only 1½ hours after the team cars crossed the line, loud knocking and banging announced the arrival of the two heroes. They had won their bet!

Nico and Pancho were naturally invited to the dinner offered by Anton von Döry to his drivers and mechanics. And when it came to the speeches, Nico solemnly presented Bela, the team's chief mechanic, with the first tool for the job he had sworn he would switch to if Nico and Pancho finished the race – a comb!

Chapter 16

Breaking records with Abarth, Opel and Mercedes-Benz

LIKE SO MANY people who have made important contributions to the automobile industry, Karl Abarth was Austrian. I remember that when we lived in Vienna I occasionally read of his motor cycling exploits in the newspapers. He was the King of the Krieau grass track, near Vienna, but he also raced successfully, first solo bikes, then home-made sidecar combinations whose notable feature was that, in the curves, the sidecar would lean together with the bike. After many successes with that machine, he had a serious accident in Yugoslavia and decided to stay there, rather than to go back to Austria, which was already 'Nazified'. There he founded a small company making parts, mainly for the bike and car industries.

When, after the war, international travel once more became possible, if difficult, he decided to visit his father near Merano, and soon joined the Cisitalia company in Turin, which, apart from small Fiat-based racing cars, was building a revolutionary flat-12, supercharged, four-wheel-drive grand prix car designed by Ferry Porsche and his team, Ferdinand Porsche Snr being still detained as a prisoner by the Allies. At Cisitalia, Abarth, who promptly Italianised his first name to Carlo, not only co-operated with the grand prix project, but was also responsible for Cisitalia's successful day-to-day racing activities. Unfortunately Cisitalia went broke, and the grand prix car, which had just been completed, never raced and is now in Porsche's museum in Stuttgart. Carlo Abarth had to start again from scratch.

'Abarth & Co' was founded in Turin in 1949 with the financial help of Armando Scagliarini, a rich farmer whose son Guido was successfully racing Cisitalias. The company retained some of the latest racing cars from the Cisitalia bankruptcy, now running as Abarths. But the company's industrial and commercial activity was the manufacture of 'go faster' exhaust silencers, beautifully styled and finished in cracked black enamel with (usually) twin chrome-plated tail-pipes, which sold like hot cakes. Abarth's main interest, however, remained racing cars, still based on Fiat models. When, in 1955, the little rear-engined Fiat 600 was announced, a model that was to become immensely popular, Abarth immediately increased its engine capacity from 633 to just under 750cc and proceeded to almost double its power. Suspension and brakes were uprated and the car was an immediate success with young drivers, both for the road and for racing. I used a test model as private transport on the occasion of the Nürburgring 1,000km race of 1956 and lent it for a short test to Mike Hawthorn, who came back just beaming! 'I wouldn't mind one of these,' was his comment.

Abarth was, however, anxious to prove that his cars were not only fast but also robust by attacking international class records; he asked Bertone to build an aerodynamic single-seat coupé body designed for the purpose by Franco Scaglione. In July 1956, on the Monza oval, the car beat the 24 Hours 750cc class record at 155.985kmh (96.927mph). Now he wanted more and, following Giovanni Lurani's suggestion, he invited six journalists who had proved their ability as drivers to team up for an attempt on class records up to 10,000km. I was part of the team together with Uli Wieselmann (then editor of *Auto, Motor & Sport*), Bernard Cahier, Walter Honegger, Gordon Wilkins and Giovanni Lurani.

As the person who suggested the formation of a journalist's team and as its senior member, Lurani took the start. After 2¼ hours he was stopped for a fuel consumption check and all four wheels were changed for examination. Those considered sound were held in reserve for another stint. Meanwhile Abarth directed the pit crew, who were wildly turning round the car, shouting to everyone in his inimitable broken Italian and repeating 'Calma, tutto con calma' about every 10 seconds, as if to urge mainly himself to keep calm!

I took over from Lurani. Due to the very tall gearing, it took nearly two laps, more than 4 miles, before the little car reached its maximum speed. Keeping the accelerator flat on the floor it would lap at 102mph, but we had been instructed not to do so if it was not necessary. That allowed me to lift off for over 100 yards twice each lap to give the oil a chance to creep up the cylinder bores, while still lapping at 100mph. In spite of its large tail fin, the car was not too stable on the straights. Reducing the high front tyre pressure would certainly have helped, but that would have increased the rolling resistance.

After 2½ hours Bernard Cahier took over from me. When the stops were made the precision work of the timekeepers was worth watching. As soon as the car stopped, a wooden marker lath was put on the asphalt exactly where it came to a standstill. The car was then pushed back to make sure that it could be push-started before it passed the marker. This made sure that it covered the entire distance under its own power.

I was not supposed to take the wheel again before midnight, but before going to bed I could not resist going back to the circuit to see how things were proceeding. Nearing the track, all was ominously quiet. The car had just stopped and removal of the valve cover showed that a valve was not closing. Abarth immediately took the car to Turin and announced a restart the next morning at 6.30am. Back in the factory he and his crew took the best of the production engines from the line and swapped it for the sick one. This meant that we would now have to rely on 42 rather than 47bhp, but this was of little importance as we had a large margin.

The car was back at Monza by 4.00am and before the restart chief mechanic Tirozzi ran it in for 3 hours. For the official restart I was at the wheel because I absolutely had to leave in the afternoon for the start of practice for the Reims 12 Hours, where I was to co-drive Olivier Gendebien's Ferrari LWB Berlinetta. Before the start I asked to be shown my average speed for each lap, so that I could decide which was the best line to take on the banking to achieve the highest speed, which I cross-checked with the rev counter reading. Keeping the car low did not pay off because of the increased rolling resistance due to the high side force. Fastest was to get on to the banking rather high and let the car run down to the 'hands off' line. This resulted in a lap speed of 95mph, still shutting off for 100 yards twice per lap. After 3 hours I was stopped to hand over to Walter Honegger, and 27 litres of pump fuel went into the tank after my 465km (289-mile) stint. We had thus averaged 5.9l/100km (48mpg).

I participated in some of Carlo Abarth's record attempts. Here I am in 1958 in a purpose-built Pininfarina-bodied Special powered by a modified Alfa Romeo Giulietta engine. The attempt failed because the wire wheels could not withstand more than an hour on Monza's bumpy banking.

My task was now over and the attempt was successfully completed by my colleagues, though not without problems due to a defect in the charge regulator, which overcharged and ruined the battery, so that at night no lights were available and marker lights had to be installed along the track. Nevertheless six new records were broken, including those for 72 hours and over 10,000 miles, both at an average of 87.36mph.

The following year, 1957, Abarth had more ambitious targets. Pininfarina had designed and built two very beautiful new record cars, one powered by a Fiat 600-based 750 engine, but now with Abarth's twin-cam head, the other by an Alfa Romeo Giulietta SV engine, whose capacity had been reduced to 1,100cc (a class limit in those days), developing 73hp. In May Abarth asked me to take part in an attempt in the 750 in which I would be partnered by Alfonso Thiele, a successful Abarth driver from Alto Adige, the German-speaking, now Italian, part of Tyrol. Due to other engagements I could not be in Monza for the beginning of the operation, and when I arrived once again all was quiet around the Autodromo. Due to a blown tyre, Thiele had crashed, fortunately without hurting himself too much, but the car was severely damaged. It had nevertheless set three new class records, up to 3 hours, at speeds ranging from 125.5 to 122.7mph.

I had not, however, come entirely in vain as Abarth had the Alfa Romeo-engined car ready for testing and put me in charge of it. But though the car proved to be very fast, easily lapping Monza at 137mph, it proved impossible to do so for more than an hour or so. Even though in those days it was only a few years old, Monza's banking was so rough that the wire spokes of the centre-lock wheels soon began to break, and as far as I know the car was never used. There may, however, have been another reason why it never returned to the track; the many successes obtained by the little Fiat-Abarths had resulted in welcome publicity for the lookalike Fiat 600 from which they were derived and brought Abarth a lot of bonus money from Fiat. But when Fiat President Prof Valetta heard of an Abarth record car using an Alfa Romeo engine, he made it clear that he did not like it, and Abarth probably remembered that discretion is the better part of valour …

In the mid-1960s Mercedes-Benz made a hybrid model consisting of a Type 190 (four-cylinder) body shell into which they had squeezed the six-cylinder engine of the second-generation Type 220. It looked like a 190, with round headlights and a shorter bonnet, but was lighter and less expensive than a 220. It was called a 219 and though its engine had only one carburettor instead of the two of the 220, it was fast and agile. The public, however, was hardly aware of the model, and one day at some social event Robert Hayet, the PR officer of the Mercedes-Benz importers in Belgium, who was a good friend, asked me if I had any ideas on how to promote it. We still lived in Brussels and, as Suzanne's parents lived in Nice, we often commuted between the two cities. At that time only a few stretches of the autoroute were finished and quite useless, and I had my own route which I knew almost as well as the Francorchamps circuit; it completely avoided the N7, which was too busy and too infested by police, and went across the Alps over the Col de la Croix Haute. My suggestion, therefore, was, 'What would you think of an officially timed drive from Brussels to Nice Airport?'

Robert immediately agreed and the run was carefully prepared. The start from Brussels was scheduled for 7.00am, so I knew quite accurately the time at which I would arrive at the refuelling points I had chosen. The attendants were informed that I would have to be served as a matter of priority and, to make sure, the nearest Mercedes dealer was delegated to each filling station. If I remember rightly, he was instructed to save time by also taking care of the payment!

Of course, there was no question of involving the Automobile Club, as any officially timed event on open roads involving speeds above 60kmh (37mph) was forbidden, so to get some sort of authentication a justice assessor certified our time of departure from our home, on the edge of Brussels, and another awaited us at Nice Airport to check our arrival time, together with a photographer.

From the beginning it had been decided that I would do the journey with Suzanne, but at the last minute Philippe de Barsy, whom I had known as a very young boy and who was now at the beginning of his very successful career as a motoring journalist, asked if he could come with us, and we agreed.

As far as I can remember we did the run in May, starting at exactly 7.00am with a minimum of luggage, a few sandwiches, some chocolate and a bottle of water on board. It was a fine day and it stayed so all the way. Everything went strictly as scheduled and we made excellent progress. The 'pit stops' could hardly have been quicker, but there was one thing we had not rehearsed: changing a wheel. Near the top of the Col de la Croix Haute I was unable to avoid a rock hidden around a corner, and 50 yards later we had a flat right-hand front tyre! We had never seen the Mercedes's jack before, and by the time we had discovered how it worked minutes had been lost. The change took 7 minutes – at least 3 or 4 more than it should have done – and I was glad we had Philippe with us to help.

The second-generation post-war Mercedes still used drum brakes, and about 90 miles from Nice, still in mountainous country, I began to notice an unmistakable sound: the brake linings were finished! As they were new when we started, it gives a clue as to how hard I had been driving, now for over 600 miles. Nevertheless, I was surprised that they wore so quickly! From that moment on I nursed them as well as I could, and we reached Nice Airport safely, where we were expected by the man with the watch and his wife. The total time for the drive was exactly 10 hours and 33 minutes, and would have been well below $10^{1}/2$ hours without the puncture. I can't remember what the exact distance covered was, but I do recall that after correcting the odometer reading, the overall average speed was around 73mph with a car whose top speed was a mere 100mph. I never knew if the drive boosted Mercedes 219 sales, but we all had good fun!

In the spring of 1972 Opel invited me to participate in a record attempt taking place on the oval of the company's proving ground in Dudenhofen, near Frankfurt. Diesel-engined cars were becoming more popular thanks to their low fuel consumption, and Opel was about to launch its first model using that type of power plant. To publicise the event, a turbocharger was added to what was to be the future 2-litre production engine and dropped into what was basically a production Opel GT coupé, which had been lightened and from which all the superstructure had been cut off and replaced with a flat deck and a Plexiglass 'bubble' above the driver's cockpit. The run was to attempt diesel records up to 10,000km. I had come with Suzanne and our niece Anne-Marie and we were accommodated in the luxurious Kempinski Hotel in nearby Gravenbruch, occupying a suite with a view over a lake on which families of baby ducks enjoyed the early days of life.

The attempt was kept secret, so the party was quite restricted, with no press around. The drivers included two girls, Marie-Claude Beaumont, champion of France, and Silvia Oesterberg from Sweden. The others were Henry Greder, who raced Corvettes and rallied Opels, former rally driver Jochen Springer, Giorgio Pianta, an Alfa GTA driver who later became responsible for the motorsports activities of the entire Fiat Auto Group, and myself.

The attempt took two days and a few hours and was certainly the least eventful in which I have participated. The weather was fine all the time, at night the track was fully illuminated and the car ran like clockwork at just under 125mph. Meanwhile Suzanne, when at the track, kept filming, and Pianta, when not driving, kept himself busy telling jokes and attending to our 16-year-old niece. Several records were broken and the event was quite widely publicised.

In 1978, at the age of 61, I did not expect to be offered a place in a team selected to take part in long-distance record attempts during which the average speed would exceed 190mph. But that is exactly what Günther Molter, at that time responsible for Mercedes-Benz's press relations, offered me, and I am still thankful for it. The venue was to be the newly built Nardo 12.6km circular track in Southern Italy, and the car would be a new, special version of the C111 experimental machine powered by a special version of the company's 3-litre, five-cylinder turbo diesel. Of course, I accepted on the spot.

Originally six mid-engined C111s had been built as high-speed development coupés for Wankel-type rotary engines, but after the Wankel programme was discontinued, one of these cars was adapted to successfully take diesel records at speeds between 150 and 155mph. However, all six existing C111s had been designed as road cars and now two new models, using the same basic technique, had been built strictly with records in mind. They were a lot narrower, had a long tail and a large stabilising fin. With these cars, which had a drag coefficent below Cd=0.19, absolute world records were to be attacked with an engine developing not more than 230bhp. The drivers were to be Dr Hans Liebold, the car's project leader, development engineer Guido Moch, former racing driver Rico Steinemann, at that time PR manager for Mercedes-Benz Switzerland, and myself.

In 1978 I was part of a crew chasing records at the banked Nardo track in Italy with the Mercedes-Benz C111/3, which was powered by a 3-litre, five-cylinder turbo diesel engine. The drivers (from left) were Guido Moch (of the passenger car development staff), myself, Hans Liebold (C111 project leader) and Rico Steinemann. The car took nine absolute world records at speeds around 200mph, with a fastest lap – as shown on the electronic display – of 327.3kmh (203.4mph).

At Nardo one of the new cars was to be used for practice, the other for the attempt. The works crew had already practised on the track some time before to finalise the car's specifications, which led to a modification of the front air intake, increasing the maximum speed by about 1.5mph.

When I arrived with Suzanne, having driven from the South of France in our Porsche, the team had been at work for a few days with the two cars. Senior company executives such as development chief Hans Scherenberg and chief of engine development Karl-Heinz Göschel were present for the occasion. The cars were beautifully made and finished, with an instrument panel, seat and steering wheel almost to S-Class standards! When I arrived I was immediately asked to get into the car, to see if I could find a comfortable driving position in the adjustable seat and to do a few practice laps. As the steering wheel was on the left, it was decided to run anti-clockwise, so that should contact be made with the guardrail on the outside of the banking, the driver would be as far away as possible from the impact. I had never driven at speeds of more than 300kmh

(186mph) before, but the car was perfectly stable and I felt absolutely at ease.

The attempt was to go up to 20,000km (12,400 miles) and the start was scheduled for midnight. Being the senior member of the team, I had the honour of doing the first stint, which was to last for about 1 hour 40 minutes at lap speeds consistently above 320kmh (200mph). Even though the 12.6km perfectly circular track was banked, at that speed the car was still submitted to a side force of some 230kg (over 500lb), not enough to be disturbing, but nevertheless requiring the car to be held on course. I was in constant radio communication with the pit crew, to whom I regularly reported the water and oil temperatures, the boost pressure, etc. After an hour I got the news that I had broken the much-coveted hour world record, then shortly before I pitted I heard that I had broken the world 500km record – all very gratifying.

Pit stops, including changing all four wheels, filling the fuel tanks, topping up with oil and checking the coolant, took less than a minute, which did not leave the drivers much time to get out and back in, including the closing of the safety harness; after four or five stints the engine oil was changed. At the beginning of a daylight stint, lap speeds started around 202mph, dropping progressively to just below 199 as the fuel temperature increased, reducing its density.

Everything went according to plan until the following night. With Steinemann at the wheel, a rear tyre tread blew off, severely damaging the body and part of the suspension. Full marks went to the driver, who was able to keep the car on the track without further damage.

It was immediately decided to do a second attempt with the well-worn practice car, to which a new engine was fitted before operations began, just in case … This time Liebold took the start and, with the well-run-in car, he immediately proceeded to break my two personal records established the previous day by a few hundred metres! Everyone took their turn at the wheel, and after about 12 hours it was time for my second turn – at night. Everything was fine until, after an hour, I heard an unfamiliar noise and felt a vibration. I only just had time to lift off and call the pit crew when there was a big bang and no drive; a drive shaft universal joint had broken and damaged several chassis tubes.

This put a premature end to the attempt, but we had nevertheless broken nine absolute world records from 100km to 5,000 miles and from 1 to 24 hours, including the last few still held by Ab Jenkins, a hero of my schoolboy days, at speeds ranging from 195 to 199mph, with a fastest lap at 203.4mph.

Chapter 17

Road testing

As I have already mentioned, most of my English was learned as a result of my parents sending me to England, where I discovered the magazines *The Motor*, *The Autocar* and *Motor Sport*; most of my progress in English came from reading them from cover to cover! The first articles I read were the road tests, and when I left Vienna to go to Brussels University I began writing down the performance data obtained by the testers in a little booklet, which I still have. I even illustrated them with a photo of the model concerned, usually cut out from the used car advertisement pages of the magazines. That was before the war.

Immediately after the war I began my activities as a motoring journalist, but it was not until around 1950 that I began to test cars myself, originally for the Belgian magazine *Belgique Automobile*, which ceased publication around 1967. I remember that my first test car was a Peugeot 203, quite advanced for its time with its well-streamlined, fastback-shaped monocoque body, independent front suspension, rack-and-pinion steering and 1,300cc engine with hemispherical combustion chambers. The valve gear copied from the pre-war Talbot Lago. Unfortunately all records of this first road test have been lost, but I remember thinking that this car made the 1939 2½-litre SS-Jaguar saloon that I had bought from my father seem rather dated.

Though thorough research would probably bring to light some of those very early test reports, the booklets I keep in my library include tests from 1955 onwards and go through to the early 1990s, when I stopped writing complete tests and taking performance figures, etc.

As related in Chapter 5, on some occasions I joined the test crew of *The Motor*, usually made up of Laurence Pomeroy Jr, Joe Lowrey and 'Bunny' Tubbs, when they came to the Continent to take performance figures on what is today the Ostend-Brussels motorway with a car that they felt was too fast for testing in England, where suitable stretches of road were non-existent at the time. Up to the early 1950s this road was known as the 'Jabbeke' autoroute and was ideal for the job as it was dead straight and level. Being still unfinished, it started nowhere, near the village of Jabbeke, ended nowhere, and was almost completely free of traffic.

Their testing methods were quite crude: they exactly measured a quarter-mile stretch, over which they timed the maximum speed and checked the speedometer. All the acceleration figures were obtained with a two-finger stopwatch, according to corrected speedometer readings, the results published being the average of several two-way runs. They also used a Tapley accelerometer to obtain the gradients the car would climb in the various gears. That was in fact incorrect, as it ignored the effect of 'squat' and of the car's inertia, though for a slow car the result obtained in top gear would not be too inaccurate.

When I began to test seriously, I copied their technique, though I soon dropped the Tapley because of the misleading figures, but I must confess that, up to my last test, I stuck to the stopwatch and corrected speedo system and never used a Correvit or other modern system, mainly because I found it too complicated to attach the instruments to the various cars. Only the stopwatch itself changed. In the early days a famous watchmaker – I think it was Heuer – produced a stopwatch with a single hand that carried a diminutive reservoir containing a drop of non-drying ink, and all you had to do was push a button, which deposited a drop of ink on the dial. This allowed you to get the time required to reach 60, 80 or 100kmh up to any speed in a single run. Later that watch gave way to an electronic stopwatch with a memory, and of course my base was 1 kilometre rather than a quarter-mile, carefully marked out with a 50-metre tape with the help of a friend or my wife. In the course of my testing activities, I had a measured base on the Jabbeke stretch, three successive ones near Brussels and one near Nice.

From about 1953 until the late 1960s, my tests were published in a daily paper called *Les Sports*, which had a weekly 'Sports Moteurs' supplement; this meant that I wrote an average of at least three road tests per month. Among the early ones I remember being amazed by the 175kmh (105.6mph) for a two-way run reached by a Porsche 1500 Super developing only 70bhp. Another car I remember was the original 375cc version of the Citroën 2CV, which had a maximum speed of 66kmh (41mph) in both third and fourth gears. But it was a genial car in every respect. During its lifespan of more than 30 years, power was increased from 9 to 29bhp, capacity from 375 to 602cc, and speed from 41 to 75mph. I loved it and even had one myself.

My earliest full notes begin in 1955, the year in which one of the most interesting cars of all time, the front-wheel-drive Citroën DS19, was first produced. Its high-pressure hydraulic system operated its revolutionary self-levelling hydro-pneumatic suspension, the semi-automatic gearbox, the clutch and the brakes, varying the front/rear pressure distribution according to the load in the car. Chapter 6 deals with that remarkable car.

A very nice car to drive was the 2-litre Alfa Romeo 1900 Super, which handled well, felt very solid and was quite fast for its time, with a maximum speed of 163.5kmh (105.6mph), but today its time of 35.7 seconds for the standing-start kilometre would be acceptable only for a small popular car. I was also very courageous in those days: I not only drove fast cars, I even travelled 2,000 miles in a Fiat 600 having a maximum speed of 60mph!

Compared with modern times, popular cars of the second half of the 1950s were pretty slow. The very popular 845cc Renault Dauphine took 36.2 seconds for the 0–100kmh (0–62mph) sprint. The Issigonis-designed Morris Minor 1000 took 29.6 seconds and the original Mini 850 took 27.1 seconds. Even the twin-cam 1,300cc Alfa Romeo Giulietta saloon needed 21.2 seconds, and required 40 seconds for the standing-start kilometre. One of the most brilliant small cars was the Fiat 1200 (in reality 1,221cc), a more luxurious version of the Fiat 1100, which achieved 18.2 seconds and had a maximum speed of 137kmh (85mph), 2kmh better than the Alfa. In their time these were really top cars in their class. Compare this with the 0–100kmh time of 32.5 and 44.4 seconds required for the standing-start kilometre by the very popular 948cc Austin A40, times just matched by the Mercedes 190 diesel.

One of the fastest American cars obtainable in Europe in those days was the spectacular 5.2-litre V8-engined Plymouth Fury Hard Top Sedan with a three-speed transmission and about the largest rear fins ever seen. It had a manual gearbox and did 0–100kmh in 10.6 seconds, which in 1959 was flying! I took one to the Montlhéry track, near Paris, for the maximum speed runs on the oval, where it did 114.3mph, very fast for a comparatively cheap car in those days. But when I tried a crash stop from near that speed, the car slowed down to around 60mph, after which it just rolled on – the brakes had faded away almost completely!

When Mercedes-Benz produced the third-generation 220 with fin-shaped rear fenders, they had two versions, the 'S' with twin carburettors and 'SE' with

The Fiat 600 was very popular in its time, but I would not like to drive a 60mph car again for 2,000 miles across Europe! The Abarth version, however, was rather fun, with capacity increased to 750cc and twice the original power.

continuous-flow fuel injection. The latter was slightly more economical when driven fast, but was only marginally quicker. It did 0–100kmh in 12.7 seconds, the standing-start kilometre in 33.9 seconds and had a rather impressive 170kmh (106mph) maximum speed.

The press launch of these cars took place in Besançon, in the French Vosges region, and I remember that Bernard Cahier and myself went out with Rudi Uhlenhaut, the Mercedes development chief who used to test his racing cars and was as fast as the works drivers. We had a wonderful time taking turns at the wheel and discussing cars. Those third-generation 220s were very lively for their time and handled quite well on their low-pivot swing axle suspension, but the steering was too 'rubbery'. As was then fashionable, the gear lever was under the steering wheel and the speedometer looked more like a domestic mercury thermometer than anything else.

A page of my road test booklet is devoted to the BMW 600, a sort of four-seat Isetta in which the front passenger entered from the front. It was quite slow, only just reaching 100kmh (62mph), and almost spelled the end of BMW. The MGA Twin Cam did a dicey 111mph on an Italian road with too much traffic, though acceleration was not spectacular, as indicated by the standing-start kilometre time of 33.5 seconds. I nearly ruined the engine because I only looked at the oil level at the second refuelling stop, by which time the dipstick showed no trace! From then on I added a litre every time I refilled with petrol!

I had a glorious period in the spring of 1958 when, in quick succession, a 5.8-litre Facel Vega HK500, a Mercedes-Benz 300SL Roadster, a Jaguar XK150 3.4 Coupé and a competition Ferrari 250GT LWB passed through my hands. As expected, the Ferrari, the only racing model of the lot, was easily the fastest at 245kmh (152mph), frightening a few people I overtook in the process, the Jabbeke road no longer being as traffic-free as it had been. From 0 to 100kmh took 7.6 seconds, and the standing-start kilometre 26.9 seconds, but both figures could have been improved if the clutch had allowed a good racing start, for which it was too weak. The Jaguar did exactly 200kmh (125mph) but its times for 0–100kmh and the standing-start kilometre of 10.8 and 31.7 seconds respectively are bettered today even by not-so-hot popular hatchbacks.

In spite of its weight of 1,900kg with its 100-litre fuel tank full, the Facel Vega was, at the time, the fastest real road car you could buy. It just beat the Mercedes 300SL Roadster with a maximum speed of 218kmh (135.5mph) compared with the SL's 217kmh (134.8mph) and a 0–100km time of 7.4 against 8.1 seconds, in spite of rear axle tramp making the start quite difficult. The Mercedes got its own back over the standing-start kilometre with 27.9 seconds against the Facel's 28.1, the latter being an air brake in itself. At the time I often urged Facel boss Jean Daninos to add rear torque arms to prevent leaf spring wind-up, but he never did. In those days Europe ignored power steering and with its big lump of American cast iron in the front the HK500 was quite a handful even though the steering was very low-geared, but it handled quite well on its mandatory Michelin X tyres.

One of the fastest and surely the most elegant Euro-American GT cars of the 1950s and early '60s was the Chrysler-powered Facel Vega. Stopping was a problem before disc brakes were adopted.

And when it acquired disc brakes, it could at last be stopped! The Mercedes 300SL Roadster was heavier and not quite as exciting as the gullwing model, but thanks to its low-pivot swing axles it handled much better and here, too, the disc brakes were a vast improvement.

Shortly after the Facel Vega test, Jean Daninos asked me to drive an HK500 over an officially timed flying and standing-start kilometre. Because the times would rank as Belgian class records, the runs were done in Belgium and timed by the Royal Automobile Club of Belgium on an unfinished autoroute near Ghent. The car was fitted with an underpan, but Daninos swears that it was otherwise completely standard. The day was typical of the Belgian climate with ceaseless rain, but we had no choice and I was very surprised when we took the class record at over 237kmh (147mph), and even more so when in those abominable conditions we even took the record for the standing-start kilometre in 28.57 seconds. I wonder what the car would have done on a dry road!

After the demise of the Facel company, I had not seen Jean Daninos for more than 20 years when we discovered that we lived only about 12 miles apart in the South of France, and he soon became a very cherished friend. For years now we have been meeting very regularly, usually for dinner, when we often have passionate discussions on the most varied of subjects. He is ten years older than me, but still drives his Porsche over surprisingly long distances.

In 1959 General Motors came up with a completely new range of compact cars, the controversial Chevrolet Corvair with a six-cylinder, air-cooled rear engine (obviously a Porsche-inspired car), the Pontiac Tempest, the Buick Special and the Oldsmobile F85. I tested them all, except for the Oldsmobile, which was mechanically identical with the Buick.

I must quite frankly confess that I rather liked the Corvair. Certainly it did oversteer, but it was easy to catch, even though the steering was too low-geared. It was not fast at 140kmh (87mph) maximum and 0–100kmh in 16.1 seconds with its three-speed manual box. But I never felt that it was dangerous; the oversteer was clean and predictable and it was good fun, though technical journalist Harry Mundy, who knew what he was talking about, thought it the worst-handling car he had ever driven. Maybe my judgement was influenced by the fact that, at the time, I ran my Porsche 1600 Super 90 and I liked the idea of GM trying to do a Porsche, even if they did not quite succeed!

As for the Pontiac Tempest, that was a really bad car. It was powered by a big, rough ohv 2.7-litre four-cylinder engine, and instead of having a two-piece propeller shaft to allow a low rear passenger floor, it had a *flexible* shaft with a centre bearing pulling it down in the middle to form an arc! And if that was not enough, it had swing axle rear suspension that jacked up as soon as you tried to corner a little faster than the average American driver. That was a *really* dangerous car, altogether one of the worst I have driven. Its performance was also less than exciting. It was the Tempest that should have been Ralph Nader's scapegoat, not – or to a lesser extent – the Corvair.

The 1961 Pontiac Tempest was one of the worst cars I ever drove. Its engine was rough and handling was disastrous.

In complete contrast, the Buick Special, powered by an all-aluminium 3.5-litre ohv V8, was a remarkably good car, and its engine, suitably developed, still powers today's Range Rover and some Morgan and TVR models. It was completely straightforward, handled reasonably well and, in its manual version, went like a flash, achieving 0–100kmh in 10.8 seconds, very good for a comfortable saloon of the period.

At the time, the late 1950s, Jean Dieudonné, father of the later racing driver Pierre, owned a resplendent 4.5-litre Talbot Lago Record saloon and was very proud of it. When I told him that I was testing a Buick, which, I felt sure, would easily outperform it, he was incredulous. So we went to a quiet, straight road, put the two cars side by side and had a go, then another and yet another. Every time the Buick made the larger-engined and twice-as-expensive Talbot eat dust. A few months later Jean sold the Talbot – but he did not buy a Buick!

I don't remember what he bought, but the car to beat the Buick would have been one that has meanwhile become a treasured collector's item – the 3.8-litre Jaguar Mk 2. In the early 1960s there were not many four-door cars to beat it, and the Jag proved it in touring car races and such events as the Tour de France. But even in standard form it was a pretty quick vehicle, achieving 0–100kmh (0–62mph) in 8.8 seconds, the standing-start kilometre in 30.6 seconds and was good for 200kmh (125mph). And the car I tested was a very ordinary example, not one of the factory demonstrators, which were always surprisingly quick. The Mk 2 also handled quite well in spite of its somewhat vague steering. It was a much better car than its successor, the S-type which had independent rear suspension along the lines of the E-type, giving a rather 'floating' rear end, weighed 200kg (440lb) more (goodness knows why!) and was correspondingly slower. But both would be easily beaten by a modern Honda Civic VTI or Peugeot 306 16V.

In the 1960s, on the occasion of one of the London Motor Shows at Earl's Court, Rolls-Royce required a story for a forthcoming catalogue featuring the Silver Shadow and suggested that a drive from Belgium to Monte Carlo and back would be the thing. This was organised in the following spring and, apart from catching a severe cold from the powerful air-conditioning system that my wife loved, we had a very pleasant trip. Everything went smoothly until we arrived back home with the car facing the door of my underground garage, when I could find only one gear – reverse! It must be remembered that the Rolls's GM-made automatic transmission had an electric selector lever under the steering wheel, rather than the usual mechanical selector. As until then the gearbox had not given the slightest sign of weakness, I suspected an electrical rather than a hydraulic problem and had a look at the superb owner's manual, where I discovered that there was a contact breaker in the electrical selector system, hidden somewhere under the dash. For some obscure reason it had been over-zealous and a push on the button solved the problem. This happened more than 30 years ago and I have driven and tested many Rolls-Royces since and always found that even though their handling has improved considerably in the meantime, they are cars that encourage even me to adopt a relaxed driving style.

Early Porsche 356s were certainly quite remarkable (not really in a good sense) for their problematic handling, but not for their performance. In 1958 an enthusiastic owner lent me his 1952 1300 Coupé to take performance figures, and though the car was in good shape it needed 20.9 seconds to reach 100kmh, admittedly on a rather windy day, and it required 39.9 seconds to cover the kilometre from a standing start. This compared with the corresponding figures of 11.5 and 32.0 seconds achieved in May 1960 by my own 1600 Super 90, which also did 187.5kmh (116/5mph). My previous 1600 Super was 9kmh (5.5mph) slower, but only 0.2 second slower to 100kmh and 0.7 second slower to the kilometre mark, thanks to lower weight and drag.

In the late 1950s and up to around 1970, Dante Giascosa and later Oscar Montabone were responsible for car development at Fiat. Aurelio Lampredi, after ten years with Ferrari, headed the engine department, and in that period Fiat produced a number of very interesting models at very competitive prices. One of them was the beautiful Ghia-styled 2300 S Coupé, which impressed me so much that I bought one, the 62nd off the production line, to replace my Porsche 356B Super 90. In acceleration the Fiat was a match for the Porsche, but it had a higher maximum speed that increased from 191kmh (118mph) at 10,000km to 198kmh (123mph) at 41,000km, all timed over the same base.

The 2300S was a much nicer car than the contemporary Alfa 2600 Coupé, which was a bad understeerer, had very heavy steering, and was no faster. In the 1960s Fiats were notable for at least equalling the performance of comparable Alfas, which also did not handle any better and were notably more expensive. The Fiat 1300 with its Corvair-inspired body was just as quick as a Giulietta saloon, and Fiat's 1500 version of the same car was, at 149.5kmh (92.8mph), faster than a Giulietta TI, which could not match the Fiat 1500 over the standing-start kilometre covered in 37.7 seconds, compared with the cheaper Fiat 1500's 36.0 seconds. But admittedly, the Alfa lent itself better to tuning.

The real quality car among the Italian sporting trio in the 2.5-litre class was probably the 2.5-litre (later 2.8-litre) short-wheelbase Lancia Flaminia, of which I drove all three versions, Pininfarina's Coupé, Bertone's GT and Zagato's Sport, which was the lightest. I tested a GT over a fairly long distance and liked it very much. It reached 100kmh in 11.0 seconds and the standing-start kilometre took 32.2 seconds, but strangely I have not written down the maximum speed – around 190kmh (118mph) – in my little book.

The Lancia Flaminia was the work of Prof Antonio Fessia who, before the war, had been the Technical Director of Fiat. He was an artist in the engineering world and his designs took little notice of manufacturing costs; he regarded engineering in much the same light as Ettore Bugatti.

A few Soviet Russian Volgas were sold in Belgium. They were rather rough, horrible and slow, being powered by a 2.5-litre four-cylinder engine giving a maximum speed 129kmh (80mph) and a standing-start kilometre time of 42.2

seconds. I wished that I had a mask to avoiding being recognised at the wheel of such a car!

The early 3.8-litre E-type Jaguars were the hottest in every respect. The factory coupé I drove from Brussels to Rome with my eldest daughter did 237kmh (147mph), 0–100kmh in 6.9 seconds and the standing-start kilometre in 26.6 seconds, figures never bettered by the later 4.2 -litre models that had to conform to the early American emission regulations. Only the much later V12 could do very marginally better, respectively 240kmh (149mph) and 6.6 and 26.3 seconds.

The 3.8 was also the hottest in terms of cockpit temperature. Heat insulation was so bad that after a fast run you could not hold your hand on the gear lever, and intense heat was dispersed from the central tunnel into the cockpit. In Italy, at an outside temperature of over 30°C and the sun blazing on the black car, the heat became just unbearable, even with open windows. The car had come from Coventry on Dunlop racing tyres, but after it had gone through *Quattroruote's* test procedure, a new set had to be bought for the return journey, fortunately in cooler weather. Another problem with the E-type was the brakes. They were discs, but too small and not sufficiently cooled. On the way to Rome I stopped in Modena to drive it on the Autodromo, where Ferrari and Maserati used to test, and I had to stop after a few laps because the hydraulic fluid began to boil and it took the brakes more than half an hour to recover.

Here I am testing a Jaguar S-type, which replaced the Mark II and had independent rear suspension. The S-type was more comfortable, but performance suffered from the extra weight and handling was disappointing. (Van Bever)

Another car I drove to Rome was an Aston Martin DB4 Vantage GT. This was a regular DB4 2+2 powered by the more powerful engine of the GT. One thing I remember about it is that I averaged 214kmh (133mph) from kilometre zero of the Autostrada del Sole in Milan to kilometre 155 in Modena on a very traffic-free day in November 1962. The Aston handled very well, better than the Jaguar, and was also 20kmh (12.5mph) faster, but being 150kg (357lb) heavier it did not better the Jag's acceleration times, being in fact 0.2 second slower over the standing-start kilometre. I covered a distance of over 3,000 miles with the car, but it was expensive fun and luxury: the overall fuel consumption worked out at 23.4l/100km (12.1mpg)!

At the time there was quite obviously a problem with *Quattroruote*'s maximum speed timing strip and the Jaguar was credited with 256.4kmh (159.2mph) and the Aston with 278.8kmh (173.1mph). The speeds I quote were therefore those I obtained in two-way runs over a kilometre with a stopwatch, but the magazine printed the higher figures and it took some time before they found the source of the error.

In my opinion the finest Aston Martin in the context of its time was the DB2, which was also the best looking. It later evolved into the DB2/4 2+2 with a tailgate, but the requirements of the rear headroom spoiled the harmony of its lines. I tested a 2.9-litre in 1955, and was very enthusiastic about it. It was my fastest test car that year, the only one to beat 10 seconds for the 0–100kmh sprint (9.7 seconds), and its maximum speed was 183kmh (113.7mph). Later cars with a V8 engine were of superb quality, but too heavy and too ponderous in their handling.

Among the most troublesome tests were those of Rolls-Royces and Bentleys. A test of a Silver Wraith remained unpublished because, as mentioned in an earlier chapter, the car left me stranded on the autoroute in 1954, and an S-type Bentley only just made it to Ostend at 12mph for the last 6 miles, and had to be pushed into the plane that flew it back to England. The problem was the same in both cases: the seal at the tail of the GM automatic transmission had failed and all the oil had escaped. I presume that the seal had been blown out by the heat-induced pressure built up in the gearbox when the car was driven at maximum speed for long distances.

The first-generation Chevrolet Corvette was a lame duck. Performance only arrived when GM dropped the small-block V8 into it, and only with the Stingray did it become a serious sports car with performance to match the E-Type and the Aston Martin tested a few months earlier. As is well known, the man behind the evolution of the Corvette was Zora Arkus-Duntov, whom I had first met in New York in 1949 when he was still making the ARDUN cylinder heads for Ford V8 engines. The Corvette's 5.3-litre V8 had fantastic torque, its handling was up to the standards of the time and its Borg Warner four-speed manual gearbox was a delight. Another Corvette, now with the ponderous big-block 7-litre engine, came my way in 1968. Maximum speed was limited to 230kmh (143mph) by low

My wife, Suzanne, and I with Piero Taruffi – the 'Silver Fox' – after a test outing with an Austin 1100 automatic. (LAT)

gearing, but it did a standing-start kilometre in 24.9 seconds and, in a straight line, would probably have stayed with today's remarkably good Corvette, but unfortunately its heavy engine spoiled the handling. I kept in contact with Zora and his charming wife Elfy and spent fascinating hours with them in Europe and in Grosse Pointe, a fashionable residential district on Lake Michigan, near Detroit, until Zora's death in 1997.

The most entertaining cars are not always the best. A good example was the Sunbeam Tiger, a Sunbeam Alpine Roadster whose 1.8-litre engine was replaced with a 4.3-litre, later 4.7-litre, Ford V8 engine. The engine was, as they say, much faster than the chassis, which was of the leaf spring and rigid rear axle type. But weighing only 1,180kg (23.2cwt) it went like a rocket and Suzanne and I had immense fun driving one to Greece to cover the Acropolis Rally, adding some days for touring the country and a part of Yugoslavia. The torquey engine was good for 189kmh (117.5mph) for the flying and 29.5 seconds for the standing-start kilometre. In all I covered over 5,500 miles with it, averaging 15.3l/100km (18.5mpg).

Testing Porsches was always fun and impressive. Even though I did not take figures on all of them, I drove almost every 911 model, starting with the very first. No 911 was ever slower than the 207kmh (129mph) achieved by a 911T, and from the start there was always a model needing less than 30 seconds to cover the standing-start kilometre.

In 1966 I timed a 911S at 6.8 seconds for the 0–100kmh sprint, 17.7 seconds to 160kmh (100mph), 27.55 seconds for the standing-start kilometre, and a maximum speed of 222kmh (138mph) – staggering for a 2-litre road car at the time and still pretty quick today. Sure, the engine was noisy and had to be kept at high revs, and the handling was still a bit tricky, but the car was immense fun. Much better handling came with the longer-wheelbase 1969 models. The 2.2 and 2.4 'S' models that followed were even faster, not to mention the famous 2.7 RS, which clocked 25.4 seconds for the standing-start and 240kmh (149mph) for the flying kilometre, times that its immediate successor, the 3.0 RS, did not quite manage to equal in spite of its additional 20bhp.

The next really outstanding Porsche was the 911 Turbo, especially the 3.3-litre of 1978, the first road car in my book (and in any road test I had read) that achieved the standing-start kilometre in 24 seconds dead, beating even the Ferrari 365GT (Daytona) and the Lamborghini Miura by a few fractions of a second, though at 258kmh (160.3mph) the Porsche had a lower maximum speed. Over the years the Turbo put on some weight and became fractionally slower. But the next car to beat 24 seconds was again a Porsche belonging to the 911 family, the fabulous high-tech 959, which posted a resounding 21.7 seconds and a maximum speed of 317kmh (197mph). In its factory-uprated 430bhp version, the 1996–97 993 series Turbo is in the same league, with a time of 21.8 seconds.

The German firm of Glas was an enterprising little company specialising in agricultural machines, which, in the early post-war years, produced a small 300cc two-stroke-engined car called a Goggomobil and later came up with more serious small cars bearing the Glas name. Glas was the first manufacturer to put its faith in a toothed belt to drive an overhead camshaft, and so made history. In 1966 its 1304TS, a little 800kg (15.7cwt) car powered by a 70bhp 1,300cc engine, was the ancestor of all GTIs. No small car could beat its 0–100kmh time of 10.9 seconds or its 32.6 seconds for the standing-start kilometre, though with only 39 per cent of the weight on the driven rear wheels, it was quite a handful, particularly in the wet. Renault soon responded with the R8 Gordini 1300, which achieved 10.8 and 31.7 seconds and a maximum speed of 168.5kmh (104.7mph) – one up on the Glas. Both were as aerodynamic as a brick wall and the Renault had an incredibly vague five-speed gearbox.

Glas had the same engine and later also a 1,700cc 100bhp version in a beautiful Frua-designed 2+2 coupé, which performed very well (achieving the standing-start kilometre in 31.7 seconds), then they put two of the 1,300 engines together to make a very nice V8-engined coupé. But with this they overestimated their own strength and the company was bought by BMW, which is how BMW acquired a factory in Dingolfing, some 100 miles east of Munich.

An interesting car I got hold of in 1965 was a 'High Performance' version of the 4.7-litre (327cu in) Ford Mustang Coupé, which had won the Marathon de la Route on the complete old Nürburgring, a 84-hour event with strictly limited times for maintenance. Jacky Ickx had been among its drivers. It was a big brute, harshly sprung and fitted with a brutish and noisy ZF self-locking differential, but it handled acceptably well and had bags of power and a non-standard four-speed gearbox (I believe by ZF). I took it as an instructor in a driving course back to the scene of its exploits, which gave me an opportunity to drive it for several laps of the 'Ring. Its maximum speed was 205kmh (128mph), 20kmh faster than the standard version I also tested, with its bonnet vibrating and pulling on its locks, a sure indication of strong lift forces, and it was good for a standing-start kilometre in 27.8 seconds, 2.2 seconds quicker than standard. I also took it to the Zolder circuit, where it lapped in 2 min 04 sec, good for a big car.

I also tested many Ferraris and Lamborghinis. In contrast to most people, I never found the Dino V6 particularly beautiful, but it was certainly a delightful little car to drive and just a match for its Porsche 911 S contemporary, both in acceleration and maximum speed. I remember taking one to England for a test drive of a BMW-engined Chevron B17, a beautifully made and very rewarding little racing car to drive. The venue, I think, was the Snetterton circuit.

Both the Ferrari 365 GTB4 and the Lamborghini Miura were good for standing-start kilometre times in the 24-second bracket, but the Ferrari that I took over the Mille Miglia passes of Futa and Raticosa required strong arms on those winding mountain roads. Its handling was nevertheless much more predictable than the Miura's and it was also, by a small margin, the faster of the two. I timed a Miura at 278kmh (172.5mph) on the Autostrada del Sole, a rather dicey adventure because the aerodynamic lift on the front wheels reduced the latter's grip to almost zero, but the Ferrari's 282.3kmh (175.4mph), timed on the Bologna-Ancona autostrada, remained unbeaten by any production car for the next 18 years. The mid-engined Ferraris of the BB family were marginally slower due to the introduction of emission regulations. The 365 BB did 278kmh (173mph) and took 24.9 seconds for the standing-start kilometre. All figures are two-way averages.

The Ferrari 365GTB 'Daytona', with which I reached 175.5mph on an Italian autostrada in 1969, remained the fastest production car that I had timed for 18 years.

Concerning the Miura, it is only fair to say that Gianpaolo Dallara, who was responsible for its mechanical design, was aware of the chassis limitations and was desperately anxious to develop a racing version from which the standard car would have benefited. But Lamborghini would not hear of racing and Dallara left the company to found his own business specialising in racing cars, which today reign supreme in Formula 3 and are among the best in Formula 3000 and Indy car racing.

The first car to beat the 365 GTB was the Porsche 959, which achieved 317kmh (197mph) in a two-way, electronically timed run, and a rousing 21.6 seconds over the standing-start kilometre on Volkswagen's high-speed track, a feat overshadowed on the same day in 1989 by Alois Ruf's now-famous 911-based 'Yellow Bird', which did 339kmh (211mph). Meanwhile this was beaten, though only by 1kmh, by a standard Jaguar XJ220 and an experimental Bugatti EB 110S devoid of external mirrors, which did 342kmh (212.5mph), the fastest speed at which I have driven a car, in 1994.

Within the Ferrari family of cars, it took 21 years to see a Testa Rossa beat the 365 GTB4's speed with a run at 291kmh (181mph), while on the same day an F40 did 324kmh (201.3mph). I remember two exciting days in Germany with photographer and motoring journalist John Lamm, driving an F40, looking both for comparatively traffic-free autobahn stretches and interesting roads. Out of town this was a highly exciting car, but in city traffic the almost solid clutch pedal and the lack of rear and three-quarter-rear visibility were a nightmare. I also had opportunities to drive F40s on the excellent Mugello circuit, on a very wet day, when I was an instructor in an advanced driving course organised by Auto Becker, Ferrari's leading German distributor, and found that they were not the handful one might expect when driven fast in those circumstances.

Early Ferrari road cars were fast, but they were not nice cars to drive. They were harsh, had bad steering, a difficult gearbox and tended to understeer excessively. The first serious attempt to make a practical car was the 250 GT 2+2, followed in 1963 by the 4-litre-engined 330 GT, the last Ferrari with a rigid rear axle. Its speed of 234kmh (145.4mph) and a standing-start time of 27.1 seconds over the kilometre set the minimum performance standard for all later front-engined Ferrari models over the following 30 years. All those cars had a maximum speed of up to 245kmh (152mph) and took around 26 seconds for the standing-start kilometre, except for the much faster 365 GTB/4 'Daytona'.

The Lamborghini 400 GT and Jarama (same chassis, different body) were in exactly the same bracket, and I cannot decide whether I preferred the cars from Maranello or from Sant'Agata. Lamborghinis had independent rear suspension from the start. But I hated the Countach, which was utterly impractical, handled abominably and was terribly erratic at speed. The Diablo is better, especially since, at last, it received power steering. It is outrageously fast – we timed one at 325kmh (202mph) on the VW speed track in 1991, a speed equalled in 2000 by a 6-litre version, in spite of much stricter emission laws. But it is too wide, too large and too heavy for fun.

Mentioning the 400GT reminds me of the visit I made to the factory with Suzanne to drive one of those cars. We were welcomed by Paolo Stanzani, at the time a still very young engineer who worked with Gianpaolo Dallara. The car was ready and as the intention was to have lunch with him slightly later, he came with us, taking a very uncomfortable place in the cramped rear seat. Off we went in the direction of Bologna on a fairly narrow, dead straight country road, bordered on both sides by fields. There was no reason for hanging around and with the V-12 singing happily, we were proceeding at anything between 110 and 120mph when, driving over a hardly noticeable brow, I was suddenly faced with a sharp right angle left turn on to a stone bridge. I braked as fiercely as I could and just managed to scrape over the bridge without hitting anything. After recovering from the emotion, I turned to Stanzani and asked: 'You know this road, why didn't you warn me?' 'I know you are a competent racing driver,' he said, 'and I was anxious to see how you would manage!' Nearly 30 years later Stanzani was responsible for the design of the V-12, four turbo, 60-valve, four-wheel-drive Bugatti EB 110 built in Campogalliano, near Modena. Unfortunately disagreements with the company's President Romano Artioli forced him to leave as the development of the car had hardly begun.

In the late 1950s the six-cylinder Maserati 3500 GT was a nicer, more usable and more comfortable car than the probably slightly faster contemporary V12 Ferraris, though I never had a chance to put a watch on it, nor on its 4-litre successors, of which the Mistral did not handle very satisfactorily. For the later Ghibli, Indy and Khamsin, the six-cylinder engine, which had been developed from the 3000S racing engine, was replaced by another race-bred engine, a four-cam V8 of 4.7-litre and 4.9-litre capacity. The Ghibli was a fabulous-looking car, but the Indy, a rather roomy 2+2, in spite of its quite ordinary chassis with a rigid rear axle on leaf springs, was probably the best-handling of the front-engined Maseratis and a very potent car that I liked very much. The V8 engine also powered the mid-engined Bora, a much underrated car.

The Bora was one of the cars that passed through my hands in February 1972, which was quite an exciting month as far as high-performance cars were concerned. Starting from Brussels at the wheel of an early V12-engined E-Type Jaguar Coupé, I first drove to Nice, incidentally driving the longest distance I ever covered in 1 hour on public roads – 206km (128 miles) according to the kilometre stones on the A7 autoroute – just before speed limits were imposed!

From Nice I drove to Modena, where I stayed for a few days and visited Maserati, Ferrari and De Tomaso, taking cars out for a day to get performance figures for a Bora, a 365 GTC/4 Coupé and a Pantera respectively, and, of course, for the Jaguar. All performance figures were taken, two-way, on the Bologna-Padova autostrada and showed that all four cars were pretty evenly matched:

	Max speed (kmh/mph)	0–100kmh/ 62mph (seconds)	0–160kmh/ 100mph (seconds)	0–200kmh/ 125mph (seconds)	Standing-start km (seconds)
Maserati Bora	250/155.3	6.8	15.5	26.5	26.3
Jaguar V12	240/149	6.7	15.6	26.5	26.3
Ferrari 365 GTC	240/149	7.2	16.5	29.5	27.2
De Tomaso Pantera	237/147	6.5	14.9	26.0	26.5

A few months earlier an Aston Martin DBS V8 achieved very similar figures with a speed of 240kmh (149mph) and a standing-start kilometre in 26.8 seconds.

Looking at these figures, it must be borne in mind that those for the Bora were taken on a rainy day on a wet road. The car was surely good for 260kmh (161mph) and a time under 26 seconds for the standing-start kilometre. The Jaguar's performance is quite impressive compared with those of the other much more expensive cars, though it was in no way an inexpensive car to run; for the 2,500 miles or so I covered with it, the average fuel consumption came out at 24.4l/100km (11.6mpg).

The Pantera was fun and an acceptable substitute for a road-going Ford GT40, but its 5.3-litre Ford V8 engine did not make the right noises and the shift mechanism of its ZF five-speed gearbox was terrible, quite apart from the fact that the build quality was rather doubtful. However, for its time it handled quite well, in contrast to its forebear, the Mangusta, which was a lot lighter and

The mid-engined Lamborghini Miura is still one of the most beautiful cars ever made. I timed one at 173mph, but handling was rather tricky.

accelerated even faster, but was a very dangerous car. A few months later I picked up a 5.7-litre GTS version of the Pantera, which did 257kmh (159.7mph), 5.8, 13.4, 22.1 and 25.3 seconds respectively.

The Ferrari 365 GTC/4 was designed to be a more comfortable and more flexible car than the contemporary 365 GTB/4 ('Daytona'). In contrast to the latter, it had its gearbox in unit with the engine instead of the differential, and it was, to the best of my knowledge, the only Ferrari in which the intake pipes were between the camshaft instead of inside the 'V' formed by the two cylinder banks. It had more room for luggage and was quieter and more comfortable than the Daytona, but quite a lot slower, which is not what Ferrari customers want, even if most of them never exploit their car's performance.

I liked the Bora, which I found to be a nicer car to drive than the early mid-engined Ferrari 365 BB of a year or two later. It was a better road car and also handled better. Giulio Alfieri, its designer, also produced a single competition version, which I test drove on the Modena circuit and found to be very good.

Alfieri was a brilliant engineer and racing cars were his passion. He had developed the Colombo-designed 2-litre Maserati single-seater into the grand prix-winning 250F and produced a masterpiece with the Tipo 61 'Birdcage' sports racing car, a real model of spaceframe technology. It was only unfortunate that in the late 1950s and 1960s Maserati lacked the money for proper testing and development.

As a road car, however, the Jaguar was probably the best of the lot, its main virtues being top performance, quietness, comfort and more than acceptable handling. But the performance of the 2.4-litre Porsche 911 S, which I had driven to Rome a few months earlier, and of the 2.4-litre Ferrari Dino, which I took to England on the occasion of the test drive of a Chevron B17 mentioned earlier, makes one think twice about the justification of those high-powered and heavy supercars – apart from 'one-upmanship'.

Also in the 1970s BMW produced the striking M1 Coupé with a plastic body on a tubular spaceframe; it was to be homologated as a GT car, but that never happened. The car handled beautifully, was powered by a four-cam, straight-six 280bhp engine, and could cover the standing-start kilometre in 24.9 seconds, a match for the Ferrari 365 BB; even though its 261kmh (162mph) top speed was some 17kmh slower, that was largely offset by much better handling.

The first Ferrari with a four-cam V8 engine in the central position was the Dino GT/4, the only production Ferrari that came with a Bertone body. This 3-litre version was the ancestor of all V8 production models, up to the current 360 Modena. Its performance just bettered that of the Dino 246 with a standing-start kilometre time of 26.8 seconds, but at 243kmh (151mph) it was 10kmh faster. I remember taking it to the launch of the VW Scirocco, a few months before that of the identically engineered Golf I, at VW's proving ground in Ehra-Lessien. At the time the now-retired VW PR officer was the very enthusiastic Anton Konrad, who used to race an Audi 80 with Hans Novak, an Audi technician well known by journalists. When I told him that I was testing the Ferrari, he immediately took it away from me and came back 90 minutes later with a full set of performance figures taken on VW's fabulous high-speed track – and the Ferrari's fuel tank full to the brim.

But not everyone can afford a Dino or a Ferrari, and an inexpensive car that really provided performance at a bargain price, with the added advantage of four seats, was the Ford Capri 2600 RS, powered by a very ordinary pushrod V6 engine. I timed one at 203kmh (126mph) and it took 7.3 seconds for 0–100kmh and 28.35 seconds for the standing-start kilometre – very good if you remember its bargain price and the fact that this was in 1971. It handled well, was great fun to drive, but, my goodness, was the suspension hard!

In the early 1970s Japanese cars began to enter the picture, but their manufacturers still had a lot to learn about suspension, acceptable handling usually being obtained only at the cost of rather severe discomfort. The otherwise quite nice first-series Toyota Corolla, the quick Toyota Trueno GT and the Mitsubishi Celeste were typical examples. The engines also became quite rough when approaching the usually unrealistically high red line. But as a rule Japanese gearboxes were excellent and the cars were reliable, which, together with their attractive prices, forged their success.

By far the most impressive Japanese car I tested at the time, in November 1971, was the Datsun 240Z. It was really elegant (thanks to Mr Goertz), performed and handled well, being let down only by a rather rough and agricultural engine, for which there was no excuse with a straight-six. But I nevertheless enjoyed it and it achieved 197kmh (122.5mph), 0–100kmh in 8.7 seconds and the standing-start kilometre in 29.9 seconds. None of the straight-six-engined Z cars that followed was as likeable or fast.

Cars need not always be very fast to be interesting. A typical example is the NSU Ro-80, the first full-size car to be powered by a Wankel-type rotary engine and which, for good measure, also featured an automatic clutch and a torque converter. Unfortunately the engine still lacked reliability and the car's performance was not spectacular enough to focus the public's attention. Mazda achieved a complete contrast with the R100; in that case the engine was again rather faster than the chassis. But it certainly made an impact, allowing Mazda to persevere and to make the engine reliable and more efficient. Unfortunately the company did not exploit its Le Mans victory of 1991 as it should have done and the current RX-7 is much underrated, and practically unknown in Europe.

In the mid-1970s Ferdinand Piëch, at the time responsible for development at Audi, lent me a very interesting Audi 100 in which the five-cylinder engine had been replaced with a twin-rotor, 170bhp Wankel rotary engine of 750cm3 chamber volume. It was fast and supremely smooth running, but the investment required to launch it would have been too high and a five-cylinder turbo replaced it in the original Audi 200.

Another car interesting for its role as a pioneer was the Dutch DAF. This was the first car to feature an automatic continuously variable transmission (CVT). It used conventional V-belts in connection with variable-diameter pulleys. Powered by a 600cc air-cooled flat-twin engine, it was nearly as slow as a contemporary 2CV Citroën, but while the Citroën was still fun to drive because you had to work the gearshift hard to keep up any speed, the DAF was a terrible bore because you just sat there, waiting for things to happen. This model was followed by a car powered by a Renault 1,108cc and later 1,289cc engine, which became the Volvo 66 when the DAF car division was taken over by the Swedish company. DAF even built a Formula 3 racing car using the system in a Ford-engined Brabham chassis, which did quite well in Monaco. I even test drove it on the Zolder circuit and found it very interesting and easy to drive, but the extra weight of the CVT and the lower maximum speed on the straights, caused by the friction of the belts, were a serious handicap.

The inventor of this Variomatic system was Hub Van Doorne, who with his brother founded DAF (which stands for van Doorne Automobiel Fabriek), then went on to concentrate on the development of today's steel-belt-driven equivalents.

Another highly interesting development was the Audi Quattro. A year after he had let me drive a very early prototype without a central differential, Piëch invited me in the winter of 1979–80 to try a more advanced prototype in the Austrian Alps. As the final coupé version had not then been announced, the Quattro machinery was built into a normal Audi 80 body that used the same platform as the Quattro. The snow was falling hard and, before we drove the car on the

This prototype lightweight Lamborghini Countach was hugely impressive, but it was never put into production.

roads, he suggested that I should try to take a number of comparison cars – a Mercedes 280E, a BMW 528i and an Audi 100 – up a steep forest road covered by a deep layer of snow, all the cars being on identical winter tyres. I first tried the two rear-wheel-drive models, the Mercedes and the BMW, which both stopped after about 100 metres. The front-driven Audi managed about 30 metres more.

'Now try the Quattro,' said Piëch, and I romped up to the top of the road, even having to ease up because of the severe bumps in the road.

'Fantastic,' I said when Piëch met me at the bottom of the hill.

'But that car was on summer tyres,' he said. 'Now you must try it on winter tyres!'

After the car was announced I drove Quattros of the original coupé models for more than 12,000 miles for short and long-term testing, for TV and for a film Audi used in various motor shows. It was a wonderful car to drive, especially on wet roads, not to mention snow, and had a steering feel that no other Audi would reproduce for the following 15 years. Its five-cylinder turbo engine had a splendid sound and powered the car to a 28-seconds standing-start kilometre, and to a 225kmh (140mph) maximum speed – virtually a dead heat with the BMW 635 CSi coupé.

The Lancia Stratos, powered by Ferrari's Dino V6 engine, was in its day an almost unbeatable rally car in the hands of Sandro Munari and Bernard Darniche. It even won the Targa Florio, after which I drove the winning car on the Monteferrato circuit; I had driven there in a Porsche Carrera RS 3.0, which proved to be the more difficult of the two. But the production Stratos was a disaster. Not only was the workmanship of the body terrible, but if you lifted the

Nearly 3,000 miles with a 450bhp, four-wheel-drive Porsche 959 was a fantastic experience. The car is seen heading for Castellane in the French Alps.

My best time around the 'real' Nürburgring was achieved with this Honda NSX 'Type R'.

throttle when taking a curve fast, it would not just tuck in – you had to take very quick action to avoid a spin! I drove at least two examples and they were both the same, plain dangerous cars.

Another interesting Lancia I kept for nearly a year was a Gamma saloon. It was quite unconventional in having a 2.5-litre flat-four engine overhanging the driven front axle, had one of the nicest power steering units ever and handled well. But it was a commercial failure because, rightly or wrongly, people who buy an expensive car want more than four cylinders, and initially the engine was not reliable enough, the one in my long-term car had a porous cylinder head.

Though the Porsche 928 ended its career as a remarkably good car, early models were not very convincing. It was rather slower than the contemporary 911 and its engine was not as smooth as a V8 should be. On a journey with this car from the South of France to Belgium via Stuttgart, I met heavy snowfalls. The car was on summer tyres and, the autobahn being blocked by cars vainly trying to drive up a slope, I tried my luck by taking a short cut. All went well until the road went downhill and uphill again. I tried hard, but whichever direction I chose I could only produce wheelspin. I had to leave the car at the bottom and walk up the road, hoping to find somewhere to stay overnight. I was very lucky to come across a small hotel less than a mile away. Next morning the sun had come out

At an empty Francorchamps circuit on the occasion of the launch of the Dodge Viper GTS in 1996.

and I had no difficulty in driving away. I stopped at Porsche's Technical Centre in Weissach to have snow tyres fitted and came back the following day to pick up the car. The night had been very cold and the engine just would not start. It was Saturday morning, but fortunately Peter Falk, the development engineer, came to my help with a mechanic who happened to be there. They tried everything, checked the ignition and the fuel injection, and replaced the electronic control unit and several parts. At noon they gave up, and I still don't know what the problem was. Finally, as I had to proceed to Brussels, Development Chief Helmuth Bott gave me an experimental 911 that he normally used himself, powered by a one-off 3.5-litre K-Jetronic engine, which developed massive torque. It was on winter tyres and really opened my eyes to the tyres' merits.

Meanwhile the Japanese were progressing quickly, even if a Nissan Silvia I tested in 1980 was one of the worst cars I ever drove: it was very uncomfortable, had a harsh and noisy engine and handled horribly, quite a contrast to the very much underrated 300 ZX that behaved very well when I drove it on the Nürburgring a few years later. Another car that impressed me was the little 1,400cc Mitsubishi Mirage (Colt), which was quick, agile and very well made. I also liked the last of the rear-wheel-drive Corollas; the 1,600cc 16-valve-engined coupé was nice to drive, had a beautifully smooth and lively engine and was really quick.

One day in July 1981 I was asked by the Yokohama Tyre Company to come to the Nürburgring. The surprise was that the object of the visit was a car, a Mitsubishi Lancer 2.0 Turbo, rather than tyres. And another surprise was that, in spite of its rather agricultural chassis with a rigid rear axle, it was quicker around the 'Ring than the BMW 323 available for comparison. When tested it did 202kmh (125.5mph) and a standing-start kilometre in 27.7 seconds.

Two years earlier I had tested a first-series Mazda RX-7 for German TV. It was a very nice car indeed and everyone who drove it on that occasion was impressed by the smoothness of its rotary engine. The later turbocharged models were very quick and the third series is one of the few cars that I could take around the Nürburgring North circuit in under nine minutes. The only others were a Porsche 944 Turbo and 911, Viper GTS and Honda NSX. On several occasions I took an NSX around the 'Ring, both the standard and the Type R. Even in its latest 3.2-litre six-speed version the NSX may not be quite as fast as a Porsche 911/993 or 996, and is certainly slower than a Ferrari F355 or 360 or a Porsche 911 GT3, but few high-performance sports cars are as well balanced and easy to drive fast as the all-aluminium NSX.

For the price of a McLaren you could buy 28 Honda CRXs. This was a delightful little car from the first 12-valve model onwards and became even better with the introduction of first the 1,600 16-valve engine, then the independent rear suspension. The later VTEC engine made it only marginally faster at 215kmh (133.6mph), but it is incredibly smooth at high revolutions, and autobahn cruising at 6,500–6,800rpm is quite normal, not to mention the fun of revving it to 8,000rpm in the lower gears. I did long-term tests of every model, except for the 'Del Sol'. The last of the test cars, a coupé with the VTEC twin-cam engine, I liked so much that I acquired it and, after ten years use, I never regretted it.

Among the cars I have tested, very few were powered by diesel engines. Whenever I tested a new model, I usually chose the highest powered version – just because it's more fun. If I chose a diesel, it was only out of professional integrity. But things have now changed. Thanks mostly to the prodigious progress achieved by electronics, the modern direct-injection turbo-diesels are catching up quickly with spark ignition engines. As I write this they are still heavier than petrol-fuelled power plants and will probably remain so because of the higher mean effective pressure at which they operate. Their specific output is still slightly lower, though even today the BMW-Alpina 2.9-litre engine develops 81bhp per litre, which is more than most production petrol engines. Where the turbo diesel scores heavily, however, is in specific torque and fuel economy, an advantage inherent in its working principle that it is likely to retain whatever advances are made in spark-ignition engine technology.

I take no risk in predicting that the diesel engine will steadily increase its market share in coming years, with important gains also in the luxury car classes.

Chapter 18

Putting experience into practice: Monica and other stories

THE MAN WHO initiated the current method of launching new cars and giving the motoring press an opportunity to drive them in such conditions that a fair judgement can be made is Bob Sicot, formerly responsible for Renault's and later Ford's press relations. On the occasion of the announcement of the Dauphine, in 1955, he managed to persuade the company's management to fly members of the press to Corsica for – if I remember correctly – two days, where the car could be driven for several hundred kilometres on the island's wonderful and demanding roads. Some of the engineers responsible for the car's development would also be present for discussions and to answer questions, and the launch was an immense success. The journalists loved it and filled more columns than had ever before been devoted to a new car launch. Other companies had no choice but to follow Renault's example.

It did not take long for the development engineers of the companies involved to realise that some of the feedback they could get from the more experienced journalists could be worthwhile, and so it came about that, back in 1971, Fiat's chief of development, Luigi Zandonà, asked me to go to Turin to give an assessment of a steering problem on the mid-engined X1/9, just before production began. This was the beginning of a long period of consulting work.

In the late 1960s and early '70s I used to go to Italy and drive the latest products from Ferrari, Lamborghini, Maserati and de Tomaso. At Maserati I became quite friendly with Giulio Alfieri who, at the time, was both Managing Director and responsible for car development. On one or two occasions he came with me as a passenger, and while I drove we discussed the car, occasionally continuing the conversation over a glass of Lambrusco in Modena's famous Ristorante Fini. He apparently liked the way I drove and on several occasions asked me to come to Modena to try some cars. Where handling was concerned he seemed to have more confidence in my judgement than in the opinion of his own people, who had few occasions to drive competitors' cars.

One episode I remember vividly was when he asked me to test drive a Merak (virtually a mid-engined Bora in which the big 4.9-litre V8 was replaced with the

Alfieri-designed V6 used in the Citroën SM). I found the car much too nervous, particularly in fast bends; as soon as the steering wheel was turned through a small angle the car would turn in more, and also more suddenly than expected. That made me aware of the importance of the steering geometry. Apparently in that car, when the front suspension was compressed, toe-in increased. Alfieri modified the shape of the steering arms to make the wheels slightly toe out under compression, and within a day and a half we had a car whose handling was highly praised in *Motor* and *Autocar* road tests.

I enjoyed these fascinating tasks and also enjoyed driving such fast and interesting cars as Maserati Bora, Merak, Indy and Khamsin, but unfortunately it all ceased when Citroën, who at that time owned Maserati, sold it to de Tomaso, and Alfieri left the company.

But my most fascinating job as a consultant in those years was to be involved in the development of a most interesting new car, which unfortunately never saw the light of day – the Monica, named after the wife of its promoter, Jean Tastevin, an industrialist who headed a railway wagon factory in Balbigny, in the Lyon area. He loved good and fast cars and intended to add the manufacture of a luxury car to the activities of his company.

I first saw the car in the Paris Motor Show of 1972 and it looked quite impressive. In fact it was more British than French; it used an advanced single-cam V8 engine, originally designed by a certain Ted Martin for use in a Formula

The Maserati Merak was one car for which I was used as a test driver to improve the handling.

1 car. For road use it had been detuned and its capacity increased to 3.5 litres, but 220 horsepower was still not enough for the car's weight which, in spite of its aluminium body, had finished up at least 200kg (440lb) more than expected. The chassis designer, also responsible for the overall project, was Chris Lawrence, the designer of the short-lived but interesting Deep Sanderson mid-engined sports car and well known as a Morgan racer and tuner. He had done a fine job with a platform made up of tubes and a welded-on steel floor, a double-wishbone front suspension with inboard coil springs, a coil-sprung de Dion axle located transversely by a Panhard rod, and rack-and-pinion power steering. The rear axle came from the Salisbury parts bin and the five-speed gearbox was a ZF.

Soon after the Paris show it was decided to solve the weight problem by using a 5-litre Chrysler V8 tuned in the US by a certain 'Racer Brown' to provide 360 horsepower SAE gross, which probably meant a realistic figure of around 285bhp DIN.

In the spring of 1973 Tastevin invited some journalists to try the car on the Paul Ricard circuit, both to get some publicity for his project and also to hear their comments. The car still had many flaws, but a number of them could be easily remedied, and there was no doubt that performance and handling were good for the period. At the end of the test a luncheon party had been organised and I was invited to share a table with Tastevin and his wife. We discussed many points, and when I asked him what the car would cost to the customer, he gave me a figure that was about twice the price of a Jaguar XJ6. My immediate reaction was, 'But who would buy a car of that class, with no pedigree whatever, at twice the price of a Jaguar?' He looked as if, in his enthusiasm, he had never thought of that!

A few days later came a letter asking me to come to Tastevin's Paris office to discuss some form of co-operation. He wanted me to drive prototypes at regular intervals and report to him about how the development progressed.

A car was ready for me in the garage and I took it out for a drive of about 100 miles in the Paris region, just to get a few impressions. Though many more or less important aspects still needed attention, the design was basically sound and the performance was very good in the context of 1973. There was a slight tendency to oversteer, though this would obviously have been easy to correct. But the car felt solid and inspired confidence.

Among the Monica's unusual features were the electric door locks. Both inside and outside the door handles were just switches, requiring virtually no force to operate, and Tastevin literally cherished them. They were to be a special attraction for eventual customers. As the car had a Chrysler engine, the United States should have been an important market for the Monica, as it had been for the Facel Vega, but in America Ralph Nader had already drawn a lot of attention to safety. I was convinced that the American authorities would never certify a car on which, in the case of an accident affecting the electrical network or a short creating a fire, the doors could not be opened. But Tastevin insisted that these catches were part of his car's unique features, and though I kept trying to persuade him to change, it was the last thing he was prepared to do.

The oversteer problem was soon solved and further, more extensive drives revealed that the car handled almost like a big sports car, but at the cost of a suspension probably too stiff for a luxury saloon. However, at the stage the model had reached little could be done about it because the rear suspension did not have enough travel, and even with two up and some luggage it occasionally hit the bump stops on some of the typical French secondary roads. One partial solution might have been to add a self-levelling device, but cost was an obvious problem.

In October 1973 a longer-distance test drive was organised. A mechanic, a pleasant and competent young man called Peter Dodds, drove from England where the development took place, to pick me up in Brussels where I still lived at the time. We were to put the car through its paces on a round trip including a drive on normal roads to the South of France, mountain roads and autostrada in northern Italy, and back north to Belgium and England. The trip was to be full of adventure.

We had hardly entered France when the clutch began to slip. The obvious reason was that the pedal had no free play, so that was quickly fixed by Peter who crawled under the car to make the required adjustment. About 125 miles later I noticed a warning light indicating that the alternator had packed up and the battery was therefore not being charged. It was late in the afternoon and the sun was getting low. I knew of a decent hotel, the Hotel du Commerce in Bar-sur-Aube, about 40 miles away, but we would have to use the headlights for part of the way to get there. Fortunately we managed it.

Just outside the town I showed Peter a service station where the proprietor's wife had been elected 'Miss Bar-sur-Aube' a few years earlier, and told him that was the place to go and get the battery charged. First we drove to the hotel to unload the baggage, of course keeping the engine running. I stayed with the luggage and Peter drove to the garage. But when he got there the battery was so flat that neither the electric door catches nor the electric windows would work! Imagine an English mechanic who does not speak a word of French trapped inside a car, gesticulating and trying to explain to a French garage man who knows not a word of English and who has never heard of electric door catches, that he cannot get out of the car unless a charger is put on the battery! We had been very lucky that the doors still opened when we stopped at the hotel!

Fortunately the bonnet lock was cable-operated. Peter pulled the handle, the garage man opened it, and, with the bonnet open, Peter was able to make it clear that the battery was to be charged. After all, the English word 'battery' and the French 'batterie' are not so different!

Of course, we now had to change our plans. The Balbigny factory was not so far away, and with a fully charged battery we would easily make it and have the alternator changed. We had a very kind reception from M Tastevin who invited us for lunch at his country house. When we told him our story, he began to realise

The Monica, powered by a modified Chrysler V8, was never put into production, mainly due to the 1973–74 oil crisis. Performance was good, with a 142mph maximum speed, but fuel consumption was horrendous.

that, maybe, I had some good reason for not sharing his enthusiasm for electric door catches …

After lunch we were on the road again, the battery was charging and we headed for Turin on those wonderful French secondary roads, just the thing to reveal any flaw in the handling department, and a joy on which to drive a good car. We entered Italy, taking the Monginevro Pass, where the disc brakes gave a good account of themselves.

After a night in Turin, the morning was dedicated to taking performance figures on the Torino-Ivrea autostrada where, at that time, Fiat had a well-marked base of 5 exactly measured kilometres on a dead straight, level stretch of road. The figures I wrote down were a maximum speed of 226.5kmh (140.66mph), 0–100kmh in 8.0 seconds, 0–160kmh (0–100mph) in 18.6 seconds, and a standing-start kilometre in 28.65 seconds. But as the test runs finished, so was the alternator again; it was probably revolving too fast and unable to withstand the frequent and prolonged high engine speeds we had been using.

So we decided that the time had come to drive back to France, where we joined the Lyon-Paris autoroute and changed the battery for a new one every time we filled up, which meant quite often, even with a 100-litre tank. Adding things up, we found that we had averaged 32.8l/100km (8.65mpg)!

I was part of the team that laid down the specifications for Pininfarina's Ferrari-based 'Sigma Grand Prix' Formula 1 safety project. Many of its features were subsequently introduced in the F1 regulations.

At that time the horrendous fuel consumption would not have been considered as catastrophic as it would be today, and apart from the alternator problem, which could have been quite easily rectified, the car had given quite a good account of itself, even though my memo contains an impressive list of little faults that should have been rectified. It had never objected to sustaining speeds of around 200kmh (125mph) on the then still unrestricted French autoroutes, with the speedometer indicating an overly optimistic 220.

But before the Paris Motor Show of 1974 came the oil crisis, bringing in its wake higher fuel prices, speed limits (which were later lifted only in Germany), and general pessimism. Nobody wanted big and expensive cars any more. These were gloomy times for Jean Tastevin, who desperately needed dealers to sell a car that nobody wanted any more. But the Monica was now so near the production stage that he gave the car a last chance. It still needed a final shake-down before going into production on a line that was by now nearly completed in the Balbigny factory. He asked me to give the car a final, thorough test and the plan was to drive – again with Peter Dodds as companion – to Calabria, in the extreme South of Italy, and back, after which I would hopefully relate my experiences not only to him, but also in the motoring press.

It was late October when I picked up a fully run-in but otherwise brand-new car in Balbigny and we headed for the Moncenisio Pass to reach Italy. However, too much snow already covered the road and we came to a hairpin that stopped us with spinning wheels. We therefore drove back to Modane to put the Monica on the shuttle train. Fortunately the customs officers were probably not aware that the trade plates adorning the car did not allow us to leave France. Next morning we soon reached Turin where, in a heavy downpour, we took the autostrada to Milan. The recently implemented speed limits were not taken too seriously in Italy (they still aren't!), but it rained so hard that we could not drive much faster than maybe 160kmh (100mph). Suddenly, about midway to Milan, there was a loud noise and a big blue cloud appeared in the mirror. There was no choice but to summon the *autostrada* rescue service and call Balbigny. Peter obviously had to stay with the car and, while we had a well-deserved lunch, I called the ever-helpful Maria Rubiolo at the Fiat Press Office who sent me a car – a 1500 L – to drive home.

A valve had dropped into its cylinder due to a broken valve retainer, which had proved before to be unreliable and had meanwhile been replaced by a modified type. Why this engine happened to have the old type, apparently nobody knew. But it struck Jean Tastevin the last blow and the Monica was never put into production. It is said that in all 17 units were built from the first very different prototype to models little different from the final specification. How many are still around is difficult to say. Jean Tastevin kept one, which, as shown in an

An important feature of the Sigma Grand Prix was the rear 'bumper' to prevent wheels 'meshing' causing cars to 'jump' each other in the case of a collision.

article published in 1991, is in pristine condition, and Chris Lawrence has kept one in England.

With a little more development it could have been a very fine car, and its beautiful shape, the work of a young Rumanian designer called Tony Rascanu, who unfortunately died before he could see a complete car, would not be outmoded today.

Also in the mid-1970s I was invited to be part of a team of consultants guiding Sergio Pininfarina in the structural design of a Grand Prix car providing a much better crash protection for the driver than was the case with the Formula 1 cars of the period. The idea had come from Robert Braunschweig, the legendary editor of the Swiss *Automobil Revue,* and Sergio, who is a very keen follower of the sport and a great Ferrari fan, immediately responded to the idea. The consulting group comprised Braunschweig, who was a sort of project leader, Prof Fiala, at that time Chief of Development at Volkswagen, who was responsible for calculating the crash structures and taking care of the driver's protection generally, and myself. My responsibility was to represent the driver's point of view and make sure that he could operate under the best conditions. We had several meetings, first when the car, called the Sigma Grand Prix, was being designed, then when it was being built around Ferrari Formula 1 mechanical units. It was a very interesting task and a pleasure to work with such competent and interesting people as Pininfarina, Fiala and the witty Braunschweig.

Inevitably the car was heavier than contemporary Formula 1 cars and some of its features were not compatible with F1 regulations. The Sigma Grand Prix never raced, but it was operative and was demonstrated on several occasions. It

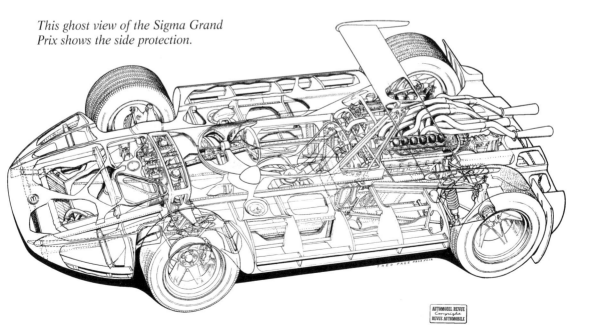

This ghost view of the Sigma Grand Prix shows the side protection.

created a lot of interest, showed the FIA that motor racing could be made distinctly safer than it was, and inspired many of the regulations that ultimately resulted in the very safe grand prix cars of today.

Thirty years on, the Sigma GP's riveted aluminium construction is completely obsolete. Because their monocoque construction in carbon fibre composites meets the very demanding resistance requirements of FIA, modern racing cars provide driver protection that could only have been dreamed of at the time that the Sigma GP was designed. But two of its features that have not been adopted, though they would certainly further improve driver safety, were its full-width body and the shields behind the rear wheels.

In 1973 I became a member (and for some time later, also Vice President) of the Technical Committee of FISA, the motor sport division of the FIA. I had been proposed by the Royal Automobile Club of Belgium thanks to the recommendation of Pierre Ugeux, at the time President of FISA and appointed, as the rules required, by FISA's General Assembly made up of motor sport personalities of the five Continents, each representing his country. The Technical Committee was, at the time, presided by Curt Schild, the President of the Sporting Committee of the Automobile Club of Switzerland. It had 10–12 members, all delegates from different nations, all appointed for one year, but indefinitely re-eligible. I remained a member for 12 years. The task of the Committee was to write or amend the 'on car' technical regulations, or make proposals according to a set order of the day prepared by the President of FISA, Pierre Ugeux in the early years of my mandate and later by the controversial Jean-Marie Balestre. The decisions of the meeting would then be submitted to the FISA General Assembly for approval. A small group of three or four members of the Technical Committee was also responsible for car homologations.

There were several other committees operating according to the same pattern, such as the Sporting Committee, responsible for sporting regulations (the starting procedure, the various flags etc), the Safety Committee, responsible for track safety (guardrail size and position, run off areas etc), a Rally Committee and so on. They each met four times in a year, usually in Paris.

While I was in the Technical Committee I defended two cases with considerable involvement. One was that the World Championship for Manufacturers should be based on races in which the competing cars are based on their manufacturer's actual production, ie GT cars for which at the time, a minimum production of 5,000 units in 12 successive months was required. The corresponding 'Group 5' regulations were actually implemented from 1976 on, but interest for the formula soon faded, mainly for two reasons. One was that the regulations suited the 911-based Porsche 935 so well that the other competitors, headed by BMW, finally gave up the challenge. The second reason is that, as a rule, regulations are carefully written by four or five persons, but as soon as they are published, they are read even more carefully by a hundred persons or more trying to find loopholes. As a hundred brains are obviously more sagacious than a mere four, loopholes were always found. The proof is the famous Porsche 935 'Moby Dick' of which the 911 origins would be hard to find. Eighteen years later, another attempt was made to give priority to GT cars by creating the GT1 Group, this time, requiring that at least one car certified for road use be built, but it went exactly the same way.

The other case for which I fought like a lion was a new formula for Endurance Races of the Manufacturers' World Championship series: the result was a formula based on a fuel consumption limit, which was implemented in 1982 for a duration of eight years. Up until then, when cars powered by a turbocharged engine raced against cars using an atmospheric engine, the capacity of the turbocharged engine was multiplied by the 'equivalence factor' of 1.4. This had come out of the blue because there is no technical, scientific or logical reason why a turbocharged engine should be equivalent to a naturally aspirated engine of 1.4 times the capacity. Later the factor was changed to 1.7, just because the 'Turbos' had been running away from the atmospheric opposition! And as a higher capacity involved a higher weight penalty, this led to some monstrously overweight small cars. Such so-called 'equivalence factors' which cannot be calculated on the base of technical facts are pure guesswork. Their real name is handicap and handicaps have no place in world championships.

Another such case was the Mazda Wankel-type rotary engine. By principle it fires three times for every two turns of its output shaft, as against one combustion for every second crankshaft revolution in a conventional four-stroke engine. In this case there is a purely mechanical equivalence between the two types of engine, the factor being 3. This is easily explained. In two revolutions of its crankshaft, a conventional piston engine aspirates a volume of air equal to its cubic capacity. In the Wankel, the rotor which turns at half speed of the output shaft contains three combustion chambers which in one rotation aspirate a volume of air corresponding to their total capacity. Consequently to aspirate the same volume of air or mixture as a four-stroke engine for the same number of output shaft revolutions, the combined capacity of the Wankel's three combustion chambers must be equal to the total capacity of the four-stroke engine. So the equivalence 3 x Wankel chambers volume = Total capacity of four-stroke engine is correct.

But it is also true that this equivalence gives the four-stroke a power advantage: the rotary engine has clear advantages of perfect balance, low weight and low bulk, but its efficiency suffers from the unfavourable shape of its combustion chambers. Mazda and several members of the Technical Committee requested a reduction of the equivalence factor to make the rotary engine more competitive and a lower factor was finally adopted thanks to a vote. At the time I had an excellent relationship with Mazda, specially with its President and later Senior Adviser, Kenichi Yamamoto, and 'Koby' Kobayakawa, but this did not deter me from my conviction that any equivalence formula must conform to the realities of physics and engineering and I always refused to compromise it.

With atmospheric, force-fed and rotary engines now competing in World Championship Endurance races, something better had to be found to give them a fair chance without having recourse for guesswork.

Look at this problem as you like, there is no other way of giving such a mixed bunch an equal chance than allocating them a given quantity of fuel, the same for all, for a given race distance. I was determined to get such a formula adopted and spent a lot of time explaining my point of view to the other committee members, writing to them and to the persons responsible for motor sport in companies interested or likely to be. I particularly stressed the fact that such a formula would be an incentive to develop more fuel-efficient engines, just what was required after the trauma of the fuel crisis, and as fuel prices were rising sharply. Keith Duckworth (co-founder of Cosworth Engineering and responsible for the hugely successful Ford DFV grand prix engine) who was consulted, suggested the cars should be equipped with a fuel-flow meter limiting the flow of fuel to the engine. But a device meeting all requirements did not exist and too much time would have passed before one could have been designed and tested. Many members of the Committee suggested that to give cars of different engine capacity equal chances, the fuel tank size should be small for large engined cars and large for small engined cars, giving these the advantage of fewer pit stops. Again, this would have been pure handicap guesswork and fortunately, basing my argumentation on the performance and fuel consumption of large and smaller cars at Le Mans, I could demonstrate that unless the big cars were allowed only a ridiculously small tank, or unless the fuel flow from the refuelling plant was absurdly slow, the system would always favour the larger engined cars, specially on fast circuits. Fortunately, Committee President Schild was convinced and from then on I got his full backing for a formula in which all cars would get the same fuel allowance for a given race distance.

But once the Committee had accepted the principle, the amount of the fuel allowance was still to be decided. My idea, based on the fact that, before the fuel consumption was limited, Ford-Cosworth DFGV engined cars had won Le Mans twice, using less than 30 litres for every 100km, was that the allowance should not exceed 350 litres for the usual 1,000km distance of the typical Endurance races of the time. But before a decision was taken, we had a special meeting with the motor sport chiefs of the constructors likely to be interested, and while some would have been quite happy with a consumption target of 35 litres/100km, others, who obviously wanted to continue to use existing thirsty engines, flatly refused to accept less than 60 litres/100km. This we were forced to accept for fear of getting only one or two-make fields when the formula was implemented in 1982, but the manufacturers were warned that, after the first two years, the allowance for 1,000km would be reduced by 10 per cent. For us, the worst vexation was that in the end, those who had been loudest in requiring 600 litres for the 1,000km race distance never came.

The fuel consumption formula also had the advantage that fuel efficiency rather than high specific power was the target. Very high revolution rates were not required any more and racing engines could be developed from standard production engines, and from 1982 to 1989, all eight Le Mans races were won by engines based on production engines, six times by Porsche and once each by Jaguar and Mercedes. A problem with the excessive fuel allowance was that it was difficult to persuade the public that races in which the cars were allowed to swallow first 60, later 54 litres per 100km, could be an incentive for manufacturers to develop techniques which would later be applied to make production cars use less fuel! And a bigger problem was that to use all the fuel available, engines developing at least 600PS were required, which prevented manufacturers who did not have sufficiently large engines in their programme from participating, unless a special engine was developed at great cost. The formula nevertheless attracted many manufacturers to Endurance sports car racing. Ford, Lancia, Jaguar, Sauber-Mercedes, Toyota, Nissan and Mazda, in addition to the faithful Porsche, all participated at one time or another.

Unfortunately, only the manufacturers were happy with the formula. Drivers do not like fuel restrictions because it can sometimes force them to slow down to save fuel; the public does not like to see their favourite stopping with an empty tank in view of the finish and organisers do not like it because fuel limitations require too much policing to prevent cheating. So now we have a formula based on air restrictions of which the diameter varies according to engine capacity, number of valves, car weight, the presence or not of forced feeding ... and why not the driver's age? This may be a more sophisticated system than a simple 'equivalence factor', but it nevertheless looks very much like a handicap system.

I much regret that nobody ever tried my own formula for fuel consumption-based racing, which would solve all the problems just mentioned. In a 1,000km race, for example, all cars would get the same fuel allowance for the first 500 kilometres. For the second part of the race, fuel consumption would be free but no modification of the engine tune would be allowed. In this way, you would never have cars stopping with an empty tank in view of the finishing line. Those who had to save fuel to reach half distance could slow down, knowing that in the second part of the race, they would hopefully be able to make up for the time lost, which could lead to exciting finishes. The drivers and public would be happy and the development target set by the fuel limitation would be reached. Only the organisers would still have reasons to complain. But must we make everything so easy for them?

Chapter 19

Influencing development

SOME TIME IN 1975 or early 1976 I had dinner with Sandro Fiorio, Lancia's Public Relations Manager, in Turin's famous restaurant Il Gatto Nero (The Black Cat). Sandro, father of Cesare Fiorio who for so long masterminded Lancia's rally successes, was a very refined and cultivated person and also a real enthusiast who, in the 1950s, had driven Lancias in rallies, taking, among other achievements, fourth place in the gruelling Liège-Rome-Liège marathon.

For some time I had felt that, interesting as my activity as a motoring journalist was, it was not creative. This left me slightly frustrated, and in the course of our conversation I told him that I thought I could put some of the experience I had gained in my profession as a journalist, car tester and in racing to good use when it came to developing new cars. This he quickly picked up, and a few days later I was asked to return to Turin, and our co-operation began with assessing current Lancia production models. At the time they were Betas and variations on the base model, such as the coupé and its stretched, four-passenger version, the HPE, all with the excellent Lampredi-designed twin-cam engine in sizes extending from 1,300 to 2,000cc. About once a week I drove from Vence, near Nice, where by then I lived, to Turin to pick up another model, put it through its paces and write reports that were discussed once or twice a month.

The biggest problem of the Beta, especially of the saloon, which had a softer suspension than the sportier models, was severe torque steer caused by unequal-length drive shafts. The shorter shaft was the left one, and when the car accelerated and the front rose it pulled severely to the right. It was so bad that, when accelerating out of a right-hand bend, the steering would not return to the straight-ahead position without help, while in a left-hand bend it would return so violently that, if it was not checked, it would overshoot and start to oscillate with ever-increasing amplitude, a very dangerous situation.

Right *Taking part in the development of the Lancia Thema from the early prototype stage was a very interesting task, and its project leader, Bruno Cena, was a fascinating person to work with.*

The build quality was disastrous, both in terms of the body and the mechanics; cars were leaving the factory with, for example, incorrectly set wheel geometries, causing them to oversteer in right-hand bends and understeer in left-hand bends and vice-versa.

When the Gamma went into production I was given one for a long-term assignment. Its 2.5-litre flat-four ohc engine was pleasantly torquey, it handled very well, had the best power steering I had experienced up to then, but again it was let down by poor quality – in this case a porous cylinder head and oil leaks. Quality, however, was not the only reason for its commercial failure; for the price asked, people expected more than four cylinders and the engine proved troublesome anyway.

It did not take long before Fiorio asked me if I would help develop prototypes of new models. This is what I was really interested in. The first car I was asked to drive was a Gamma-engined version of the mid-engined Lancia Monte Carlo with bigger brakes and fatter tyres than the standard 2-litre model. It was much quicker than the 2-litre, but oversteered quite badly in fast bends. I remember that I suggested one modification, which could be done in half a day, and when we took it out again it was an altogether different car. From that moment I gained the confidence of Ing Barp, at the time responsible for Lancia development, and we established an excellent working relationship. Unfortunately, due to the problems experienced with the Gamma flat-four, the Gamma Monte Carlo never reached the production stage. It could have been quite a nice sports car.

When I began the job the Delta was still at the development stage and I followed it until production began. I liked that little car, except for its too 'rubbery' gear shift mechanism and its steering; it was not power-assisted, but struck a nice balance between the effort required for parking and its feel and accuracy. However, like the Beta, if when accelerating out of a corner you left the wheel to return to the straight-ahead position unchecked, it would overshoot and begin to oscillate. It took me years to persuade the team to do something about it, for instance to add a steering damper, which they only did when the faster GT model was introduced.

Several years earlier Ferdinand Piëch had let me try an early Audi 50 (which soon became the VW Polo), the first car he developed for Audi. It had the same problem. When I told him he tried the car himself and said, 'You're right – we'll look at it and it will never happen again.' The problem was soon fixed and I never encountered it in any Audi I drove thereafter. The difference of attitude is significant – and look where Piëch is today! As Chairman of Volkswagen AG, he is not only a brilliant engineer but also a first-class driver, who personally tests all the VW Group's new models before they are marketed; he has been known to delay a launch because the model concerned is not up to his demanding requirements.

After the Delta came the Thema, for which the project leader was Bruna Cena, later responsible for the development of all cars of the Fiat Auto Group – Fiat, Lancia and Alfa Romeo. He is a brilliant engineer as well as a brilliant driver who, when he was a student, raced in Formula Abarth, an equivalent of today's Formula Ford or Lotus.

The Thema started as a common project with Saab, the idea being to use a common platform and as many common parts as possible, as for example for the suspension. Prototypes were built with Lancia's strut and three-link rear suspension and with Saab's rigid axle located by Watt's linkages, both laterally and longitudinally. Cena and I went out with both cars on demanding roads and we finally agreed that the strut suspension made the car more agile. So finally the Lancia Thema and the Saab 9000 were fitted with different rear suspensions.

My co-operation was soon extended to the Fiat brand, when I became involved in the development of a large number of models and reported to Ing Porro, who had been Cena's boss at Lancia, to Ing Canavese, now retired, and later to Cena again, whose responsibilities had been extended. Evaluation of handling, comfort, road noise absorption, steering, engine noise and gear ratios was what was mainly asked from me. When assessing handling, there were two points that I always considered essential: a car should understeer, but only as much as was required for its stability, its behaviour should be affected as little as possible when fully laden, and, when the accelerator is lifted, it must react by moderately tucking into a corner while the car is submitted to a fairly high side force.

Except for two sessions on Alfa Romeo's Balocco proving ground, when it came to evaluating various programmes of four-wheel steering and four-wheel drive systems under exactly similar conditions, all testing for Fiat and Lancia was done on public roads. Both development teams had their pet roads, but with traffic making things increasingly difficult, I set out to find a better route, which was soon adopted by both. It included stretches of autostrada and of badly surfaced road, some fast bends with good visibility and a winding mountain road. Secrecy does not seem to be as important to the Italians as it is in America or Japan, though in the early stages prototypes were usually quite heavily camouflaged. But after the press had published spy photos, less care was taken and a dull black paint was usually considered enough.

Prototype testing is not without its dangers. In 1984 I was asked to try a prototype that I had already driven before, and whose rear suspension design I did not like anyway. Some modifications had been made but not tested. From the outset I felt that the car understeered much too much, so I did not go very far. On the way back I came to a fairly fast bend that I had taken a thousand times before. Knowing that the car handled badly, I slowed a lot more than I would normally have done, but nevertheless there was a monumental understeer, the car hit the guardrail, bounced back across the road and landed in a field below, making a complete roll. The car had no safety belts and the mechanic who, as usual, had come with me, was thrown out and lay motionless on the grass. You can imagine how horrified I was. People stopped and called an ambulance, which took him to hospital where he was found to have a broken shoulder. I was taken to a nearby place where other mechanics were waiting for us in another car and was finally also taken to a hospital in Turin, where they diagnosed seven broken ribs. Ever since, all Fiat prototypes have been equipped with seat belts.

Though I think that road cars should be tested and developed on the road, some testing on a good racing circuit is nevertheless useful to finalise a car's behaviour at the limit of adhesion, the amount of tuck-in when lifting off in a bend, etc, but if too much emphasis is put on track behaviour, a car tends to become uncomfortable. What the priority should be – in terms of comfort or handling – of course depends on the sort of car being developed.

For many years I was a consultant for a reputable tyre manufacturer. Tyre testing is a real speciality, and not an easy one. Modern tyres must comply with an impressive number of requirements, which sometimes seem irreconcilable. Most of the tests in which I was involved took place on the famous northern loop of the Nürburgring, now reduced to 20.5km and the nice thing about it was that the cars on which the tyres were tested were invariably fast machines, such as the Porsche 911 and 911 Turbo or 944 Turbo (a much underrated car), BMW Alpina and M5, Honda NSX, etc. Such tests usually took place three times per year, each involving lapping the 'Ring anything between 12 and 20 times at a rate of two laps per set of tyres – a good way to keep in practice. Each two-lap test was followed by a short discussion, and sometimes a list of about 15 questions, prepared by Porsche, had to be answered in writing regarding only the handling on a dry road, which was quite difficult because several questions seemed to be the same, just using different words.

I made it a rule never to ask anything about the tyres fitted, to avoid being influenced in my judgement. There was one occasion when I was asked to go to the 'Ring to test tyres on a big, fast car whose manufacturer was not satisfied with the tyres that had been provided by my part-time employer. To have a basis for comparison, I first did three laps with the tyres judged unsatisfactory. They were, in fact, nothing exceptional. Then a new experimental set was fitted, which, I felt, were slightly better but not much. Another, different set came on and after two laps I came back saying, 'These have a marginally better response, but the difference is very slight.' A third comparative set was then fitted, and I reported that I could not notice any difference. 'Now try these,' they said. I went out again and after two laps came back with a big smile. 'Now, this is what we want!' I said. But there was no smile on the face of the development crew. 'These are not ours,' they said. 'They are from our biggest competitor ...'

For many years I acted as a consultant to Mazda. How it came about I cannot exactly remember, but what I do know is that I was very interested in the Wankel engine, and that when I first went to Hiroshima, in 1971, my primary aim was to meet the engineers who had put their faith in that type of engine, especially Kenichi Yamamoto. He was then Director of R&D, and had done a great deal to make the engine reliable and was also anxious to further improve it and make it comply with ever-stricter emission laws.

I was very impressed with the cleanliness of the offices and the factory, and was given a chance to drive various models on the short track along the seashore. After the drive a meeting with a number of engineers and marketing people had been arranged, during the course of which many opinions were exchanged. It appeared that, in common with other companies, the Mazda people were anxious to sell cars in Europe, but knew very little about European tastes and driving habits, and what was important and what was not.

I was happy to have learned more about the Wankel rotary engine and the Mazda people must have found the meeting useful, for in 1976 they invited me back to Japan, this time with my wife Suzanne, for further testing and discussions. It was also on that occasion that we met Takaharu Kobayakawa who was then in charge of Mazda's public relations. He spoke fluent English (which was then still an exception) and we soon became very friendly.

There were more such visits over the following years, full confidence was established between us, and we were shown mock-ups of future models for appreciation. At the time two alternative front grilles for the future 323 (the last rear-drive model of the series) were still under discussion. I remember that Suzanne was asked what her choice would be. She immediately opted for the one with horizontal bars, which was promptly adopted for the final export model, launched in 1977. We were also taken to the Miyoshi proving ground where I was invited to drive a prototype of the first-series RX-7, which I liked very much. It

My relationship with Mazda ended shortly after the launch of the third-generation RX-7, a real sports car that was much underrated in Europe.

gave me great pleasure to drive it on what was at the time Miyoshi's only handling course, so small that I soon came to call it the 'Mickey Mouse' course, to the great amusement of the Mazda crew. On the high-speed track, however, there was a slight tendency to oversteer when cornering very fast on the flat (non-banked) part of the curves. As I thought the car's agility on the slower-handling course should not be spoiled, I suggested the addition a small rear wing, which was eventually fitted, with good results for the up-market models.

It was quite obvious that both parties benefited from such meetings and testing sessions, and from the subsequent discussions, which mostly concerned development, engineering, handling, styling and marketing. They had started in 1971 as a journalistic operation, but as the inputs were mutual a logical conclusion was to make the working agreement official. This involved not only regular visits to Japan, but also testing Mazda prototypes in Europe, often in direct comparison with what I thought to be the best equivalent European car of the time.

Fearing leaks about new models, Mazda had hardly ever developed its prototypes outside Japan, but mostly on its own proving grounds, which, in those years, were completely inadequate. I am convinced that cars must ultimately be developed in the environment in which they will have to perform. Even if the roads, the climate and the driving habits are not the same in northern Germany and in southern Italy or Spain, the differences are much less than between Europe and Japan. A suspension tuning, a heating and air-conditioning system, a tyre type or a wind noise level perfectly suitable or acceptable for Japanese conditions are unlikely to be what is really required in Europe. I think that I had some influence in persuading Mazda to adapt the export models better to local conditions by taking prototypes abroad, at least in the final phases of the development of such items as suspensions, power steering, gear ratios, and interior and exterior body trim details.

The fact is that in the following years many Mazda models were taken to Europe at an advanced stage of their development before they were finalised. This included a visit to my home in the South of France and a drive with the test crew over my favourite test routes, including mountain roads, motorways and typical rough and fast French secondary roads. Back home we then had an extensive discussion and the day was usually rounded up with dinner in a nice restaurant.

On one occasion the test team brought over two cars, one prototype and one for further development. It was a beautiful December day and at around 10.00am we set off for a 125-mile drive, beginning with the Col de Vence, a pass leading to the southern Alps, at an altitude of over 3,000 feet. When we started the weather was so mild that I never expected that once we had reached the top some stretches of road not facing south would be icebound. I was driving quite fast and round a corner the road was just black ice. There was nothing I could do and we crashed the prototype heavily into the banking. Fortunately both my companion and myself wore seat belts and neither of us was hurt. But after the car was rescued, two members of the development team took a big hammer and completely destroyed what was left of it to avoid anybody taking photos of the new model. Needless to say, I was not happy!

What I prefer to remember is that, on the occasion of one of those visits, it was on my big dining-room table that the shape of Miyoshi's 'Global Course' was discussed, which led to an additional fairly fast bend being included in it.

I also have pleasant memories of the many meetings we had in Hiroshima, in which opinions were exchanged. Any suggestion I made was always duly considered, and I never felt that any of them were rejected as 'not invented here', as so often happens. I know that sometimes I did make errors of judgement. One instance was when I suggested that a small family car with rear-wheel drive would be quite acceptable. That was because, as a driver, I prefer rear-drive cars. But it was just like swimming against the tide. Another regret is that during its development stage I only drove the third generation RX-7 on closed tracks, at Miyoshi and Nürburgring. When I drove a production model on the road I found the suspension too hard for my liking. But there is one thing I am proud of: several times during our meetings I insisted that there was a niche to be filled, the niche vacated by the traditional, affordable British sports car with a front engine and rear-wheel drive, of which the elegant Triumph Spitfire was the last representative. No doubt I was not the only person to hint at that niche – but who knows what would be left of Mazda today without the MX-5!

Working relationships also extended to America, where I followed the development of the Chrysler Neon from its early stages and did my best to contribute to making the road behaviour of the Voyager acceptable for European customers, successfully persuading Chrysler to revise its front-end styling, which was more suggestive of a domestic appliance than of a car. But here again, all dynamic testing was done on proving grounds, without input from the real world.

Chapter 20

Exciting cars
for road and track

WHEN, IN THE early 1970s, emission laws were implemented almost worldwide, with disastrous results for performance and driveability, and for good measure most European countries imposed ridiculous overall speed limits, it seemed that the era of exciting cars and fun at the wheel was over for good. Fortunately, things are not quite as bad as expected. For one, the ever-increasing fuel prices and the corresponding efforts to improve fuel economy have resulted in much increased attention to the reduction of air drag, bringing about steep increases in maximum speed. This is hardly logical in view of the speed limits implemented, but is nevertheless a welcome trend. After all, police cannot be everywhere at the same time! I write this without shame because speed is not dangerous in itself, but only where it is excessive in any given context. It is also my experience that driving over long distances at speeds much below the safe speed for any given car in any given context is responsible for lack of concentration and for sleepiness. There are many cases when a higher speed requiring more attention and reducing the journey time would definitely benefit road safety.

That said, look at the cars we have today and compare them with those of 30 years ago, regardless of their class. A good example is the Porsche 911. Of course you can't buy today's 911 at the same price as an early one, but the prices of all cars have gone up in similar proportions. Even disregarding the Turbo, the performance of the 911 has increased regularly and steadily over the years, except for a short period in the late 1970s, despite the ever stricter emission and safety regulations. In the late 1960s a Jaguar Mk 2 3.8 was the quickest and most exciting saloon you could buy at an affordable price, but on any sort of road, including a German autobahn, a modern hot hatchback meeting all current regulations, such as a Peugeot 306 16V, would leave it standing, and is much more fun to drive. And even if, some day, fuel consumption will be severely limited, you will still be able to have fun; the Lotus Elise is the best proof of that, and costs little more than a hot hatchback. And where could you find, 25 years ago, anything as exciting as a McLaren F1 or a Ferrari F50?

This brings us to what this chapter is really all about: which were the most impressive cars I drove during, say, the last ten years or so?

Quite a few stand out, and for different reasons, including in some cases for being far from perfect. One of the latter is the Bugatti EB 110, a wonderful piece of engineering, which would have required much more development and was completely spoiled by abominable styling and even worse packaging. There were many reasons for this. The wonderful mechanical part, including the carbon monocoque carrying a 60-valve V12 engine fed by four turbochargers and driving the four wheels through a six-speed gearbox, was the work of former Lamborghini chief engineer Paolo Stanzani. Following a dispute with the company's President, Romano Artioli, he left Bugatti before the car had hardly ever run. In the two following years four development engineers followed him in quick succession, including Mauro Forghieri who, for 20 years, had run Ferrari's racing department. None of them stayed long enough to have any impact on the much-needed development of the engine, which had bags of power between 5,500 and 8,000rpm, but was as flat as a kipper below 5,000rpm.

Certainly the car handled as a sports car should, was not overly uncomfortable and had beautiful power steering. But the visibility was so bad that reversing and parking were a nightmare and luggage accommodation was just non-existent. On one occasion when I had an EB 110 S for two days, a photographer who came

The Bugatti EB110S was a mechanical masterpiece but under-developed and very impractical.

to spend half a day to get good photos of the car could not even find space to put her little bag containing cameras, lenses and films, and had to follow me with her own car! At the time when Artioli was still optimistic about the future of his company, he organised a big rally to Venice for Bugatti cars of all ages and kindly invited me to participate with Suzanne in a car that he would put at my disposal, adding that another car would carry our luggage! But there is no question that the car was fast; I drove one through the timing strip of Volkswagen's fabulous high-speed track at a two-way average of 341.5kmh (212mph).

On the same day I did 339.5kmh (211mph) with a Jaguar XJ220, though I would call this a draw with the Bugatti as the Italian car cheated by not having external mirrors, which, at that sort of speed, would surely account for at least 2kmh. The Jaguar also accelerates at least as fast as the Bugatti, but its V6 engine is much less involving and, at that sort of speed, did not feel quite as stable as the Bugatti. While the Italian car is commendably compact, reminding you what lies under its skin, the Jaguar is almost 5 metres long and it is therefore even less excusable for having virtually no luggage accommodation …

The Ferrari F40 and F50 are no better in this respect and when, together with my friend and colleague John Lamm, I spent two days with an F40, we had to decide to leave the emergency-size spare wheel in the garage to be able to carry his cameras and our overnight necessities. I have driven several F40s, including one on a very wet day on the excellent Mugello circuit, and I disagree that it is hell to drive on wet roads. As with any very powerful car, some feel when operating the throttle is required, but I had a lot of fun trying to accelerate as fast as possible out of bends with the tail well under control. However, the F50 is a

At Fiorano, Ferrari's test track, with an F355 and a line-up of eight Formula 1 cars. (Road & Track)

more serious attempt to put pure racing car technology on the road, with a real carbon monocoque and suspension pivoted on spherical Unibal joints. It is not any more practical than the others, but it is a magnificent car to drive, as far as I could judge by taking it for several laps around the Fiorano circuit.

In the face of all this, far and away the best and most genial of the real exotics is the McLaren F1. It is the most compact of all of them – at 4.29m (14 feet) long and 1.83m (6 feet) wide, it is little larger than a Porsche 911 – takes three people, has useful luggage room and is the fastest of them all. It may be a little heavier than claimed, but it is very reasonably comfortable … and in 1995 it won Le Mans in almost standard form! On the road it is perfectly tractable; its BMW V12 engine so flexible that it could manage with two rather than six speeds, and it offers everything you can reasonably wish from a road car. But yes, I know – for the purchase price of one of these cars you could buy 12 Porsche 911s or 35 Lotus Elises …

One million dollars is also the price of a Porsche 911 GT1 in its road version. Road version it may be, but it felt much more at ease on a racing circuit than on the road! As a road car the Porsche cannot hold a candle to the McLaren. If you have never driven a proper racing car and desperately want to get the feel of one on the road, the 911 GT1 'Road Version' is for you (if you can afford it). You get the performance, though with a turbo engine little more than half the size of the V12 BMW, it does not provide the immediate push-in-the-back of the McLaren; you get the handling, but you also get the noise, the lack of comfort, the bad three-quarter-rear and zero rear visibility and the difficult access to the seats of a racing car. To be quite frank, having driven almost all versions of the 911 ever

The McLaren F1 is the fastest and most sophisticated road car ever made. Spending 36 hours with one was a memorable experience. (Philippe de Barsy)

made, I found the much more compact, real-911-sized-and-shaped 911 GT2 'Road Version' much nicer than the GT1 and, on the road, the difference in performance is hardly noticeable. Opting for a GT2 rather than a GT1, I could make myself very popular by buying one for myself and presenting my wife and each of my three daughters with a standard Porsche Turbo, still with some money to spare! Homologation Specials have seldom been nice cars to drive.

The main reason why, as a road car, the 911 GT2 is a much nicer and more practical 'pleasure tool' than the GT1 is that it was developed from a genuine road car – the 911 – whereas the GT1 was designed as a pure racing car from which a road version was derived for homologation purposes. Though racing definitely improves the breed, it does not mean that racing technology should be transferred straight to the road without further development and adaptation.

A perfect illustration of this was the fabulous Porsche 959, of which some 250 units were built from 1986 to 1988. It incorporated all the developments and experience gained in racing and rallying the 956/962 and modified versions of the 911. At the time a comparison was organised on Ferrari's Fiorano track between an F40 and a 959, the first two production cars capable of exceeding 300kmh (186mph). As expected, the F40 was the faster of the two around the track, but as practical road cars there was just no comparison. With the Porsche you could not only have immense fun, but also take a companion in full comfort for a week's touring holiday.

Large saloons can also be fast and impressive. Today we have become accustomed to cars like the BMW M5 and the AMG-Mercedes performing at Porsche and Honda NSX levels, but in 1991 the tremendous but increasingly

Even though this is the 'road' version of the Porsche GT1, it is much more at ease on a racing circuit than on the road.

smooth and effortless performance of the 5 Series-based BMW-Alpina B10 biturbo, which I drove over long distances, came as a real shock. In acceleration it was a match for a contemporary Porsche Turbo and achieved a two-way maximum speed of 288.5kmh (179mph) at 5.00am on a German autobahn on a Sunday morning. It was just incredible. It had only one serious competitor and, believe it or not, that was an Opel! The very standard General Motors Opel Omega model had its twin-cam straight-six engine and all its running gear attended to by Lotus Engineering, owned at the time by GM, and was called the Lotus-Omega. I drove one on the road, though over shorter distances than the Alpina, which it could very marginally outdrag (0–160kmh in 10.9 seconds against the Alpina's 11.5 seconds, a standing-start kilometre in 23.8 seconds against 24.0 seconds), though its maximum speed, at 279.5km/h (173.7mph) was slightly lower. It was a very exciting car, but it lacked the Alpina's smoothness and feel of quality. Neither the contemporary BMW M5 nor the Mercedes-Benz 500 E were a match for those two exceptional four-doors.

Today, the German 'Big Three', Audi, BMW and Mercedes-Benz, have agreed to limit the maximum speed of their fastest models to 250kmh (155mph), but none of their current four-doors accelerates faster then the B10 Alpina and Lotus-Omega because of the increased weight resulting from improved crash resistance and added comfort and safety equipment. Only the 290kmh (180mph) V12-engined BMW Alpina B12 can break the 24-second barrier over the standing-start kilometre, complete with automatic transmission and lavish luxury equipment.

Only when Audi produced its first direct injection turbocharged 'TDI' diesel engine in 1989 did I begin to look at diesel engines with some interest. Until then I always found them too rough and noisy for the benefit they provided in fuel consumption. The Audi-VW TDI engines were a huge improvement over any diesel seen before. But the progress made in the last ten years of the 20th century was no less spectacular thanks to common rail systems ensuring high pressures from low engine revolutions, injector pump systems ensuring injector pressures up to 2,000 bar, sophisticated electronic managements allowing the accurate split of the injection between pre- and main injection, and electronically controlled variable geometry turbochargers. The best of the latest turbo-diesels are as silent as spark-ignition engines, have a much better fuel efficiency and a much higher specific torque, but have a smaller useful revolution band, a lower specific power and are heavier. But future developments will bring further progress.

The best of the current common rail turbo-diesel engines develop 60–65bhp/litre, but the 2.95-litre BMW Alpina, which operates with the next-generation 1,600-bar common rail system and twin turbochargers with electric motors operating the variable-pitch vanes, develops 245bhp and 500Nm of torque, equivalent to 80bhp/litre and 170Nm/litre. And even more sophisticated electronics and piezo-electric injectors will bring further progress in efficiency, refinement and environmental friendliness. Diesel-engined cars have been raced successfully by BMW and VW, and racing developments will accelerate the diesel's rate of progress. Today I am fascinated by the progress made by this type of engine.

Performance is, however, only one aspect of efficiency. For many people it is important to regard it in terms of fuel economy. Here the diesel is unbeatable among internal combustion engines, if only because the power output is regulated by the quantity of fuel injected into the cylinders, while the air intake system always remains wide open, reducing the pumping losses to a minimum. Even in lean-burn petrol engines, this is the case only at low loads.

What can be achieved by a modern diesel-engined car is demonstrated by the VW Lupo 3L, which, in the European cycle, has an overall fuel consumption of less than 3l/100km (better than 94.7mpg). I recently drove such a car from Oslo via Copenhagen to Brussels, a journey of just under 1,000 miles, during which the fuel consumption was measured with the utmost accuracy. There were two of us in the car with luggage for two nights (in Oslo and Copenhagen). The drive was mostly over motorways, speed-limited in Scandinavia to 100kmh (62mph), in Benelux to 120kmh (75mph), and unrestricted in Germany. These speed

On five occasions the American magazine Road & Track *has organised maximum speed tests on Volkswagen's fabulous high-speed track, with Phil Hill and myself driving. In 1987 200mph was exceeded for the first time by a Ruf-Porsche CTR (centre) with a two-way speed of 211mph. The standard Porsche 959 (right) achieved 197mph. Fastest speed to date by a production car was 211.5mph by a Jaguar XJ220 in 1994.* (Road & Track)

limits were loosely observed, and in Germany we drove at speeds varying from 75 to 90mph. The resulting overall fuel consumption was 3.46l/100km (82.02mpg). Nine other similar cars participated in the event, and the average consumption of the entire group was 3.34l/100km (85.2mpg). Two crews tried really hard and got down to 2.634 and 2.677l/100km (108.01 and 106.27mpg)!

The cars were strictly standard and were some 150kg (330lb) lighter and aerodynamically optimised compared with ordinary Lupo TDIs. They were powered by a 1.2-litre three-cylinder injector pump direct injection all-aluminium turbo-diesel and weighed around 850kg (16.7cwt) without crew and baggage.

Whether efficiency is exploited to improve performance or economy, it reflects only a small part of car development over the years. The preceding pages say little about the progress made in the fields of braking, road-holding, tyres, ease of driving – think of the relief brought by power steering – and active and passive safety generally. In the last 25 years the development of electronics has made by far the largest contribution to the progress made in all aspects of automobile technology, from the design stage through to production and on board the vehicle itself. Electronics have been essential in developing crash-resistance, and they have cut the design and development time of cars from five to three years. The are essential to such safety systems as anti-lock brakes, traction control, dynamic stability programmes, differential control and every sort of airbag, and have largely contributed to the progress of automatic transmissions of all kinds. Meeting current and future emission regulations would be simply unthinkable without their contribution; they protect engines against abuse and, in the very near future, will help drivers maintain a safe distance from other vehicles, automatically applying the brakes and working the steering if the driver fails to do so.

The measure of the progress achieved in the field of safety in the last 25–30 years is given by quite simple figures: traffic in Western Europe has multiplied by about 2.5 since the early 1970s, but the number of fatal road casualties has not only steadily decreased ever since, but is also now less than half the initial number. It is, incidentally, also completely unrelated to the enforcement of speed limits.

Moving on to track testing, the end of my racing career did not stop me from driving racing cars on several occasions. But even before that, during the practice sessions for the Belgian Grand Prix of 1960, Lance Reventlow offered me the chance to have a spin at the wheel of one of the two Scarabs he had entered for Chuck Daigh and himself. The Leo Goossens-designed car was beautifully built, fast and handled well, but unfortunately it had come too late – in 1970 front-engined cars were already obsolete. But I am glad to have taken it around Spa-Francorchamps for a lap or two; I don't think many Europeans had a chance to drive one of these cars, powered by a 2.5-litre four-cylinder engine, tilted almost flat to reduce the frontal area.

In all those years I had several opportunities to drive historic racing cars, among them some models I had never driven before, such as a 1955 Type W195 Mercedes-Benz grand prix car, a Type 35 Bugatti, a Maserati 250F and a 1955 Lancia D50, which reminded me of the Ferrari-badged version I drove in the 1956 Belgian Grand Prix. But my main interest was always in contemporary models.

Formula 3 and the almost equivalent Formula Renault and Formula Lotus cars have always been fun because, weighing about 450kg (8.8cwt) with 150 to 175bhp, according to type and vintage, they are quick without being awe-inspiring, they don't generate too high a downforce and are beautifully agile. I remember that on the occasion of the launch of Formula Lotus in 1988 on the new Pau-Arnos Circuit, I managed, in spite of the handicaps of age and lack of practice, to lap only 1 second slower than Derek Bell, who was also there.

In cars generating a lot of downforce, it takes a good deal of practice to brake and corner anywhere near the car's limits, which are so much higher than even the best road car or the cars I drove in my racing days, and which also vary with speed. The only really powerful modern downforce racing car in which I approached anywhere near the limits was the rotary-engined Mazda 757 sister car of the 1991 Le Mans winner in which I did 69 laps of the Paul Ricard circuit on the occasion of my 75th birthday, as related later in this chapter. But even that car did not generate as much downforce as most current racers because at Le Mans low drag is more important than extreme downforce.

Downforce has solved one big problem faced by most of the competition cars of my racing years, which became particularly acute when the engine moved from the front to the back. If a car is set up to be good in comparatively tight bends, it will become difficult to handle in fast bends due to the oversteer induced by the strong rear-weight bias. As more time can be saved in fast bends than in slow ones, cars were usually set up for high-speed stability and would consequently understeer excessively in tighter corners. Adding front and rear wings solved the problem. The wings are set in such a way that the ratio of downforce to mass on the rear axle increases faster than the ratio of downforce to mass on the front axle. This makes it possible to set up the car not to understeer excessively in slow corners but still be stable in fast bends because the rear-wheel grip increases more than the front-wheel grip as the speed rises.

In the 1970s François Guiter, who was responsible for the involvement of the Elf fuel company in motorsport and also largely responsible for Renault's involvement in Formula 1, invited some journalists several times to the Paul Ricard circuit to drive interesting cars using Elf products. In 1974 this provided me with an opportunity to drive a Formula 1 Tyrrell-Ford, when Tyrrell was still one of the leading teams. It was certainly quick, with 460bhp from the Ford-Cosworth engine in a 600kg (11.8cwt) car, but the greatest difference compared with Formula 1 cars I had raced was the incredible road-holding provided by the huge tyres and the downforce produced by the large aerofoils. After a few laps

In 1976 Elf Competitions Manager François Guiter invited a few journalists to drive some Elf-sponsored racing cars at Paul Ricard. Here I am being fitted into a Formula 1 Tyrrell-Ford. Four years later I was given a similar chance in a Formula 1 Renault turbo.

Ken Tyrrell called me in because he thought I was going too fast; he let me out again, but I was quite sure that I remained far off the car's cornering and braking limits. One thing I remember vividly is that if the revs dropped below around 4,000rpm, the engine would die instantly, which made starting rather difficult. This also happened when I was clumsy enough to miss a gear and found myself in neutral. Fortunately the car was still rolling quite fast and I restarted it easily.

Turbocharged engines are more easily managed at low speeds, and in 1976 I was invited to drive one of the new Renault-Alpine sports prototypes, powered by a 2-litre turbocharged Renault V6 engine, of the type that went on to win Le Mans in 1978. Only a few weeks earlier I had driven the Porsche 936 that had won the 1976 Le Mans, and it was interesting to compare the two cars; the Renault seemed to have a better turbo response than the Porsche's 2.14-litre flat-six. At the time both used a single turbocharger.

The single-turbo engine of Renault's 1980 RE20 F1 also suffered from a rather

Didier Pironi explains the controls of his Formula 3 Martini-Renault before a test drive at Paul Ricard in 1976.

disconcerting turbo lag but, when the boost came in, it was quite an experience! All these cars, especially the single-seaters, generated considerable downforces and it was on such occasions that I realised how much practice it would take to find their braking and cornering limits, a lot more than was possible within the relatively short time available.

Those testing sessions were always interesting and in one of them I learned to be wary of the modern wedge-shaped kerbs. I was driving a Formula 2 Renault V6-engined Alpine, normally driven by Jean-Pierre Jabouille, who had been very successful with it. Exiting a slow right-hand corner I ran slightly wide and the car's left-hand front wheel touched the wedge-shaped kerb. I did not expect anything to happen, but as the tyre ran on the kerb its outside rolling radius became smaller than the inside radius, which pulled the steering vigorously to the left and took me by surprise. I spun and slightly damaged the rear wing support. Fortunately, this was the only mishap I experienced when driving racing cars after my racing days.

Thanks to my good relationship with Porsche and in connection with my books on the company's racing models, I have driven almost every important type of racing Porsche, starting in 1970 with a session on the now-defunct Southern Loop of the Nürburgring on which Porsche did a lot of its development testing. On that occasion the fabulous 908/03 and 917 were being tested by Hans

Herrmann, with engineers Manfred Bantle and Helmut Flegl, the project leaders of the 908/03 and 917 respectively, in attendance. The lightweight 908/03 (540kg/10.6cwt) was incredibly agile, a wonderful car to drive on a difficult circuit, while the flat-12-engined 917 was more awe-inspiring and required good arm muscles!

That was certainly also the case with the 917 CanAm, which put an end to McLaren domination in the CanAm championship. The one I drove was the development car for the 917/30, and its 5-litre turbo engine developed over 1,000bhp, the most powerful car I have ever driven. To get better traction, the car had no differential and understeered heavily if you did not drive fast enough. But if you really got going the wheel on the inside of the bend became sufficiently unloaded to allow the car to corner in a fairly neutral attitude. On less than perfect track surfaces, the solid drive resulted in poor straight-line stability, as one wheel or the other lost grip and the opposite wheel took over the drive. But the improved traction was more important and for the following 15 years all Porsche racing cars had a solid driving axle.

The so-called Turbo Carrera, a much-modified 911 developed to acquire experience in view of the new formula for the Manufacturers World Championship, was an ultra-lightweight 450bhp freak with probably more than 70 per cent of its weight on the rear wheels; it was based on the modified production GT car regulations, scheduled for 1975 but postponed to 1976. Thanks to its hugely wide rear tyres, it was less difficult to drive than expected. Performance was astounding and it finished second in the Watkins Glen 1,000km and at Le Mans, competing against such full-blooded machinery as

My long and happy association with Porsche has led to the opportunity to drive many of the company's racing models. Here I am in the 911 LM Turbo that crashed at Le Mans but dominated the GT class throughout 1993 and '94.

In the late 1980s, Porsche raced the 962 with the semi-automatic PDK gearbox. I drove one at the Nürburgring and found it very worthwhile.

V12 Matras and 312P Ferraris. A much nicer car to drive was the mid-engined open 936, using the same 2.14-litre turbo engine, which Porsche had built in great haste along with the 911-based 2.85-litre turbo-engined 935, fearing that the production car-based formula might not get off the ground. It did, but was not a lasting success, due to excessively loose regulations, exactly as happened

In 1987 and '88 Porsche participated in the American CART series, winning one race with the 2.65-litre turbocharged V8. I was among those invited to try one of the cars at the Nürburgring.

On the occasion of my 75th birthday, in February 1992, Mazda prepared one of its Le Mans cars for me to drive at Paul Ricard. It was a wonderful day on which I took most members of my family for a two-lap ride of the circuit.

later with the GT1 cars. Both the 935 and 936 were very successful, the 935 winning Le Mans in 1978 and the 936 in 1976, 1977 and 1981.

From 1982 the formula limiting fuel consumption was implemented, and the turbo-engined Porsche 956 and the almost identical 962 were unbeaten at Le Mans from 1982 to 1987. Early cars had a 2.65-litre turbo engine, later increased to 3 litres. I was invited to drive a 1982 model at Hockenheim at the end of the season. It was a great car with a remarkably flexible engine, but very heavy steering. The geometry was later modified and the 962C I drove in 1989 required less muscular force. That car was fitted with Porsche's PDK twin-clutch semi-automatic gearbox with a choice of control, either by a stalk or two buttons on the steering wheel. It shifted up and down without interrupting the drive and without the use of the clutch pedal, which was used only for starting, thus saving a lot of time compared with the conventional Porsche synchromesh box.

Another interesting Porsche was the turbocharged V8 single-seater, based on a March chassis, which was entered for the Indycar races of 1988 and 1989. It scored one victory and took one pole position with Teo Fabi at the wheel. In later years I was invited to the Paul Ricard circuit to drive the cars Porsche was developing for the 1994 Le Mans, and in 1996 I had a chance to try the 911 GT1 at Hockenheim – a great experience in the first Porsche endurance racer with a dog clutch gearbox.

But probably the most exciting drive I had in a powerful racing car more

After my 75th anniversary drive, with Hugues de Chaunac (on my right), owner of the ORECA racing team which prepared the car, and Pierre Dieudonné (on my left), together with the ORECA crew.

recently was when Mazda, who had won Le Mans in 1991, prepared one of the team cars for me to drive on the Paul Ricard circuit early in 1992, for my 75th birthday. On that occasion I invited my daughters and nieces with their husbands and my then teenaged grandchildren to show them that 'Grandpa was not really 75'. It was a wonderful day and, after seven or eight practice laps, I taxied each of them and several friends for two fast laps of the circuit. After that, the tyres were changed and I had ten wonderful laps on my own. In all I did 69 laps, which allowed me to get much nearer to the braking and cornering limits of a downforce car than I had done before. Everyone had a great time and I hope I convinced them all that there had really been a mistake with my date of birth!

My warmest thanks to 'Koby' and to team manager Hugues de Chaunac for making it possible!

Chapter 21

Japan

SOME TIME IN 1967 or early 1968, when I still lived in Brussels, a letter arrived from a Japanese car magazine called *Car Graphic*, of which I had never heard. It was signed by Jack Yamaguchi who, at the time, was a member of its editorial staff. They had read a road test report of a Ferrari 330 GTC that I had written for the British magazine *Motor*, and suggested that I should send them articles in the same vein as those I regularly wrote for the UK. Thus a contact was established that has now lasted for more than 30 years and will hopefully continue for many years to come. This Japanese connection was to have a considerable influence on my professional life.

My racing career had ended only seven or eight years earlier and someone at *Car Graphic* must have heard that I had been an instructor in sports and race driving courses, for during the winter of 1968–69 I was contacted by a young Japanese called Isao Watanabe, who was a student in Brussels and the younger brother of Takao Watanabe, owner of the Nigensha Publishing Company that published *Car Graphic*. On behalf of his brother he asked me if I would be interested in being the instructor in advanced driving courses being organised by *Car Graphic* on the Suzuka Circuit. The courses would last two weeks and the invitation would be extended for a further week to enable me to see more of Japan and visit several Japanese car factories, so that I would gather a lot of interesting material for my journalistic activities. Remember that at that time very little was known in Europe about the Japanese motor industry and Japanese cars. All this was very tempting and Suzanne would also be invited. I enthusiastically accepted.

In the second half of April 1969, after an 18-hour flight that included a stop in Anchorage, we were met at Haneda Airport (Narita did not then exist) by *Car Graphic* editor Shotaro Kobayashi and Jack Yamaguchi, and after staying one or two days in Tokyo and taking the opportunity to admire the giant Buddah at Kumakura in a snow storm, we moved to Suzuka to stay for 18 days instead of the originally planned two weeks because the courses had to be interrupted for a national sports car race to be held at the circuit. (The race was won by a quite impressive V-8 engined Toyota 7, driven by a certain Kawai who, I understand, unfortunately had a fatal race accident some time later.)

The participants in the courses drove their own road cars and there were one, two- and three-day courses for groups of about 20 cars. The morning was dedicated to theory, the afternoon to driving exercises. As I did not speak a word of Japanese, I lectured in English and was given an interpreter called Shigeaki Asaoka (now an esteemed motoring journalist and a good friend), who at the time was employed by the Isuzu car company as a racing driver. At the time his English was little better than my zero Japanese, but as he knew what I was talking about, we managed. For my driving demonstrations I was lent a brand-new little Honda S800 roadster with a hard top, which I just loved, and a Honda N360 for commuting to and from the circuit.

In 18 days at the circuit Suzanne and I never had a dull moment. Everything was new to us, the people, the food – which we both loved – and the cars. Those were the days of the Isuzu Bellet and its stablemate, the beautiful 117, the Datsun Fairlady roadster and Goertz-styled Sylvia, the Prince Laurel, the rotary-engined Mazda R100, the nice little first-series Corolla and the famous Nissan Skyline GTR. Thanks to the efforts of the Honda and *Car Graphic* staffs, Suzanne also had a chance to visit several places of interest in the Suzuka region, while I was able to do some laps of the circuit with Asaoka's racing Bellet and a Japanese F3 Brabham powered by a Honda S800 engine and rolling on Bridgestone racing tyres. Shotaro and Jack occasionally visited us, and even took part in one of the courses. In all, seven *Car Graphic* staff members took the course, including

publisher Takao Watanabe, and enjoyed it! We were also honoured by being invited for lunch by Mr Soichiro Honda, who spoke through an interpreter. It was a great occasion to spend some time with this highly enthusiastic and interesting great man.

While at Suzuka we visited the local Honda factory where the N360 and small commercial vehicles were made, and were amazed by the speed at which the work was done. Some workers actually ran from one point to another to pick up parts and fit them. Isao Watanabe, who had established the contact between Nigensha and myself and had now returned from Brussels, was (and still is) a great lover of Japanese art, and at the weekends he became our very competent guide in Kyoto and other interesting places.

As promised, Shotaro and Jack introduced us to various Japanese manufacturers. These were occasions for interesting meetings and for driving many different cars. Soichiro Honda himself came to watch me drive his very latest model at the time, the infamous transverse-engined, air-cooled and front-driven Honda 1300 saloon, which was very noisy and understeered wildly. But this I only found out later, the venue being just a straight strip of asphalt with a few cones on which it was impossible to form a judgement. On that occasion I must have been the first European ever to ride the brand-new four-cylinder CB 750 bike, which at the time was very impressive. On that occasion we also met the late Yoshio Nakamura, who had masterminded Honda's entry into Formula 1 and who became a cherished and respected friend. With Jack I went to drive some Nissan cars on a factory test track and remember the 2-litre four-cylinder

Left *My first visit to Japan, in 1969, arose from an invitation by* Car Graphic *magazine to be an instructor in advanced driving courses on the Suzuka circuit. A new Honda S800 was at my disposal for demonstrations. I loved it.* (Car Graphic)

Right *During that first visit to Japan I tried the air-cooled, front-drive Honda 1300 – a noisy car. Here I discuss it with Honda R&D boss Yoshio Nakamura, behind whom is Soichiro Honda.* (Car Graphic)

Fairlady. Everything was rough in that car: the suspension, the handling, and above all the engine, but performance was quite good. The 'cooking' Skyline with the single-cam engine handled reasonably well, but its engine was pretty rough too, which is inexcusable for a straight-six.

Shotaro and Jack also provided cars for me to drive on the road. I remember driving a Subaru 1100, the only front-drive car in Japan at the time (and whose flat-four engine was a successful copy of the German Lloyd Arabella), a Toyota Corolla and a Mitsubishi, which was not particularly exciting. To be honest, except for their excellent gearboxes, Japanese cars of the late 1960s were still well below international standards. Not only were most of them too small and cramped for us Europeans, their suspension was in most cases horrible and the engines were just too rough. Was it to show off that, in so many cases, the red zone of the tachometer started at 7,000rpm? The fact is that at 5,000rpm things became so loud and so rough that nobody in his right mind would have dared go further before shifting up. In those days the only really smooth engines were Honda's S800 and Mazda's Wankel-type rotary, which provided the R100 with more power than its chassis could safely use. Its performance was nevertheless

Left *I was probably the first European to ride the then brand new Honda CB750. With me is famed journalist Jack Yamaguchi.* (Car Graphic)

Right *A visit to Fuji Speedway in 1969 provided an opportunity to drive a 2-litre straight-six Nissan R380 racing car. It felt quite competitive with European equivalents but never raced against them. The gentleman with stopwatch and camera is* Car Graphic *Chief Editor Shotaro Kobayashi and the lady in the pit is my wife Suzanne.* (Car Graphic)

excellent publicity for the unconventional engine, which, thanks to the enthusiasm and determination of Mr Kenichi Yamamoto, was finally developed to achieve great reliability. A rotary engine is so logical, and every time I drive a modern RX-7 I deplore the fact that its chances of survival are virtually nil because the shape of its combustion chambers is such that its fuel efficiency is unlikely ever to match that of a conventional piston engine.

Mazda was the last car company we visited, having flown to Hiroshima in a Japanese-designed and built YX 11, enjoying a splendid view of Mount Fuji on the way. We were very kindly received by Mr Yamamoto, who had very interesting things to say about the development of the rotary engine. We drove several cars on Mazda's little sea-front test track and were hugely impressed by the cleanliness not only of the beautiful administration buildings, but also of the factory halls.

One day Shotaro picked us up with a 'cooking' Nissan Skyline. He had arranged for me to drive a racing Skyline on Fuji Speedway where they had a 'free for all' testing day. Rain had been pouring down for a long time and as I carefully learned the circuit, which still included a banking at one end, cars were passing me and immediately aquaplaning off the road or just spinning for no reason on the main straight. Then I stepped into the racing version and also quickly spun it on the straight! The layer of water on the track was so deep and the tyres so inadequate for the conditions that any serious driving was just impossible.

Fortunately the following day was fine, the track had dried and I was offered

the wheel of a Nissan R380 racing coupé, a Porsche 906 lookalike powered by a 2-litre straight-six engine and based on a Brabham chassis. It was an interesting car with good handling and I think it would not have been out of place in European races. But we will never know. Another interesting car in the pit lane was a mid-engined 16-cylinder Nissan racer, built to the Japanese Group 7 regulations. It was very impressive, but I don't know whether this intended Toyota 7-killer was ever successful.

By the time we flew back to Europe I had gathered a lot of 'food' for articles, which kept me busy for several weeks and were well received, as people began to realise that sooner or later Japanese cars would become part of the European scene. At that time, however, the Japanese economy was flourishing, the local demand for cars was considerable and less than 10 per cent of the passenger car production was exported, mainly to South East Asian countries. I had been very impressed by the productivity of Japanese factories, by the loyalty of the Japanese workers to their employers and vice versa, and by the co-operation of the workers in improving quality and productivity, even going as far as the formation of 'quality groups' that met regularly outside working hours. I had been less impressed by the cars themselves, which were full of interesting details but were basically rather crude with rough and noisy engines, mediocre handling and poor, uncomfortable suspensions. Export appeal was also compromised by regulations such as the limitation of the width of passenger cars to 1.70m (about 5ft 6in), above which taxes increased enormously. At the time – remember we are in 1969 – Japanese cars were bought in Europe only because they were cheap and reliable, and only by people for whom a car was nothing but a necessary means of transport.

European interest in Japanese cars, both for the industry and its production methods, was, however, growing quickly. My articles had stirred a lot of interest and I was asked to go back to Japan to gather more information. This time I was alone, but Jack Yamaguchi was a great help in introducing me to interesting people and in acting as an interpreter, for even then, at a time when very few Japanese, even top executives, spoke any foreign language, he spoke excellent English.

By the time of my second visit to Japan excellent relationships had been established, particularly with *Car Graphic*, Honda and Mazda, and from 1976 onwards my visits became more frequent – more or less yearly – first with Suzanne, later on my own when Suzanne's health began to deteriorate. That was the year when we first met 'Koby' Kabayakawa, then responsible for Mazda's PR department, who has since become a dear friend. Many years later 'Koby' became the project leader for the third-generation RX-7, and today he is responsible for Mazda's Design Studio in California. Thanks to him, to his charming colleague Fumiko Araki and to our friends at *Car Graphic*, we had many opportunities for sightseeing and learning more about Japan and its culture.

The first time I was invited to Mazda's Miyoshi proving ground was to take the wheel of the first-generation Mazda RX-7. I was fascinated by the smoothness of its Wankel-type rotary engine, which had then become a reliable proposition thanks to the enthusiasm of Mazda's Technical Director Kenichi Yamamoto.

Our relationship with Mazda became so friendly that on one occasion – I believe it was the last time Suzanne accompanied me to Japan – on a nice, mild autumn evening 'Koby' and Fumiko Araki organised a barbecue party on the Miyoshi premises to which all the engineers and test drivers who had taken part in the test drives and discussions were invited. There was such a wonderful and friendly atmosphere about it!

Inevitably there were some episodes that in retrospect may sound quite funny, but were rather stressful at the time. One evening in 1976 or 1977 we were driving back to Tokyo on the Tomei Expressway with two cars. I was with Suzanne driving a Datsun coupé, while Shotaro and 'Koby' were, I believe, in a Mazda. As I am seldom in a mood to stick to overall speed limits and certainly not to 100kmh (62mph), they suggested that we should go ahead, leave the expressway at Gotemba and wait for them, to have dinner together. But just before the Gotemba exit a sign indicated an expressway restaurant 1km ahead, just after the exit, and I felt sure that this was where we were supposed to meet. So we drove on to the expressway restaurant area and waited for the other car to arrive. After waiting for 15 minutes we began to get a little nervous. After one

In 1989 Mazda produced a film featuring the second-generation RX-7 on the 72km Targa Florio course in Sicily. Targa winner Nino Vaccarella, journalist Jack Yamaguchi and I were invited to feature in the film by 'Koby' Kobayakawa (right), who had already been named project leader for the third-generation RX-7. Grafitti celebrating NINO were still visible, more than 10 years after the race was abandoned.

hour we were getting really worried – had our friends been involved in an accident, or had there been a pile-up that had stopped them? A police car arrived and I tried to ask its crew about an accident, but they just did not understand what I was talking about.

I went to the restaurant to try and call *Car Graphic*. Perhaps Shotaro had left a message, but who can read a Japanese telephone directory? I needed help, but not a single person in the restaurant spoke a word of English. For the same reason we could not even call a taxi to take us back to our hotel, which involved driving across Tokyo. And how would Shotaro and 'Koby' react when they could not find us? We really felt as if we had just landed on a desert island in the middle of the ocean. So imagine our joy when, after an hour and a half's anxious waiting, the Mazda appeared! I will never forget 'Koby's' demonstration of relief when he saw us waiting anxiously, neither will I ever know which of the four of us felt more relieved! And so we all proceeded – this time in convoy – to the Gotemba exit and to the intended restaurant!

I never went to Japan without also contacting Honda and vividly remember driving the second-generation Accord coupé, the one that was a VW Scirocco clone, with Yoshio Nakamura and Hiroshi Kizawa, who was later to take over as Honda's chief passenger car development engineer.

Yoshio asked me, 'What do you think of the performance?'

'It's quite good,' I answered in good faith, as in my opinion the Accord was never supposed to be a sports car.

Yoshio countered this with, 'It's not fast enough'! That was typical of the man who had played an important part in the development of Honda's first-generation Formula 1 car.

My relationship with Honda was excellent and in Tochigi I drove many interesting cars, such as a Prelude with the first-generation four-wheel steering. Some time later Kizawa invited me to Helsinki to drive the car on snow, where the system proved its worth. But that early, very ingenious and entirely mechanical system had a problem: the additional rear wheel steering added too much friction to the mechanism, which had a detrimental effect on the steering feel. This was rectified later by electronically controlled and hydraulically operated systems, but I never felt that all-wheel steering systems were really worth the extra cost, weight and complication, this being confirmed by later experience with Mazdas, Mitsubishis and BMWs using similar systems.

On the occasion of my visit to Japan in 1984, Kizawa invited me to try the new Civic range on the Suzuka circuit, and when the car became available in Europe he let me have a CRX with the 12-valve engine for a long-term test, asking me to send him a complete report on my experience. It proved to be a delightful little

The RX-7 in the pit area of the Targa Florio, near Cerda.

car with a smooth and lively engine and a superb gearbox, its suspension being its weakest point. The procedure was repeated when new models were announced, and when it came to the 1.6-litre VTEC coupé, I was even asked by Honda R&D in Germany how I wanted it equipped. As I wanted it to be as light as possible, I took it without air-conditioning and power steering. I finally liked the car so much that, when it came to handing it back, I acquired it. You will learn more about it in the next chapter.

With an average of about one trip to Japan per year for more than 20 years, I have seen a lot of the country, including Hokkaido, which I visited twice, once to drive the Lexus LS400 (Celsior) on Toyota's proving ground before it came to Europe, and once, in 1996, to drive various cars on Honda's excellent testing circuits. The last time Suzanne came with me we spent a weekend on Kyushu, driving a Cosmo coupé and being guided by a young member of Mazda's PR department, Kenichi 'Ken' Terasaki, who speaks French as well as English, a rare thing in Japan. Unfortunately we saw little more than rain. It was worst of all in Nagasaki, but we nevertheless went to visit the villa where 'Madame Butterfly' was supposed to have lived.

It is now over 30 years since I first visited Japan and many things have changed, not only in the car world. All major manufacturers have their own

Good friends meet in Yokohama (from left): Akira Kawamura of Car Graphic, *John Lamm of* Road & Track, *Mrs Kawamura and myself.*

factories and development centres in Europe and the US, not to mention smaller branches in other parts of the world. In 1969 less than 10 per cent of car production was exported. Today, exports and cars built in so-called Western countries account for the majority of those wearing a Japanese badge. In the early 1970s Japanese cars were bought in Europe because they were cheap, well-equipped and reliable, even though they were rough and uncomfortable. Today they are expensive, sometimes more expensive than equivalent European cars, but they are still more reliable and some of them set such standards of refinement, silence and comfort that even a company of Porsche's know-how and prestige recently sent a group of engineers to Japan to get more information on how the Japanese's unequalled productivity is achieved at no expense in quality.

Honda took six Formula 1 World Championships in a row and has swept the board in the American CART Championship for the last four years, while the rally world is dominated by Toyota, Mitsubishi and Subaru. A lot has been said in Europe and America about the unfair competition of the Japanese manufacturers competing almost without restriction with domestic products, while the Japanese authorities protect their industry by high import duties, high taxes and endless red tape. That was true 30 years ago, but progressively things have changed. The cost of labour in Japan is now also more comparable with average European rates. What is not said, however, is that the Japanese made the European and – even more so – the American car industry wake up to reality. They have shown us what *real* workmanship and quality look like. European and American cars would not be what they are today if the Japanese had not applied pressure on our industries.

Chapter 22

My own cars

As a MOTORING journalist I began serious car testing in the early 1950s, including taking a full set of performance figures, and for about 40 years I had at least one, sometimes more, test cars waiting for me in front of the house or in my garage. During that period I could almost have done without a car of my own. Prior to that the war had almost stopped any driving activity, which explains why over a period of 60 years since I obtained my first driving licence in Vienna, I have not owned more than 20 cars.

The first was the Belgian-made six-cylinder Imperia of which I was the fifth owner and which I bought from a friend who had crashed it just before the war;

My Ballot 2LTS as I bought it in 1947.

When my father bought a 3¹/₂-litre Jaguar Mark V, I bought his 1938 2¹/₂-litre of which I was very proud.

during the war I straightened and rebuilt it. The second was the 1925 2-litre type 2LTS Ballot that I bought as a chassis in 1947 and first drove as it was, with two bucket seats, before having a primitive open touring body made for it. Both have been discussed in earlier chapters.

I reluctantly sold the Ballot, which I considered an old friend, my father having owned four cars of that renowned make before the war, when, in 1950, he bought his third Jaguar, a Mark V. I made an offer for his 1938 2¹/₂-litre when he wanted to sell it. It had been stored during the war, and when it was put on the road again I had carefully looked after it. With rigid axles front and rear and ridiculously small suspension travels (common to all pre-war British cars), it was hardly up to date in 1950, and its Burman worm-and-peg steering with a transverse drag link was far from being a model of accuracy, but the car was one of the most elegant of its time and a quite potent performer, even though I would have preferred it to have had the 3¹/₂-litre engine under its long bonnet. But when I began serious professional testing, I better realised the limits of vintage suspension and steering and sold the Jaguar to a cousin, buying a grey type 103 Fiat 1100 in 1953.

By that time I had been introduced by Jacques Ickx, Jacky's father and a respected journalist, to Fiat's PR department, led at the time by Giovanni Pestelli, who was soon to be superseded by the legendary Maria Rubiolo. I was personally introduced to the then brand-new Fiat 1100/103 by Fiat's Technical Director,

Dante Giacosa, one of the most famous car engineers of the century and an immensely kind and respected person. I had been quite impressed by the performance of the little four-door when I first drove it, and it was not too expensive to buy or run, so it was an obvious choice. Unit body construction, independent double wishbone front suspension and a willing ohv engine with a four-speed gearbox made it a truly modern car at the time. The worm-and-roller steering with a complicated linkage was not too accurate and the car understeered too much on its skinny tyres, but I still liked it. It was quite well made for a popular car and even had cast-iron-lined aluminium brake drums.

A year after I bought my 1100, Fiat produced the 1100 TV, a faster version that developed 50 rather than 36bhp, and I decided to tune the engine of my own car to get more power. Intake manifold and ports were carefully matched, the compression ratio was raised, washers went under the valve springs and a new carburettor with a larger choke size and an accelerator pump was adopted. Maximum speed went up from 120.5kmh (74.8mph) to 131kmh (81mph) and 0–100kmh acceleration went down from 28.5 to 22.3 seconds. This may sound very slow today, but was very good for a popular 1,100cc car at the time. Unfortunately, the connecting rod bearings did not like the extra power. They did not last more than 10,000km and I could not use the TV's lead bronze bearing shells because the basic 1100 did not have a hardened crankshaft.

When Alfa Romeo produced the Giulietta, its engine boasting a five-bearing crankshaft, linered aluminium cylinder block and twin ohc, I thought that this would be the answer to my hard driving over long distances, which was very

In 1956 I changed my tuned Fiat 1100 for an Alfa Romeo Giulietta Sprint – the most unreliable car I have owned.

When I sold the Giulietta, I went straight to its most feared competitor and bought a Porsche 1600 Super. I am seen driving it to victory in the Journalists' Slalom at the Nürburgring on the eve of the 1958 German Grand Prix. I changed the car for a 1600 Super 90 two years later.

common in my racing days. My idea was to buy a four-door Berlina, but the Alfa importer persuaded me to take the Bertone-designed Sprint coupé, which was much more elegant and had an engine producing 65 rather than 50bhp. There was still room in the back for my three young daughters and I was never without a test car anyway. However, as mentioned in an earlier chapter, the Giulietta was a disaster. Not only did she understeer far too much (I had not had a chance to drive one before I got mine), but she broke almost everything that can break in a car. Not even the engine was trouble-free. After a time the hate predominated in the love/hate relationship I had with the car, so I sold it and turned to the Giulietta's worst enemy in GT racing and rallies – a Porsche 356.

But before turning to the Porsche, I should mention that, in 1954, when it became known that the 569cc Fiat 500C Topolino would be discontinued in favour of the rear-engined 600, I bought one, just because I thought that Giacosa's first creation (back in 1936) was a genial and wonderful little car. I used it quite often and – probably on an occasion when the Giulietta had yet another problem – even drove it from Brussels to Modena and back to visit Ferrari! Then I finally stored it to become an 18th birthday present for one of my daughters, but unfortunately it was written off a year later when a large lorry skidded into it while it was parked in front of the house. Ever since then I wanted to get another one, which I was able to do more than 20 years later when I bought one from Italian friends who were the first owners, and who had stored it for 11 years. This is a 1950-model wooden Giardiniera (station wagon), which was kindly fully restored by Fiat and which I occasionally drive in and around Monte Carlo, where I now live, and where it gets more attention than a Ferrari!

My aforementioned first Porsche was a blue 75bhp 356A 1600 Super, the first model that did not use a front suspension straight from the Beetle, had a properly sized front anti-roll bar and 4.5J15 wheels. The 4.5 rims had been recommended by Helmuth Bott, then a young test engineer, and Porsche had to accept responsibility for them; the tyre companies declined because they were considered too wide! The 1600 Super was a wonderful little car, with a maximum speed of 178kmh (111.5mph) – nearly 20kmh faster than the 1,300cc Giulietta – and very reliable as long as you stuck to the 5,500rpm limit (which a journalist to whom I had lent the car for a lap of the Montlhéry circuit did not, resulting in bent valves and damaged pistons). I soon regretted parting with it in favour of a 356B Super 90, also blue, which was only marginally faster, and less comfortable because of its centrally pivoted, single-leaf transverse rear spring, which was supposed to improve the handling. But the improvement was not worth the loss of comfort – at least not on the road – and the gearbox had to be rebuilt after 25,000km.

The Super 90 performed only slightly better than the 75bhp 'Super' … and was louder, not as reliable and altogether less civilised. (Van Bever)

After the Super 90 I needed something more roomy and bought a Fiat 2300S Coupé, a Ghia design. It had a wonderful-sounding and powerful Lampredi-designed straight-six engine allowing a maximum speed of 120mph, and there were disc brakes all round. The only weak point was rather vague and sticky steering. I kept it for six years.

I well remember that on one occasion when I was driving in northern France between Avesne and Reims on one of those typically irregularly surfaced French secondary roads, I was pondering on the Porsche's discomfort and noise. At that time you could find cars that were fun to drive, performed at least as well and were more comfortable. Fiat had just introduced the 2300 S Coupé, which also had a larger rear compartment, and I decided to get one. I kept it for six years and 90,000km. It had a wonderful 136bhp six-cylinder pushrod engine with hemispherical combustion chambers and twin Weber 38 DCOE carburettors, designed by ex-Ferrari wizard Aurelio Lampredi; it even sounded like a Ferrari and very nearly reached 200kmh (125mph) after the engine was completely loosened. That was my first disc-braked car and it was very reliable. While it was in my possession I added (then very new) long-range halogen lights, which made an enormous difference to night driving; Nardi added his short-lever, remote control gear-change mechanism (to replace the standard long-cranked lever); and Oscar Montabone, who had succeeded Giacosa, exchanged the standard 5J15 wheels for wider-rimmed 5.5J wheels, which reduced the rather excessive understeer.

Simultaneously with the beige metallic 2300 S I also had a beige 2CV Citroën as a family hack, which I found great fun to drive. I have always loved clever popular cars. In 1962 I took it on a summer holiday to Italy with my first wife and the three children, plus luggage for a month. It is incredible how much luggage you can get into a 2CV! The car ran for ever and on crowded holiday routes, especially in the mountains, you never got impatient behind slow-moving columns of cars. It was you who decided on the speed of the column … behind you!

Meanwhile Fiat produced the 124 Sport model with, initially, a 1,438cc twin-

I foolishly changed the Fiat 2300S for a first-series 1438cc twin-cam Fiat 124 Spyder, the only convertible I have ever owned. It handled beautifully (better than later models) and its Pininfarina body was very pretty, but was not fast enough.

cam engine, also a Lampredi design. With Suzanne I drove a Spyder version from Turin to Sicily and back on the occasion of the Targa Florio in 1967 and liked the car so much that I ordered one and sold the 2300 S. I soon found out, however, that what amounts to a holiday trip to Sicily is a very different thing from long professional journeys across western and central Europe. For fast long-distance driving a closed car is best but, with the soft top in place, the wind noise in the green Pininfarina-styled 124 Spyder was very tiring. Driving on the winding coastal roads to Sicily, at a time when the *autostrada* did not yet exist, I had not really noticed that the car, which had a maximum speed of 170kmh (106mph), was not fast enough after I had been used to Porsches and the 2300 S. But for an open car it was commendably rigid and it handled beautifully – better than later cars that had a different rear suspension and understeered more. In the end, for long journeys, I preferred to take the long-term-test light blue Flat 125 S saloon, which had a 1,608cc version of the same twin-cam engine developing 100bhp and later even 110 after Montabone endowed it with a twin-choke Weber carburettor installation. Excessive understeer was cured by running the car with zero front camber (the best that could be done) and rear tyre pressures lower than the front pressures.

Shortly before we got the 124 Spyder, a blue Fiat 850 saloon was added to the stable, mainly for Suzanne to go shopping, and we both liked this cute little rear-engined car very much. Its only problem was that it was not watertight, and it was worse when the car stood still than when it was driven. After a night in heavy rain you would find water 2cm deep in the rear footwells. I tried very hard to stop the water coming in, but in the end I gave up and punched a few holes in the floor, which solved the problem!

Then, some time in 1968, I took to Italy for a *Quattroruote* road test a car that I just could not resist: a 180bhp BMW 2002 Alpina, which I picked up with Suzanne from the then still very modest Alpina premises in Kaufbeuren, Bavaria. Its performance was incredible. Up to 170–180kmh (105–110mph) it easily matched any Ferrari or Lamborghini, and its suspension was very well sorted. We had immense fun with it and a few laps of the Vallelunga circuit were a revelation. I simply had to get a car like that, and Alpina boss Bovensiepen built one for me from a yellow 2002 TI I got from BMW. But – probably wisely – he insisted that, for the road, I should take a 160bhp rally engine, rather than a full racing engine. Performance-wise it did not seem to make much difference, as the car weighed only 950kg (18.7cwt) and it was officially timed, in full road trim, at 25.2 seconds over the standing-start kilometre, and at a maximum speed of 204kmh

A BMW Alpina test car I drove to Rome with Suzanne convinced me that this was the car for us. It was a real rocket: without any preparation it took the Belgian class record over a standing kilometre in 27.25 seconds. Only the opportunity to buy a Porsche 911S 2.4 from Weissach persuaded me to part with it.

(126.7mph) in spite of a drag coefficient I don't care to think about. It had its problems, one being rather poor brakes, because the rear ones hardly did any work and the front end was very sensitive to tyre balance. I also burned a piston and broke one or two of the standard aluminium rockers (probably caused by the stiffer valve springs). But after that, Bovensiepen sent me another engine, which proved 100 per cent reliable. At that time we often commuted between Brussels, where we then lived, and Nice to visit Suzanne's parents but, as the car was rather low-geared, I felt I should not fully extend it on the motorway for a long period, so I usually kept the speedometer around the 180 mark, rather frustrating when you feel that the car is longing for more!

Meanwhile I had tested a number of Porsche 911s, which became better and better as they were steadily developed, and I finally realised that a 911 S was the right car for me. I sold the Alpina to Pierre Dieudonné, who used it for many years without any serious problem, until it fell victim to rust, and bought my first 911 from Paul Hensler, the engineer responsible for Porsche engine development. It was a blue 1972 model to which he had fitted the 'duck's tail' spoiler and the 7J15 rear wheels of the just-announced Carrera 2.7. It was a wonderful car. Its 2.4-litre engine was just longing for revolutions and the car handled beautifully. It was several years before Porsche made such a good car again, except for the legendary Carrera 2.7. But, as I have mentioned in an earlier

Left *After my 911S was stolen in Italy, I bought a 1976 Carrera 3.0. This was the year Porsche pioneered fully zinc-coated body structures. It had much more torque than the 911S, but only 10bhp extra. It was nice to drive, except in dense traffic where the combination of Bosch K-Jetronic fuel injection and fuel cut-off when coasting made smooth progress difficult. This 911 was also stolen, this time on a short visit to Brussels.*

Right *Having become a Porsche addict, I replaced the stolen Carrera 3.0 with a 'pre-series' Carrera 3.2 that I kept for 11 years – until I could not resist a new 993. The 3.2 now belongs to one of my daughters and is seen with my 993.*

chapter, I had agreed to be a guinea-pig for the factory, and after about a year the 190bhp 2.4 S engine was replaced by a still-experimental 175bhp 2.7 K-Jetronic engine, which produced good torque but did not rev nearly as freely. In the end the car was stolen in Bergamo and never found again.

It was replaced by a 1976 Carrera 3.0. Its 200bhp provided a much better performance than the rather optimistic 175bhp of the 2.7, and its flat 'tea tray' spoiler further improved the high-speed stability. The only problem I had with the car was the failure of a timing chain tensioner, which happened twice. This was an old problem and it seems strange that it had not been attended to before. The valve timing was probably also a little too extreme for the K-Jetronic injection system, which gave rise to irregular pulling when driving at low speed and low load. Zinc coating ensured freedom from rust and I would surely have kept the car for more than six years if it had not also been stolen – this time on the occasion of a visit to Brussels when I was already living in the South of France. Five years later I was informed by the police that the car had been retrieved, but I never saw it again.

It was followed in 1983 by an early metallic grey Carrera 3.2, which I drove for 120,000 trouble-free kilometres (70,000 miles). It certainly was the best performer and also the most economical of all the Porsche 911s I had owned until then, but after ten years its limitations became more and more obvious: the

old-type 915 gearbox had become really dated and on bad roads the kickback in the steering was really excessive by today's standards. The 964 series was already a considerable improvement, but when I had a chance to drive the 993 series, I decided that the improvement was such that I could resist no longer.

But before that, another car had joined the Carrera 3.2 in my garage and still keeps the 993 company. Ever since Honda added the CRX to the Civic range, one has been left with me for a long-term test of several months. One after another I had the first-series three-valve 1.5-litre, then a 1.6 four-cam, followed by its differently styled successor, and finally a similar car with the 1.6 VTEC engine. I liked it so much that when the Del Sol model, which is slightly larger and heavier, was introduced, I decided that I would keep the black coupé, which I have now had for more than eight years. The odometer has just turned 100,000km and, apart from one replacement of the constant velocity joints, a change to a later type of shock absorber (because they are much better), replacement of the front brake discs (because they were warped) and skimming them once, the car has been absolutely trouble-free, down to the smallest details. It has been more reliable than any car I have ever owned. I had always said that (apart from the 2CV Citroën, which is a freak among cars) I would never own a front-drive car. Now I will have to eat my words.

The latest car to join the Honda, the Porsche and the Topolino is a 1995 Chrysler Voyager V6 automatic, which is mainly driven by Suzanne. Several years ago Chrysler sent me a fairly early model for assessment before it came to

Since the Honda CRX has been in production, Honda have let me have one of each successive model for several months on a consultancy basis. But when the 1990 model with the 1.6-litre, 8000rpm VTEC engine came along, I liked my loan car so much that I acquired it. Now on 70,000 miles, it has been utterly reliable and I enjoy it as much as on the first day.

I bought this 1950 Fiat Topolino Giardiniera (station wagon) in Italy after 11 years' begging of the family of the first owner, a family I have known since childhood. The car, which had not been touched since its lady owner died, was completely restored for me by Fiat in Turin.

Europe. It was summer holiday time and we had a full house with the children and grandchildren, just the right conditions to appreciate the merits of that sort of vehicle, and when Chrysler later attended to the front-end styling and took care of the handling, we decided to have one, and have not regretted it.

Life goes on and automotive technology continues to progress, and some day will probably develop in completely different ways. After dedicating my life to cars, I am still hugely interested in their development and what lies ahead. And I still like driving in spite of all the measures the authorities take to spoil the fun. As to the future I can no longer look too far ahead, and I don't think that I will see many cars on the roads that are radically different in their technology from those of today, and I am sure I will still enjoy driving them.

Some day cars will probably be powered by some new source of energy, and, once on a motorway, will carry their occupants from A to B just at the push of a button. I am glad that I will never see that day.

Epilogue

WHAT AMAZES ME is how quickly cars evolved in less than 30 years after Carl Benz built his first tricycle, in 1886. Within 20 years, the current architecture of modern cars with a front engine driving the rear wheels through a clutch, a gearbox, a propeller shaft and a differential, had already firmly established itself and the internal combustion engine had prevailed over steam and electricity. The first car in my family, a 1906 Belgian-built FN was already a practical means of transport and my parents' first car, a 1.4-litre Fiat 501 of 1922, was an utterly reliable machine with which journeys of 300–350km on the unmetalled, dusty narrow roads of the time, often in an appalling state, were undertaken. Cruising speed on good roads was around 60kmh, 10kmh below the car's maximum speed. Cars capable of exceeding 100kmh were considered with respect, but traffic regulations were just as unrealistic as today: I remember that we were fined in a little town near Paris for exceeding the signposted speed limit of 10kmh. A virtue of Italian cars was that most of them were built in Turin or Milan and could tackle the nearby mountains without overheating. Most other cars overheated because they were tested in the prototype stage only on roads in striking distance of their factory. Today, all serious cars are thoroughly tested from North Scandinavia to Death Valley before they are marketed.

There were many significant steps in the evolution of the motor car since those early times. One was the introduction of all-steel bodies which not only made cars safer, but above all made the mass production of bodies possible, spelling the end of most specialised coachbuilders and finally leading to the complete amalgamation of the chassis and the body.

Another significant step was front-wheel drive, made possible by the availability of constant velocity joints, with a transmission layout in which the gearbox overhangs the front wheel axis making it possible to accommodate the entire power plant without requiring an excessively long bonnet, as pioneered by Citroën in 1934. The next step in front-wheel drive development was the transverse engine, as introduced in the early 1960s with Alec Issigonis's Mini, Dante Giacosa's Autobianchi Primula and the Fiat 128. The latter solution with the gearbox in line with the crankshaft is now almost universally adopted for small and lower middle class cars. Front-wheel drive however has its limits: the higher the torque applied to the front wheels, the greater the weight transfer from the front to the rear axle, reducing the grip of the front wheels. It is therefore unsuitable for car a having a very high power/weight ratio. But it saves weight and space.

Synchromesh gearboxes, first introduced in 1927 by the Cadillac Division of General Motors, removed the last real hurdle prospective drivers had to face and it was also General Motors who, in 1940, set the pattern for all modern automatic transmissions, the Hydramatic. Independent suspension was pioneered well before 1910 by Sizaire & Naudin and from the early 1920s on the Sizaire brothers marketed a successful car featuring independent suspension of a modern design, which also had rack-and-pinion steering. But the big breakthrough with this only came in the early 1930s, producing better comfort and better handling. However the biggest contribution to improved handling, arguably, came from the tyre industry, shortly after the Second World War when Michelin developed the radial ply tyre.

The contribution of brakes to improved safety came in two major steps: the first was the progressive adoption of four-wheel brakes in the early 1920s after a few pioneers like Argyll, Isotta-Fraschini and Peugeot on its 1914 grand prix car, had introduced them just before the First World War. The second was the introduction of disc brakes in the 1950s.

But probably the most important breakthrough in the car industry which I have witnessed is the development of electronics. Computers have replaced the drawing boards in the design office and made it possible to evaluate the behaviour of a car or any part of it under the stresses to which it will be submitted. They also control all the manufacturing and assembly processes, including robots which could not even have been dreamt of without their help, and computers aboard the cars control an ever-increasing number of functions, from engine management to anti-lock brakes and stability systems. Thanks to electronics, modern cars emit 96 per cent less pollutants than they did in 1970 and that will soon be further improved to 98 per cent. The recourse to electronics to further improve safety and engine efficiency will not stop here: electronic stability systems and speed control in function of the surrounding traffic are already with us and will be increasingly used to take over from the driver's responsibility in operating the car, probably at the expense of driving pleasure. And the time is not so far away when camshafts will leave the scene and valves will be operated by electronically controlled solenoids, allowing any required variations of their timing.

In the course of the last century, most power plants in which energy is transformed into a rotating movement by a piston, connecting rod and crankshaft mechanism have been replaced by rotary power plants. Steam piston engines have been replaced in ships by steam turbines, before steam was abandoned altogether (admittedly to be replaced by diesel piston engines); on railways steam and pistons have been replaced by electricity, and in aircraft, piston engines have given way to purely rotative jet engines. But for more than a century, motor cars have stuck to piston engines. Attempts have been made to replace them with gas turbines or with

Wankel-type and other rotary engines, but none of them achieved the breakthrough. In the case of the turbine this was because of its low fuel efficiency in the context of the widely varying loads and speeds at which cars are operated and, for the Wankel, because of the unfavourable shape of its combustion chambers. The main asset of the piston engine is the enormous amount of development from which it has benefited. In 75 years, the specific power of production engines has increased by 500 per cent in spite of the restrictions imposed by the emission laws, and their life expectation has increased by at least the same amount. In 1923, the best atmospherically aspirated racing engines developed around 50PS/litre. Today's Formula 1 engines develop over 250PS/litre and revolve at 18,000rpm. Such is progress to which the fuel industry has also contributed.

Witnessing such fantastic evolution and investigating the factors which made it possible was a thrilling experience. But the question today is how long will the internal combustion engine survive. Considering what has been and still can be achieved, pollution should not be a problem any more. But we all know that some day the oil reserves of the planet will be exhausted and other sources of power will have to be developed not only for road transport for which substitute power plants are under development, but also for air transport which is a much bigger problem, although hydrogen will probably provide the answer.

Life as a motoring journalist with an intermezzo as a racing driver has been fascinating and I look forward to more interesting experiences. It has brought me together with many men and women of great quality, in all parts of the world, many of which have become dear friends and have enriched my life. Some might feel that they have been neglected, but the life of a freelance is so busy! I hope they will forgive me.

The only aspect of a journalist's life which sometimes worried me is that it is more narrative than constructive. This is why I was happy when manufacturers began to take a real interest in my comments on new models and some of them involved me in their development. I am also proud of the 12 years, commencing in 1973, in which I was part of the Technical Committee of FISA, then the motor sport branch of FIA, where my efforts to enforce a formula based on the limitation of the fuel consumption in endurance racing, the only technically correct way of giving engines of any type and size an equal chance, finally succeeded. It required a lot of persuasion and I have always regretted that, having accepted the principle, the Committee, under the pressure of a majority of the manufacturers who wanted to retain existing engines, set the fuel allocation too high. But the formula certainly set the manufacturers a development target directly benefiting everyday consumers by improving the engine fuel efficiency.

Even if motor sport is not always going the way I would like it to take; even if some government regulations, like unrealistic and in most cases unnecessary blanket speed limits have spoiled the pleasure of driving a good car and have forced me to live in illegality each time I am at the wheel, I will remain interested in cars, in the constant technical progress made by the industry, and in motor sport for the rest of my life which has been and will continue to be so full of cars.

Index